Is Racial Equality Unconstitutional?

Is Racial Equality Unconstitutional?

MARK GOLUB

OXFORD
UNIVERSITY PRESS

Oxford University Press is a department of the University of Oxford. It furthers the University's objective of excellence in research, scholarship, and education by publishing worldwide. Oxford is a registered trade mark of Oxford University Press in the UK and certain other countries.

Published in the United States of America by Oxford University Press
198 Madison Avenue, New York, NY 10016, United States of America.

Library of Congress Cataloging-in-Publication Data
Names: Golub, Mark, author.
Title: Is racial equality unconstitutional? / Mark Golub.
Description: New York : Oxford University Press, 2018. |
Includes bibliographical references and index.
Identifiers: LCCN 2017031336 (print) | LCCN 2017035515 (ebook) |
ISBN 9780190683610 (Updf) | ISBN 9780190683627 (Epub) |
ISBN 9780190683603 (hardcover : alk. paper)
Subjects: LCSH: Equality before the law—United States. |
Race discrimination—Law and legislation—United States. |
Constitutional law—United States.
Classification: LCC KF4755 (ebook) |
LCC KF4755 .G65 2017 (print) | DDC 342.7308/73—dc23
LC record available at https://lccn.loc.gov/2017031336

9 8 7 6 5 4 3 2 1

Printed by Sheridan Books, Inc., United States of America

For Zoe

CONTENTS

PREFACE

This book was written almost entirely while Barack Obama was president. Its subject is not electoral politics but race and constitutional law, and the central dynamic it wrestles with considerably predates the 2008 election. Nonetheless, President Obama has become a powerful symbol of how racial politics operates in the post-civil rights era, combining high-profile signs of progress and integration with entrenched racial disadvantage. Indeed, where I once found talk of "post-civil rights racism" likely to be greeted as novel or counterintuitive, the issues soon gained easy traction under the general problematic of "race in the age of Obama." At a purely personal level, it then feels oddly appropriate that the end of the Obama era should coincide with final revisions and this book heading off to press.

In this period, American common sense on matters of race was stretched ever further to reconcile persistent disparities in social welfare, criminalization, and economic opportunity with a general understanding of itself as a "postracial" society. And as advocates for racial equality increasingly found themselves laboring simply to establish the existence of the problem, I felt with rising urgency the need for progressive scholarship not only to counter the mythology of postracial America, but to do so in a way that productively shifts the terms of debate rather than orienting around them.

As a scholar of race and law, I am often asked to comment on court cases or political events that receive attention in the popular media. For years now—as a conservative Supreme Court has repeatedly demonstrated its eagerness to curtail civil rights protections, restrict the use of affirmative action, and gut enforceable provisions of the Voting Rights

Act—when asked about the meaning or significance of such decisions, I've responded by quipping that they are bad for the country but good for my book. With the results of the November election, however, and the shocking mean-spiritedness of the campaign that preceded it, my "bad for the country, good for my book" quip seems to have turned suddenly unfunny. Witnessing the successful mobilization of right-wing populism under hypermasculinist appeals to an unapologetic white nationalism, one cannot help but wonder whether the Obama era ends with a return to something from an earlier age. In 2016, at least, racist political appeals often were explicit and open, not coded or concealed, with seemingly no need for dog-whistling subtlety.

To put things slightly differently: This book takes as its premise two seemingly contradictory facts about American politics and social relations. First, it is marked by near-universal acceptance of antiracist norms, and so at least purports to extend equal care and concern for all of its members, irrespective of their race, gender, ethnicity, color, or creed. And second, it is fundamentally structured by relationships of racial domination and subordination. How these two elements of American identity and social structure can coexist is the larger puzzle to which the book responds. Prior to the election, the first premise seemed entirely uncontroversial, while the second was likely to generate resistance or critique. After the election, it is the second premise that seems most evident, while the first is called uncomfortably into question. For many who watched the Trump phenomenon grow from comical distraction to real but unlikely threat, to new political reality, the most dispiriting part has been the realization that Trumpism reveals something about America that we either did not know or were unwilling to admit.

But this book is not about Obama or Trump. It does not seek to explain the recent election, nor does it pretend to know or predict the actions of the new president or the decisions of a Supreme Court certain to be shaped by his appointments. Rather, it marks an intervention into a long-standing debate over the meaning and possibility of racial justice in American law and society. At the heart of this debate, I argue, is the highly mythologized figure of the color-blind Constitution. That the terms of debate principally have been set through a contest between advocates and critics of something called "color-blindness" has been profoundly unhelpful for understanding either the racially structured nature of American democracy or the race-intensifying effects of a formally color-blind rule.

In naming race and constitutional law as my book's subject, I mean something greater than just case law and doctrine. Taking constitutionalism in its broadest sense of forming or constituting a political community, this book asks to what extent the American polity is created out of relationships of racial domination, and to what extent the constitutional vision of liberals and conservatives alike is shaped by an unwillingness to confront this basic premise. Accordingly, it may be understood as taking up Saidiya Hartman's painful challenge, in *Scenes of Subjection*, to theorize slavery and emancipation in terms of continuity rather than break. The figure of the color-blind Constitution, around which this book is organized, first appeared as part of a dispute over what substantive rights African Americans might claim as a consequence of slavery's formal demise. Similarly, color-blindness achieved privileged status as a symbol of constitutional equality amid contentious debate over what substantive rights African Americans might claim as a consequence of Jim Crow's formal rejection, and so suggests both break and continuity between segregation and civil rights.

So too, with the closing of the Obama era and evident inauguration of the post-postracial age. It is of course impossible to know the future of a Trump-appointed Supreme Court and federal judiciary, but the weight of American history suggests that our current moment may be understood less in terms of a return to the bad old days of open racism—registering, as it were, entirely as loss—and more as a reminder of continuities we prefer not to acknowledge. It is this underlying point of unrecognized or disavowed agreement that I mean to suggest by posing the question of this book's title: *Is Racial Equality Unconstitutional?*

The question is intended to be read on two distinct levels, corresponding to the doubled possibility of meaning carried by the word "constitutional." First, in its more limited sense, the question of constitutionality compares a particular law or policy with the requirements of the basic law, either as interpreted by the courts (as a speculative/empirical question) or as courts ought to interpret it (as a political/normative question). To pose the question in this familiar register is to ask whether some particular policy will or ought to be held in violation of, for example, the Equal Protection Clause of the US Constitution. And yet the question also serves to disrupt that familiarity, since readers are likely to be accustomed to thinking of racial discrimination, rather than *equality*, as constitutionally prohibited. In this first sense of the question, my title asks whether the pursuit of racial equality as a substantive democratic goal is consistent with the Court's current understanding of equal protection. I argue that it is not, even when pursued by facially neutral policies that do not classify individuals by race, and even though advocates of color-blind constitutionalism would surely disavow this conclusion. One of the book's contributions, in this practical sense, is to show how the logic of color-blindness compels results that even its authors acknowledge to be unacceptable, and how liberal critics of the doctrine nonetheless have been captured by its terms.

But the title also plays at a second and more fundamental level, in which the language of the Constitution marks the bringing into being of a political community or people. To ask whether racial equality is unconstitutional in this second, constitutive sense of the term is to call into question the status of the American polity as forged by racial exclusion—indeed, as *constituted* by that exclusion—and so fundamentally at odds with genuine equality and racial democracy. Posed this way, the question exceeds the domain of Supreme Court doctrine and goes to the core of the constitutional dilemma instigated by the structuring role of race in the American constitutional order.

Where virtually all existing critiques of color-blindness point to the need for greater awareness of racism's lingering effects, my argument instead calls attention to the peculiar racial logic at work in the demand for color-blindness itself. In so doing, I raise the possibility that racial equality cannot be the *perfection* of the American democratic project. I hold this view, moreover, whether racial progress is conceived as elusive, inevitable, or already achieved—and whether it is offered cynically, in claims of postracial America, or hopefully, as a call to action that we may achieve "a more perfect union." Rather, meaningful equality will require a more radical break from American constitutional order, and *refounding* upon principles of racial democracy. This book is offered in the spirit of bringing the need for such a break, and its possibility, more clearly into view.

ACKNOWLEDGMENTS

A ny book worth writing will, in the process, accumulate for its author far greater debt than can be repaid. Hopefully, this is such a book, and I am deeply grateful to all of the people whose time, energy, inspiration, curiosity, criticism, labor, and loving support went into its creation. I could not possibly thank everyone by name, but take this opportunity to express my deep gratitude nonetheless. I am especially grateful to the remarkable teachers I have been fortunate enough to have learned from over the years. Trix Rose taught me to write and was the first to let me in on the secret of writing's subversive potential. Leslie Vaughan introduced me to political theory at a time in my life when I needed it most. In graduate school, John Seery, Sharon Snowiss, Gary Shiffman, and Alan Houston generously shared insights and ideas I return to again and again. Tracy Strong and Harry Hirsch did as well, while helping me find my way in the intersection of political theory and law. Both pushed me to say what it was I thought I wanted to say, and both saw more clearly than I did what followed from my earliest venturings. That their pushing was frequently in opposite directions undoubtedly improved the clarity of my thought. Special thanks are due to George Lipsitz, whose teaching changed how I think about pretty much everything, and whose writings fundamentally inform the approach and sensibility of this book. I cannot imagine a better role model for engaged critical scholarship.

Thanks also to the many friends and colleagues who have sustained me along the way. In San Diego, many years ago, the seeds of this book took root in remarkable conversations around the kitchen table and over drinks with Tom Kim (Tommy, at the time) and Elmer Almachar. Thanks to Verity Smith, Nancy Luxon, Jason Kosnoski, and Oona Ceder for thinking together about what theory can and can't do. And to Druscilla Scribner, Eben Friedman, and Priscilla Lambert for much-needed community and friendship. At Scripps College I have been uncommonly lucky to find a Politics Department that at times feels more like a family. To Tom Kim (again) and Vanessa Tyson, our phenomenal most recent addition, and to Nancy Neiman Auerbach especially: Thank you for making my place of work a place of camaraderie, care, and intellectual engagement. I am grateful to many colleagues and friends at Scripps, for ideas cultivated in intellectual community over the years. Particular thanks to David Roselli, Aaron Matz, Rita Roberts, Paul Bucholz (eternally), Sheila Walker, Julie Liss, Michelle Decker, Tom Koenigs, Maryan Soliman, Matt Delmont, Mona Mehta, and Leigh Gilmore. Amy Marcus-Newhall offered institutional and moral support for this project in numerous ways, without which it could not have been completed. Meagan Roderique supplied outstanding research assistance. Becky Ballinger contributed administrative assistance, kindness, and exemplary strength.

This book has benefited enormously from the thoughtful comments of many readers: Marek Steadman, Joe Lowndes, the late Joel Olsen, Anna Marie Smith, David Tanenhaus, John Seery, Nancy Neiman Auerbach, Ashleigh Campi, Ainsley LeSure, Dylan Howell, and Constance Jordan each read and commented on one or more chapters. Kirstine Taylor (my most trusted interlocutor) read every page at least once, occasionally lifted me from despair, and reminded me when needed that despair also holds the power to spur new possibilities and ways of being in the world. I can't say thank you enough, for everything. The enormously helpful suggestions of two anonymous reviewers made the book substantially better than it otherwise would have been. I am especially grateful for the push toward popular constitutionalism, which brought into focus some of the implications of my argument, and which emboldened me to attempt a more direct answer to the question posed by my title.

Portions of chapter 3 appeared previously as "*Plessy* as Passing: Judicial Responses to Ambiguously Raced Bodies in *Plessy v. Ferguson*," *Law and Society Review* 39, no. 3 (2005). Portions of chapter 4 appeared as "Remembering Massive Resistance to School Desegregation," *Law and History Review* 31, no. 3 (2013). Thanks respectively to Wiley, the Law and Society Association, and Cambridge University Press for permission to reprint.

Above all, I am grateful for the support of my family in all of its various forms. Ann Roman and Rosalee Golub are not here to celebrate the completion of this book with me, but their kind spirits, good guidance and constant encouragement is everyday felt and deeply appreciated nonetheless. Edward Golub and Constance Jordan have been anticipating this book for many years. I hope they will find it worth the wait, and that I might somewhat repay their support by giving them something to kvell about. The entire Mann family has been uncommonly generous in more ways than I can count. Ami Mann was there in the mid-1980s and earlier, and for almost twenty years has been the center of my orbit. I am and will be forever grateful for all that we've made together. Zoe Mann came along in 2006 and has never ceased to inspire and amaze. It is with immeasurable joy that this book is dedicated to her.

Is Racial Equality Unconstitutional?

PART I | The Race-Conscious Logic of Color-Blind Constitutionalism

CHAPTER 1 | Beyond Color-Blindness and Color-Consciousness

DISCUSSIONS OF RACE in American law and politics remain captured by the figure of the color-blind Constitution. From its origins in a dispute over the proper interpretation of the Fourteenth Amendment, its influence extends far beyond the realm of legal doctrine and has emerged as the central metaphor of the post-civil rights era. Its symbolism profoundly shapes popular understandings of race, law, justice, and equality, and for many Americans embodies a kind of collective racial common sense. The phrase lays claim to the Constitution in the strong sense of constituting a political community, not only in terms of what the written Constitution means (or should mean), but also in terms of who we are as a nation, in what we believe, and to what we aspire. Even for those who reject its claim, the language of color-blindness sets the terms of debate, making its presence felt implicitly even in challenges to its constitutional authority.

It is not surprising, therefore, that extensive literatures in law and legal studies, ethics and philosophy, history, and the social sciences have supplied a vast array of arguments for or against color-blindness and the color-blind Constitution.[1] For its proponents, color-blindness represents an ideal of equal treatment under law and a principled rejection of policies that classify or treat individuals differently on the basis of race. The phrase itself traces to Justice John Marshall Harlan's dissenting opinion in *Plessy v. Ferguson*—the 1896 case that upheld the constitutionality of state-mandated racial segregation under the doctrine of "separate but equal." Rejecting that view, Justice Harlan famously declared: "Our Constitution is color-blind, and neither knows nor tolerates classes among citizens."[2] Discerning just what Harlan meant by this phrase is a complex question that I take up in more detail in chapter 3, but today his words are generally understood to condemn all forms of race-based decision-making by the state. Adapting Justice Harlan's phrase for the title of his book, for example, Andrew Kull's *The Color-Blind Constitution* traces the history of this "austere proposition" that the Constitution denies government "the power to distinguish between its citizens on the basis of race."[3]

The intuitive appeal of this view derives from its close connection with liberal political theory and related values of abstract individualism, moral autonomy, and procedural justice. Liberalism, and American liberalism especially so, conceives itself to be born of a fundamental abhorrence of formal status hierarchies. Historically, of course, the nation's political order has never fully conformed to these self-stated ideals. But for advocates of the color-blind Constitution, that fact simply confirms the validity of the principle itself: the meaning of constitutional equality is measured, they hold, by historical injuries sustained through lack of adherence to color-blindness in practice. The rightness of the color-blind Constitution, say its champions, is on display precisely in the wrongness of slavery, segregation, prejudice, and discrimination. Rejecting the use of race in policy and legal decision-making, it is argued, is the best and perhaps only way to achieve the color-blind ideal now and in the future. Chief Justice Roberts expresses this view in the form of a judicial maxim when he writes: "the way to stop discrimination on the basis of race is to stop discriminating on the basis of race."[4]

For some, there is evidence that the civil rights revolution has largely accomplished its goals: the unprecedented rise of a black middle class; visible signs of integration and diversity in the workplace and social spheres; widespread and sincere condemnation of explicitly racist views and public use of demeaning racial epithets; and, of course, the formerly unthinkable: the historic election of an African American president. And yet a defining element of the post-civil rights era is that these accomplishments coexist with trends that are both well known and difficult to reconcile with the optimistic progress narrative of "postracial" America: persistent or growing material inequality in almost all measurable categories of social welfare; massive and unprecedented expansion of racialized surveillance and a prison system that disproportionately incarcerates black and brown bodies; widespread public support for draconian immigration laws and militarization of national borders; indefinite detention and deportation, justified under the rubric of antiterrorism; coordinated programs of racially targeted voter suppression; the continuing vulnerability of black bodies to police violence and private acts of racial terrorism. How is it that these two trends can coexist? How are the former signs of racial progress reconciled with the later indications of entrenched racial domination? And what could it mean, then, to be "color-blind" in the post-civil rights era, when formal institutions of segregation are repudiated while material inequalities between races are steadfastly preserved?

This book is not meant to persuade those who believe, or purport to believe, in a "postracial" America where racism is largely a relic of the past.[5] Rather, I start from assumptions not likely to be shared by those who hold such a view, joining a tradition of antiracist scholarship defined at minimum by an acknowledgment that "race matters" (historically, socially, and politically rather than biologically), that racial hierarchy has been a persistent and defining feature of American democracy, and that democratic commitments as well as simple human solidarity oblige us morally and legally to confront racial inequality in all of its forms. In venturing to write about the role of law in reproducing racial subordination in the United States, my thinking both grows out of and hopes to contribute to this tradition. More specifically, my project is motivated by a concern that antiracist criticism too often has been defined by the object of its critique, and so offers inadequate tools for resisting it. Even when it is rejected, that is, color-blindness discourse sets the terms of debate, defines normative goals, and limits the scope of legitimacy for alternative formulations of racial justice.

Against its overwhelming popular and political success, for example, critics of color-blind constitutionalism have labored to justify color-*conscious* policies and legal principles. In pursuing color-consciousness as an alternative, however, this strategy concedes an underlying assumption that color-blindness marks a refusal of racial consciousness rather than its mobilization. On this view, color-blindness is understood to supply a cramped and narrow constitutional vision that serves chiefly to disqualify many of the tools that could helpfully be engaged to combat persistent racial inequality in the United States. Color-consciousness is justified, it is argued, because blindness to race risks fostering blindness to racism, and so functions to perpetuate current inequalities not easily separated from the explicitly white supremacist practices of the past. Color-blind constitutionalism renders invisible the legacy of these practices (past and present) while falsely equating race-conscious remedies with the white supremacy they aim to combat. In the post-civil rights era, say its critics, color-blind constitutionalism perpetuates racial hierarchy and undermines policies that would confront entrenched racial privilege.[6] Race-conscious decision-making is therefore justified as necessary to confront historical and present racial injustices. Justice Blackmun expresses this view in the form of a judicial maxim when he writes: "In order to get beyond racism, we must first take account of race."[7]

In what follows, I seek to disrupt the terms of this debate, rather than taking a side. For while I agree with critics that color-blind constitutionalism serves as a tool for justifying and reproducing racial inequality, I also worry that arguments in favor of color-consciousness have implicitly reproduced the underlying premises of the color-blind view. When race-based decision-making is condemned as a departure from color-blind norms, and when it is defended as a necessary alternative to them, this limiting dichotomy tends to obscure the underlying racial logic of color-blind constitutionalism itself. Both sides, that is, regard race-conscious remedies such as affirmative action as a departure from color-blind norms; whether that departure is *justified* is the subject of their dispute. It is this shared assumption, rather than their disagreement, that this book aims to challenge.

A more robust defense of racial equality begins, I argue, with an understanding of how the imposition of a color-blind rule in itself affects a heightened awareness of race, and so ought to be conceived as a particular *form* of color-consciousness rather than an alternative to it. My approach thus differs substantially from those working within the familiar terms of popular and academic debate—framed, as they are, by the stark choice between color-blindness and color-consciousness in legal and political decision-making. Advocates of racial consciousness have shown how color-blindness limits the scope of permissible state action to remedy entrenched racial inequality, and so fails to produce a racially egalitarian society. This much explains why color-blindness is normatively undesirable, and why it is preferable to "take account" of race. What it fails to explain is how prohibitions against racial classifications *already do* take account of race and so are, in themselves, already profoundly race-conscious. Color-blindness is not a meaningful option in societies structured by racial hierarchy. The choice is not between blindness and consciousness, I argue, but between two distinct modes of racial awareness: whether our racial consciousness will take the form of a prohibition or an engagement, and whether it will seek to preserve racial hierarchy or to transform it.

Viewed this way, the problem with color-blindness is not that it prohibits consideration of race, but that it expands racial consideration on behalf of purportedly victimized whites. Within its terms, the pursuit of racial equality registers as injury, loss, or constitutional violation. This interpretation inverts familiar understandings of race, rights, and the Constitution, according to which the law is figured as a protector of racial minorities against majoritarian excess. In contrast, my argument identifies racial hierarchy rather than equality as an enduring constitutional norm, thus posing the question of the book's title: *Is Racial Equality Unconstitutional?* The following sections seek to explain how and in what sense this question bears an affirmative answer, first at the level of doctrine, and then as a matter of ideology or racial formation.

Anticlassification, Antidiscrimination, Antisubordination

In legal scholarship and as used by legal professionals, the color-blind Constitution is understood to organize a way of thinking about the permissibility of racial classifications by the state. Framed this way, color-blindness refers less to a constitutional theory than to a legal doctrine, the aim of which is to establish consistent rules regarding the use of race in law and public policy. As a general principle, the doctrine has been championed by a majority of the Supreme Court but has never been adopted as an absolute rule. Even for its ardent champions, exceptions are allowed in a limited number of cases: to remedy the effects of specific, prior discriminatory state actions;[8] to promote diversity in higher education;[9] in voting, as a relevant factor in the redistricting process;[10] and in emergency situations such as prisons and matters of national security.[11] Nor has anticlassification always been regarded as the natural, obvious, or dominant meaning of antidiscrimination law. Rather, as Reva Siegel has shown, our current understanding of the anticlassification principle is in fact an "artifact of political struggles" over the meaning of antidiscrimination after *Brown v. Board of Education*.[12] Nonetheless, recent Supreme Court decisions suggest a growing consensus around some version of the color-blind principle.[13]

As doctrine, the color-blind rule can be evaluated from the perspective of three understandings of equal protection law: anticlassification, antidiscrimination, and antisubordination. According to the Court's more conservative members, anticlassification is simply a literal articulation of antidiscrimination. On this view, it is the act of classifying by race that offends the Constitution, rather than the result or purpose to which a classification is put. As Justice Thomas writes: "The Constitution abhors classifications based on race, not only because those classifications can harm favored races or are based on illegitimate motives, but also because every time the government places citizens on racial registers and makes race relevant to the provision of burdens or benefits, it demeans us all."[14] Color-blind constitutionalism thus describes a conservative judicial philosophy while nonetheless finding justification for its view in a strong version of political liberalism, with its attention to the rights of individuals, private choices, and free markets. For Justice Thomas, and others who support this view, the Constitution guarantees every individual the right to be treated as an individual. Because they "make race relevant," racial classifications are said to violate this basic principle and are therefore unconstitutional.

But liberal values of individualism and equal treatment need not imply the illegitimacy or illegality of racial classifications in some contexts. A second vision of constitutional equality, also grounded in the principle of antidiscrimination, regards race as a permissible and at times necessary basis of decision-making to ensure fair treatment and meaningful equality of opportunity for all individuals. Paul Brest's classic formulation, for example, defines the antidiscrimination principle as "the general principle disfavoring classifications and other decisions and practices that depend on the race (or ethnic origin) of the parties affected."[15] Yet, while many race-based decisions will reflect impermissible assumptions of "racial value and racially selective indifference," Brest notes, others may not, and may even constitute "desirable uses of race" such as the integration of formally segregated schools.[16] On this version of the antidiscrimination principle, the harm of discrimination adheres not in the act of racial classification, but in the injuries they traditionally have worked.

In distinguishing between color-blind means and ends, the liberal antidiscrimination position conceptualizes racial classification as instrumentally rather than intrinsically harmful. As a consequence, it also sets the terms by which some forms of racial classification could be justified: if race-consciousness is morally suspect because it treats people as members of groups rather than as individuals, and so denies them treatment with equal dignity and respect, then surely society has a compelling interest in minimizing the extent to which race correlates with traditional measures of life opportunity. In this sense, it is the failure to acknowledge and address racial injustice that violates principles of democratic individualism.[17] On this view, the legally and morally objectionable feature of discrimination is tightly drawn to the inegalitarian social order through which racial categories are imbued with meaning. Government use of racial classifications in public policy is not what "makes race relevant" today—and, to the extent that inegalitarian social organization contributes to the salience of racial categories, race-conscious policies that promote integration or minimize the racial concentration of socially valuable goods may in fact help bring about the kind of society in which race matters *less*.

On this account, antidiscrimination and race-consciousness need not be in tension. That they so often are thought to be in conflict reflects the mistaken assumption that racial consciousness is a product of the classifications themselves rather than a reflection of an unjust social organization. As Amy Guttman has argued, color-conscious policies may be consistent with the ideal of a color-blind society if they have the effect of bringing such a situation into being: "some color conscious policies and some kinds of color consciousness may minimize injustice today and make it possible to be both fair and color blind in the future."[18] Understood aspirationally, that is, color-blind ideals may at times authorize color-conscious practices. On the liberal understanding of antidiscrimination, color-blindness represents a vision of how a fair society ought to be structured, but does not justify a categorical prohibition against racial classifications in a society such as our own—that is, one in which racial hierarchy and prejudice are pervasive. Race-conscious policies that would be unfair in an ideal society may well be justified in our imperfect world, Ronald Dworkin contends, when they serve to "reduce the degree to which American society is overall a racially conscious society."[19]

At first glance, liberal and conservative formulations of antidiscrimination would appear to be diametrically opposed. After all, the liberal model is intended to justify precisely those race-conscious policies that color-blind conservatives reject as unconstitutional. And yet the arguments reveal a surprising level of agreement. Whether viewed as an impermissible introduction of race that ensures its continued relevance (the conservative view), or as a valuable method for decreasing the salience of race in contemporary society (the liberal view), the legitimacy or illegitimacy of race-conscious policies in both cases turns upon its imagined relationship to an idealized "nonracial" American society. In this sense, and despite its prescriptive justification of race-conscious policies such as affirmative action, the liberal formulation of antidiscrimination may just as easily be described as a kind of *aspirational color-blindness*. The true measure of color-blind constitutionalism's victory, then, is its implicit acceptance even by ostensible critics, who are left to justify temporary departures from a color-blind norm, and to do so on the promise of a more color-blind future.

By recognizing this underlying convergence in liberal and conservative antidiscrimination law, it is perhaps easier to see how color-blindness discourse might supply the rhetorical tools with which simultaneously to challenge *and defend* entrenched racial hierarchy. Indeed, the concern that both liberal/aspirational and conservative/anticlassification versions of antidiscrimination will prove inadequate to the task of challenging systemic inequality motivates a third approach to equal protection law: antisubordination theory.[20] Initially put forward by Owen Fiss as the "group disadvantaging principle," this view holds that the Equal Protection Clause ought not be understood to protect individuals against "discrimination"—a phrase notably absent from the Constitution—but rather is grounded in "a proscription against status-harm" that prohibits the government from engaging in practices that enforce "the subordinate position of specially disadvantaged groups."[21] On Fiss's view, antidiscrimination's limited focus on improper or prohibited treatment of individuals renders it both normatively undesirable and theoretically unable to account for the law as actually practiced. Because the great bulk of scholarly attention has focused on the normative claim, I will take it up first, before returning to the more provocative yet underexplored theoretical observation.

Why does Fiss think that antidiscrimination law must fail to challenge inequality generally, and racial inequality in particular? In part, his concern stems from antidiscrimination's origins in efforts to promote and enforce "means-ends rationality."[22] To the extent that racism is premised in irrational beliefs about biological inferiority, the requirement of means-ends rationality works to root out arbitrary and invidious discrimination as expressions of illegitimate legislative motives. The test of legislative motive is, in effect, an assessment of the goodness of fit between a law or policy and its stated purpose. The state has a legitimate interest, for example, in preventing acts of sabotage or terrorism—as it would now be called. But the targeting of Japanese Americans for restrictive curfews at issue in *Hirabayashi v. United States* (1943) is not a sufficiently rational means of accomplishing this end. It is both overinclusive, since it treats all citizens of Japanese ancestry as presumptively and indistinguishably disloyal, and underinclusive, since it does not target citizens of German or Italian ancestry.[23] By seizing upon the irrationality of prejudice and stereotypes, the antidiscrimination principle would discredit their incorporation in law. Race does not, in fact, correlate with the prejudiced assumptions assigned to it, and so makes a particularly poor proxy for almost all legitimate state purposes.

It is easy to see how this account tends naturally toward the color-blind view. By purging the law of irrational or morally irrelevant categories such as race, antidiscrimination seeks to hold decision-makers to the relevant criteria—thereby ensuring that individuals be judged fairly, on their merits, without regard to race. It is also easy to see an underlying market-logic at work here, with economic efficiency as the benchmark of nonracialized, rational decision-making.[24] The problem, as Fiss and antisubordination theorists see it, is that racial inequality is quite often advanced through mechanisms that neither violate market rationality nor require any discernible racial intent.[25] The wrongness of racist policies and practices, in other words, lies not in their deviation from individualist ideals (discrimination), but in the systemic advantaging of one group relative to another (subordination). Consequently, antidiscrimination's principled rejection of group-salience renders it inadequate for theorizing or confronting the actual social processes through which racial hierarchy is maintained.

From an antisubordination perspective, two types of cases reveal the inadequacy of antidiscrimination law in both its conservative and its liberal forms. The first involves race-conscious remedial measures such as affirmative action. As we have seen, such policies are disallowed under the color-blind conservative view because they require classifying individuals by race. Under the liberal antidiscrimination perspective, race-conscious policies may be justified in certain circumstances, when it can be shown that they do not run afoul of their underlying individualist goals. The liberal antidiscrimination approach would allow differential treatment on the basis of race, but only in a limited, temporary, and tragic way: limited, because great care must be taken that racial distinctions not be used to perpetuate inequality rather than ameliorate it; temporary, because their justification diminishes as the society they envision draws nearer;[26] and tragic, because their necessity serves as a painful reminder of the nation's failure fully to confront the systemic historical injustices they are meant to address. From an antisubordination perspective, however, there is no problem to be explained away. Even if affirmative action *is* "discrimination," as color-blind conservatives insist, neither its purpose nor its effect is to subordinate any historically disadvantaged group. On the contrary, while antisubordination theory does generate an asymmetrical application in relationship to race, permitting preferences for disadvantaged groups while prohibiting preferences for the dominant group, this turns out to be part of its appeal, since the regime of racial domination itself is by nature asymmetrical.[27]

A second type of case involves facially neutral or nondiscriminatory laws that nevertheless aggravate group disadvantage. These cases involve situations widely recognized to be racially unjust, but cannot be accounted for within the antidiscrimination framework, as they do not involve discrimination per se. A general willingness to enforce private contracts, for example, is not ordinarily understood to be discriminatory action, but may predictably result in racial exclusion. It is not clear how, on the basis of antidiscrimination, courts are authorized to prohibit the enforcement of restrictive housing covenants[28] or decline the request for a liquor license by a "whites-only" private club.[29] In neither case need the state action be motivated by race. Nor need the state even be aware of the private racist preferences advanced by the facially neutral law. The antisubordination critique thus explains why a general prohibition against discriminatory treatment on the basis of race—even if it were rigorously enforced—will fail to confront the kinds of subordinating racial practices typical of our current society.[30]

In the context of race, the antisubordination approach has been used most effectively by practitioners of critical race theory (CRT), a designation which names both a legal theory and a social movement explicitly committed to antiracist praxis.[31] In the realm of legal scholarship, CRT is unique in its grounding of race as a central analytical category rather than an instance or test of some other, purportedly more general constitutional question (discrimination, equal protection, free speech, etc.). Critical race theorists tend to regard current antidiscrimination law as preserving racial hierarchy rather than challenging it, both as a matter of doctrine and in its dissemination of color-blindness as political ideology.[32] Not surprisingly, then, critical race scholarship has at times been misunderstood as a racially essentialist, perhaps even biologically determinist, identity-politics movement.[33]

It is true that CRT is defined in part as a movement of minority law professors—and by its insistence that this fact matters substantively, thus linking the race of its practitioners to the content of its critique. Richard Delgado and Jean Stefancic call this the "voice of color thesis."[34] And critical race scholarship overwhelming is done by nonwhite legal scholars who at times claim to speak on behalf of racial minorities, give voice to minority experiences, and/or represent the perspective of "outsiders" or "the bottom."[35] But critical race theory is equally defined by its antiessentialist sensitivity to the historically specific nature of race, shifting boundaries of racial groups, and constantly evolving techniques of racial domination. Delgado and Stefancic call this the "social construction thesis," and critical race scholars are unquestionably more diligent in its practice than are mainstream civil rights liberals or color-blind conservatives.[36] So it makes more sense to approach CRT as responding to a puzzle, as do the editors of the *Critical Race Theory* anthology, who describe their project as "an effort to construct a race-conscious and at the same time anti-essentialist account of the processes by which law participates in 'race-ing' American society."[37] Without foreclosing the question of how successful these efforts have been, we might note that it is a puzzle not of CRT's own making, but one that emerges from the actual social conditions of post-civil rights American society—and one that remains stubbornly lodged at the intersection of widely embraced egalitarian ideals and persistent racialized patterns of politics and social opportunity. CRT scholarship may thus be regarded as a kind of "racial counterpublic" for legal thought.[38] The benchmark of common sense it provides for academic antiracists is indispensable for counterhegemonic intellectual work, and indeed serves as a starting point for the arguments advanced in this book.

Nor do I find much urgency in rehearsing familiar debates over essentialism, group rights, or the appropriate status of community in liberal political and legal theory.[39] Rather, I want to explore the extent to which CRT's critical and prescriptive elements might be supplemented, extended, enhanced, and perhaps at times challenged by pursuing the more theoretical and conceptual difficulties within current equal protection law, alluded to earlier. Returning to the second of two objections raised by Fiss in "Groups and the Equal Protection Clause," recall that he critiqued antidiscrimination law for its internal incoherence, and not only on the grounds that its application yielded unacceptable results. He viewed its characteristic appeals to neutrality and individualism not just as bad ideas, but as "an illusion."[40] Classification is how law works, he suggested, making it impossible to eliminate the role of groups from equal protection law—irrespective of the normative value in so doing.

For various reasons, what's critical about critical race theory has been understood primarily in normative terms, as advocacy or "praxis." Perhaps unfairly, this much-needed critical engagement has at times encouraged an overly voluntaristic approach to the law—as if scholars might simply choose between anticlassification and antisubordination approaches, or as if the power of legal advocacy were sufficient to halt the Court's steady movement toward color-blind constitutionalism.[41] But the problem is not simply a matter of which constitutional principle ought to prevail: color-blindness or color-consciousness? Rather, it concerns a more fundamental instability within those principles themselves—an instability that is obscured, I argue, by the normative pitch for recognition of the salience of groups, race, or "difference." By itself, the valorization of minoritarian identity and subject position fails adequately to disclose how purportedly color-blind approaches generate their own racial meanings, trade in their own mobilizations of (white) racial group status, and so work to sharpen rather than eliminate racial awareness. In place of familiar arguments that would condemn one and justify the other, this book seeks to demonstrate how color-blind rhetoric conceals its own decidedly race-*conscious* political commitments, and so is inseparable from the racial logic it so vocally condemns.

Color-Blindness and the New American Dilemma

At one time, there was considerable optimism that removing arbitrary and unjust barriers to individual success might usher in an era of material equality between the races—that from formal equality, substantive equality would soon follow. That this has not been the case suggests a fundamental inadequacy of the ubiquitous trope of racial progress, with its plausible but empty assurances that things are getting better while much work remains yet to be done. For what is at stake here resides not in our relative proximity or distance from past racial injustices, but in the quality of our relationship to those continuing histories, and in what manner contemporary racial inequality may be contested, justified, preserved, or transformed. Approaching the discourse of color-blind constitutionalism in this way is meant to provoke an analysis that exceeds immediate rule-bound doctrinal concerns—pressing as those concerns may be—and to encounter the law as an agent of political theory, fully engaged in the ideological contest over racial meaning in the broadest cultural sense. I take up these questions not only as a matter of constitutional law, but equally as an issue of deep significance for political theory and a defining element of contemporary American race politics.

Approaching the law in this way similarly resists treating race and racism in ahistorical or moralistic terms. Where most commentators treat color-blind constitutionalism as a fixed legal rule or principle, my project understands that concept to operate within distinct sociocultural contexts, bounded by its particular historical moment, even as it references and transforms received understandings of the past. Indeed, it deserves an explanation why historicized accounts of race and law remain the exception rather than the rule. As Thomas Holt has observed, racism tends to be figured as "an anachronistic hangover from some primitive past" and at the same time, paradoxically, "*timeless*."[42] This resistance to the historicization of race is understandable, at least in one sense, as restoring to race the time-bound quality in which it necessarily is lived and experienced would deprive certain common-sense racial narratives of their evasive power. So long as racism is understood chiefly in ideational terms, as mental error, prejudice, or irrationality, its contributions to the material organization of society need not be called too greatly into question. Little wonder, then, that how individuals think and talk about race is given greater attention and priority over and against the question of who benefits and who is burdened by particular social organizations and racial practices.[43]

Moreover, the failure to historicize race and racism leaves popular conceptions of those terms fixed in place by highly visible confrontations over segregation and civil rights in the early postwar period. In part, this registers an understandable response to traumatic events, and may even record a depth of sincere moral commitment. Those who participated in the civil rights movement are lauded as moral exemplars, just as the iconic "whites only" signs of Jim Crow have become universal symbols of injustice. But the universality of condemnation also serves to limit its meaning and application, and so to insulate current racial inequality from critique. It is as if the enormity of past wrongs renders present injustices categorically distinct and politically unrecognizable. Understood in these terms, we fail to see what Patricia Hill Collins has called the "past-in-present" quality of "the new racism."[44] We fail to heed George Lipsitz's cutting observation that "there has always been racism in the United States, but it has not always been the same racism."[45]

Since the time of its founding, premised as it was upon the untenable joining of democratic freedom with chattel slavery, a central task of American political thought has been to theorize the gap between ideals of social justice and the reality of racism and other forms of domination.[46] In the nineteenth century, this formula describes the basic rhetorical structure of the American jeremiad.[47] In the post–World War II era, it was Gunnar Myrdal's *American Dilemma* that named the distance between an American creed of individualism and equal opportunity, on the one hand, and the evident fact of Negro oppression on the other.[48] Notably, Myrdal's analysis was as hopeful as it was critical. Myrdal both recognized and condemned the pervasive nature of mid-century American race prejudice, but he also viewed the elimination of racism as a choice America seemed poised to make. For Myrdal, ending segregation was necessary to (and necessarily would) bring about the perfection of American liberal democracy. Indeed, to denounce racism as "un-American" is implicitly to assert that America, in its best and truest sense, is "unracist"—despite its failure fully to honor its own ideals. The profound optimism of this view lies in its treatment of racism as anomalous to rather than constitutive of American democratic culture and institutions.

Given the benefit of more than half a century of hindsight, we recognize that racial inequality has turned out to be far more intractable than Myrdal anticipated. Were it truly an anomaly, Jennifer Hochschild observes, "racism and its effects [would] be eliminated through normal processes of political choice and policy implementation." That this has not occurred suggests "a *new American dilemma*, whose resolution is yet unknown."[49] To pose the problem of race in nonanomalous terms is to suggest that racial domination is an expression of American values rather than a failure to comply with them.[50] It is to suggest, in Hochschild's metaphor, that racism is not the noxious weed in an otherwise healthy garden, but the soil out of which all its plants must grow.[51] It is to follow the example of Charles Mills, when he writes of the "racial contract" that it "effects a gestalt shift, reversing figure and ground . . . inverting 'norm' and 'deviation,' to emphasize that non-white racial exclusion from personhood was the actual norm."[52] It is to recognize, with Joel Olson, that "racial oppression and American democracy are mutually constitutive rather than antithetical."[53] And it is in this sense that I use the term "constitutive racism," marking white supremacy as a defining element of American political and social order.

Two important shifts in postwar racial dynamics greatly transform Myrdal's American dilemma and shed light on what is distinctive about post-civil rights discourses and practices of race: the demise of scientific racism, and the widespread rejection of explicitly racist social norms. Because these are changes in kind, and not only of degree, it is misleading to frame the issue as a question of racial progress. A more fruitful approach requires careful attention to the specific forms and techniques by which white supremacy is reproduced in an age committed to the ideology of racial equality and invested in an image of itself as conforming to that ideal. How are we to understand racism in an age where biological conceptions of race have largely been discredited? What more can be said when all reasonable people readily accept (and loudly profess) that racism is indefensible and morally wrong?[54] Taken together, these two related shifts articulate a specific form of systemic racial privilege peculiar to the post-civil rights era and set the terms of the new American dilemma: "racism without racists" and "racism without race."[55]

That many will hear these phrases as contradictions in terms attests to the enduring power of Myrdal's framework. He wrote in an era only beginning to emerge from ideas about race that today seem outlandish. "Race" had assumed the status of a scientific concept, delineating biological groups thought to possess innate and immutable physical, mental, and character traits that justified the categorical exclusion and exploitation of nonwhite groups. By mid-century, Myrdal viewed these myths of Negro inferiority as the primary mechanism through which the American dilemma was "resolved."[56] If blacks did not fare as well as whites and were unable to achieve economic advancement, the rationalization went, it must be due to lack of intelligence or character or desire to take advantage of opportunities axiomatically available to all. But this strategy is no longer available today, when explicit appeals to racial characteristics are likely to be regarded as outside the bounds of legitimate argumentation or political efficacy. Where Myrdal's dilemma was reconciled by invoking the myth of black inferiority, today's new American dilemma is "resolved" rhetorically, we might say, through invocation of a myth of white innocence.[57]

Ashley Montagu famously derided race as "the witchcraft of our time."[58] And because current race politics typically are viewed from the perspective of earlier struggles against state-sponsored segregation, the decline of scientific racism in the mid-twentieth century tends to be celebrated as a victory of humanist truth and rationalism over racist prejudice and ignorance. It would be more accurate to describe this transition as marking a shift in antiracist rhetorical strategy, from that of a moral-political orientation to a more rational-scientific framework.[59] The language of rationalism lays powerful claim to the universal, and so renders the views of recalcitrant racists not only morally contemptible (a subjective judgment about which individuals might disagree) but also factually in error, backward, objectively wrong to the point of being foolish.

To be sure, the declining stability of race as a scientific category has not been matched by a comparable transformation in social structure or dismantling of the material conditions under which racialized differences become meaningful. In Toni Morrison's phrase: "The world does not become raceless or will not become unracialized by assertion."[60] The rationalist critique of race prejudice cannot be expected to produce a raceless world, but it does nonetheless constrain the terms upon which racism and white supremacy are contested. While powerfully undermining the formal institutions of racial status-hierarchy, critiques of biological race and irrational prejudice also prioritize the denial of difference over and against considerations of how those differences are positioned within a particular legal or political structure.

Much attention recently has been paid to the international context in which American racial common sense was transformed and civil rights consensus established. In the aftermath of World War II, owing both to the association of Nazism with racial science and to growing US concerns that anticolonial struggle in the nonwhite world would foster the spread of communism, overt endorsement of white supremacist ideology emerged as a serious foreign policy liability. Racial liberalism grows from this dual political need, which Jodi Melamed describes as the "suturing of U.S. globalism to official antiracisms."[61] In content as well as timing, then, desegregation can be explained as a "Cold War imperative."[62] But the domestic incentives of antiracialist discourse should not be overlooked. For if official antiracism was sutured to the American Cold War agenda, one consequence was, in Michael Dawson's phrase, "the sundering" of black radicalism from labor and anticapitalist movements on the left.[63] Litigation strategies around school desegregation further emphasized the pursuit of formal rights over struggles against material disadvantages at the intersection of race and class. Even in victory, argues Derick Bell, *Brown v. Board of Education* foreclosed "equalization strategies" that emphasized control over resources and curriculum within black communities.[64] More broadly, the cultivation of a civil rights consensus around what Gary Peller terms "the repudiation of race-consciousness" served the dual purposes of condemning white racism while simultaneously equating that racism with more militant ideologies of black nationalism.[65] The emergent consensus around civil rights thus served to silence and disqualify calls for self-determination, taking the insights of black nationalists off the political agenda. In this sense, the retreat from race may have, from its inception, provided the intellectual resources by which both white supremacy and concrete measures to dismantle racial hierarchy could be condemned with equal force.

There is, of course, real danger in overestimating the extent to which openly racist appeals will be rejected as outside the boundaries of legitimate political discourse. As we have seen, cultural pathology arguments of various kinds (absent fathers, drug use, lack of sexual or labor discipline) continue to blame working-class people of color for the failure of formal equality to yield more substantive results. Racially coded appeals to the effects of crime, drugs, immigration, and welfare continue to mobilize electoral politics with disastrously polarizing and predictable results. Nonetheless, the very necessity of speaking in code suggests that the rules of the game have shifted in meaningful ways since the era of formal segregation. Indeed, the "past-in-present" quality of contemporary racial culture must account for change as well as continuity, and for what many encounter as the intuitive appeal of color-blind ideology.

Too often this is not the case, as when "color-blind racism" is described chiefly in its covert dimensions. Framing the issue as a problem of covert racism suggests that we are dealing with the same "old-fashioned racism" as before, only now kept carefully hidden from view. Eduardo Bonilla-Silva gives this impression when he writes that "modern racial ideology does not thrive on the ugliness of the past or on the language and tropes typical of slavery and Jim Crow. Today there is a sanitized, color-blind way of calling minorities niggers, Spics, or Chinks."[66] Similarly, Ian Haney López excoriates Republican lawmakers for their use of coded racial language, or "dog-whistle politics," which formally repudiate the use of offensive racist epithets while simultaneously appealing to a sense of racialized grievance and white solidarity.[67]

These accounts get something fundamentally right about American politics. But, in a strange way, both are actually too optimistic. If color-blind racism is primarily an expression of covert white animosity, only placed under cloaked or socially acceptable disguise, then there is still hope that Myrdal was right, and that substantive equality may ensue from the sincere elimination of irrational prejudice (not just its concealment) sometime in the future. Moreover, too great a focus on secretly held noxious beliefs—and the salacious circulation of their shameful revelation—may in fact undermine analyses of race that emphasize material relationships of domination and subordination by focusing instead on those "bad ideas" (prejudice, hate) that still infect our thinking. Covert racism can explain how an individual might denounce white supremacy while continuing to benefit from it, but its explanation is one of bad faith or deception. No doubt this fairly describes some—perhaps many—of white supremacy's beneficiaries. But it is not true of all—perhaps not even most—and cannot explain the behavior of any whites for whom the idea of white supremacy is in fact sincerely abhorrent, yet who nevertheless predictably act to preserve the privileges of their whiteness.

To a lesser extent, the same may be said of explanations emphasizing how racist stereotypes have been preserved at a subconscious level of which most people are unaware. This explanation also invokes the explanatory power of deception, but turned inward, such that racist assumptions may subconsciously be held even by the most sincere antiracists as well as members of stigmatized racial groups. Unlike covert racism, subconscious racism accounts for the perfectly ordinary quality of racial hierarchy in the post-civil rights era. It also comes backed by a substantial amount of empirical data from experimental psychology.[68] So the question is not whether its claims are true, but rather how much explanatory power follows from the truth it reveals. It is important, and for some it will be startling, to be made aware of how deep such racist stereotypes run. In the context of equal protection law, this insight reveals an additional and fundamental challenge, since current antidiscrimination law typically limits provision of remedy to those harms resulting from intentional discriminatory acts. If discriminatory behavior is both pervasive and subconscious, then proof of intentionality establishes a threshold requirement nearly impossible to meet.[69]

Nonetheless, it is striking the extent to which recent interest in subconscious racism and implicit bias remains focused on *lack of consciousness* as a primary driver of racially inegalitarian social conditions. By contrast, my emphasis on the constitutive quality of American racism is meant to reorient this discussion back to the ground of racial structure, or the material conditions that govern and maintain systems of domination and racialized social control. The law, in this regard, may be understood to perform a legitimating function similar to that described by critical legal studies scholars in regard to class domination.[70] My effort to locate legal discourses upon this terrain of ideological contestation is guided by Omi and Winant's account of "racial formation," which links structure and representation through a Gramscian framework of hegemony.[71] Ideas and representations of race are not reduced to superstructural irrelevance on this view, but their significance lies primarily in their ability to advance racial interests by rendering particular policies and practices as ordinary, unremarkable, or inevitable—what Omi and Winant describe as the production of "racial common sense."[72]

Accordingly, my reading of legal discourse will emphasize its location as a crucial site for the production of racial meaning and active participant in the struggle for racial hegemony. The reproduction of white supremacy is not principally psychological in nature, and does not necessarily require race-differentiating thoughts (prejudice) or actions (discrimination), whether in overt, coded, or subconscious form.[73] Accordingly, my goal is to demonstrate neither the depths of internalized racism, nor the failure of law adequately to address issues of implicit bias, but more broadly to understand the social processes through which racial subordination is rendered legitimate, ordinary, and just—which is also to say, how racial equality comes to be seen as a violation of white rights.

Beyond Color-Blindness and Color-Consciousness

Whether the Supreme Court and other political actors understand themselves to adopt a color-blind view of the Constitution, and in what sense that phrase is to be understood, has serious consequences for the direction of public policy and allocation of resources in any number of current disputes over education, housing and employment discrimination, voting rights, racialized patterns of poverty and economic development, immigration, the prison-industrial complex, and countless others, no doubt. And yet, despite these currently pressing concerns, the popular appeal of color-blindness discourse remains tied, in large part, to its association with past struggles against racial injustice. Beneath often bitter controversies regarding the scope and nature of contemporary racism lies a surprising degree of consensus as to what these competing visions of racial equality are meant to replace. The boundaries of legitimacy for contemporary discussions of race are in this sense defined largely by reaction against those iconic institutions of America's racist past: slavery and Jim Crow segregation.

That current understandings of racial equality remain circumscribed by the rejection of past institutional forms of racial domination suggests a desire, common to positions across the ideological spectrum, to "move past" or "get beyond" race, and so to achieve a national politics finally freed from its familiar debts and resentments. Condemnation of past injustice is thus put into the service of present exoneration, just as recognition of past racial injury is joined inevitably to the promise of future redemption, with its suggestion of national release from guilt and perfection of the democratic project to which American national identity so tightly is bound.

It is understandable then, that racial justice in America has in every era been theorized chiefly in terms of *futurity*. Pursuing northern capital for black educational institutions, Booker T. Washington counseled optimism in *The Future of the American Negro*.[74] When W. E. B. Du Bois proclaimed "the problem of the twentieth century is the problem of the color-line," he did so from the vantage of 1903, and so prophesized a future defined by racial conflict.[75] Speaking at the March on Washington for Jobs and Freedom in 1963, Martin Luther King Jr. would forever bind the promise of American racial democracy to the language of dreams. Again and again, discussions of race in America return to a vision of the future that is less racialized and more just. Typically, these elements are viewed as mutually reinforcing, such that the dream of racial equality provides at the same time a fantasy of escape from racism's historical legacy.

In his three-part essay "The Future American," Charles Chesnutt lays bare this connection between racial equality, futurity, and the desire for national redemption. Publishing his essay in August 1900, Chesnutt had reviewed Washington's *Future of the American Negro* earlier that year, so his title may be read as a kind of rejoinder to Washington's conservative racial uplift project. Displacing speculation over the future fortunes of "the American Negro," Chesnutt imagines a "future American" in which racial difference has been eliminated through a steady process of intermarriage and racial mixing. Seldom acknowledged but already underway, this "mingling . . . of the various racial varieties" promised someday to create "a new American race," notable for its homogeneous appearance.[76] The achievement of a truly "American race," for Chesnutt, implies a future in which American national identity is no longer divided by racial difference.[77] In such a future, he writes, "there would be no inferior race to domineer over; there would be no superior race to oppress those who differed from them in racial externals."[78] Racial identity is dangerously corrosive of national unity, on this view. The obvious and perhaps only solution to the seemingly intractable problem of American racism, then, would be the elimination of race itself.

Notably, Chesnutt's invocation of a mixed-race future comments less upon the community of light-skinned blacks that so often appear in his novels and short stories than upon the conditions under which it is possible to imagine racial equality being realized in the United States. Consistent with Chesnutt's abiding interest in the permeability of the color line (a topic to which his fiction so often returns), the "Future American" essays have been interpreted to propose "amalgamation"—the greatest fear of nineteenth-century white racists—as the twentieth century's salvation.[79] Chesnutt's future American is the mulatto, positioned not as a tragic outsider, but as an emerging national condition.

If Chesnutt's now century-old "Future American" fantasizes a harmonious postracial future, it also functions to satirize present efforts to achieve racial democracy, and reveals something central and paradoxical about contemporary racial discourse. According to Chesnutt, there can be "no such thing as a peaceful and progressive civilization in a nation divided by two warring races"; "homogeneity of type," therefore, is "a necessary condition of harmonious social progress."[80] Read this way, and from the perspective of a future about which Chesnutt could only speculate, his amalgamationist optimism contains also a most cutting critique. For within Chesnutt's dreamlike invocation of future Americans "with no distinguishing mark"[81] is a sobering admission as to the likely permanence of American racism. To be sure, Chesnutt's readers in 1900, and many still today, were likely to experience racial difference as natural, stable, permanent, and largely unchanging. Read this way, Chesnutt's vision for the future turns out to be rather more grim, suggesting as it does that racial equality will become possible only with the elimination of race itself—a precondition so unlikely as to be regarded by his readers principally as a source of comedy.[82]

Because Chesnutt writes of and for a future without race, it is tempting to encounter his essay as a form of speculation as to the extent or likelihood of racial progress. But this is not what interests me about the essay. Rather, the future of color-blindness may be understood not as prediction, but as a question of *racial futurity* and the role it plays in constructing a shared constitutional vision. I use the term racial futurity to distinguish my project from familiar genres of doctrinal analysis and prediction of judicial outcomes, and to signal my interest in the rhetorical invocation of imagined nonracial futures as a dominant feature of both liberal and conservative color-blind discourses. Accordingly, my approach to the future of color-blindness is not limited to the practical question of what happens next—for whatever next happens with color-blind constitutionalism is bound to take shape within a narrative framework that fantasizes a future of racial transcendence and national redemption, the ideological constraints of which are the subject of this book.

Today, it is color-blind conservatives who most obviously have adopted this redemptionist view of race, albeit stripped of Chesnutt's satirical edge. Justice Scalia, for example, transports Chesnutt's "future American" into the immediate present when he writes that "we are just one race here. It is American."[83] But judicial liberals equally rely upon ideals of progress toward the next American race. Where color-blind conservatives adopt a triumphalist narrative that celebrates how far we've come on matters of race, liberals defend color-conscious policies such as affirmative action by emphasizing how far we have left to go. By insisting that we work harder to achieve the postracial society that conservatives say already is at hand, liberal color-consciousness implicitly trades upon what I term aspirational color-blindness—as an ideal rather than a rule. For if we must "first take account of race" in order to "get beyond racism," as Justice Blackmun suggests, then it is the promise of future racial transcendence that supplies color-consciousness its present justification. The very reason for "taking account" of race, on this view, turns out to be a more fundamental desire to "get beyond" it.

In calling attention to these similarities, I do not mean to suggest that liberals have the same political agenda or constitutional vision as conservatives on matters of race. To be sure, their differences are substantial and, in my view, worth fighting for. Rather, my aim is to locate those differences within a shared narrative of racial progress and national redemption, in order to demonstrate the extent to which critics of color-blindness have been defined by the object of their critique.[84] As table 1.1 illustrates, liberals and critical race theorists both advocate against the color-blind Constitution, and would allow for classification of individuals by race for nonoppressive purposes. But liberals justify color-consciousness instrumentally,

TABLE 1.1 Color-Blindness and Color-Consciousness

	ADVOCACY	NORMATIVE VIEW	LEGAL PRINCIPLE
Conservative	Color-blindness	Triumphal color-blindness	Anticlassification
Liberal	Color-consciousness	Aspirational color-blindness	Antidiscrimination
CRT	Color-consciousness	Substantive equality	Antisubordination

on the grounds that it is necessary to achieve a color-blind society in the future. Liberal color-consciousness in this sense turns out to be a kind of *aspirational color-blindness*. Critical race theorists, in contrast, advocate for color-consciousness on the grounds of a competing value (substantive equality), which is said to demonstrate the inadequacy of color-blind norms. Crucially, on all three views, color-blindness is positioned as an alternative to color-consciousness, and so as a form of racial nonrecognition. The color-blindness that conservatives view as a moral good, liberals and critical race scholars reject as normatively undesirable. By contrast, my argument is not that color-blindness is a bad idea—unjust, unfair, or unwise (although it may well be all of these things)—but that it is conceptually incoherent and fundamentally self-deceptive. My concern with color-blind constitutionalism is not that it prevents the adoption of necessary or valuable race-conscious remedies for existing inequality, but that it mobilizes its own form of white identity politics, which then is mistaken for an absence of race.

Within the current terms of debate, then, the question of how much progress has been made on matters of race remains closely linked to an apparent choice between color-blindness and color-consciousness in legal and political decision-making. Neither of these questions, I want to suggest, proves adequate for understanding the complexity of race in contemporary law and politics. Because their positions tend to be oriented by advocacy for or against color-blindness, both of which seek ultimately to get outside of or beyond race, neither liberals nor conservatives are able to account for the peculiar form of racial consciousness required by the color-blind rule.

And yet the paradoxically racializing nature of calls to prohibit or transcend race can been seen even in those narratives of racial progress intended to redeem the nation from its racist past. For every measure of civil rights progress at the same time records a legacy of oppression. In memorializing the Emancipation Proclamation, Ida B. Wells, or *Brown v. Board of Education*, we acknowledge the history of slavery, lynching, and segregation. So too, while the election of Barack Obama was rightly praised as a milestone in African American history, and widely debated as to whether it foretold a coming post-racial age, little attention was paid to the contradictory symbolic demands being made of the president's racial status. On the one hand, Obama had to be authentically black, and defined by his blackness, in order to complete an arc of civil rights progress understood to extend from Frederick Douglass through Rosa Parks and Martin Luther King Jr.[85] At the same time, however, the purported completion of that arc and cause for celebration, beyond any immediate partisan victory, was defined precisely by Obama's ability to transcend race—and by extension the nation's, by voting for him. Paradoxically, within dominant narratives of racial progress and national redemption, Obama had to be black enough to prove that his blackness no longer mattered.

Similarly, whether invoking a color-blind ideal or imposing a rule against racial classification, we both acknowledge and codify the heightened social significance of the prohibited category. To claim, as I do, that color-blindness is not a meaningful choice is to acknowledge the effect of such a prohibition when enacted or enforced in a society structured by racial hierarchy. And this matters for reasons beyond the familiar criticism that race-conscious preferences are needed to compensate for past discrimination. In practical terms, efforts to administer color-blind rules will require for their implementation a heightened awareness of race. Recognition of this fact helps us to dislodge the association of color-blindness with race-neutrality—an association upon which equal protection law increasingly has come to rely. In their brilliant article "The New Racial Preferences," Devon Carbado and Cheryl Harris make this point by way of an audacious thought-experiment. Imagining four hypothetical applicants to law school (among them are included a young Barack Obama and a young Clarence Thomas), Carbado and Harris use the applicants' autobiographical writings to create "personal statements" such as required of most applicants to colleges, universities, and professional schools. Not surprisingly, each of the personal statements contains implicit and explicit references to race: reflections on growing up marked by racial difference, confrontations with white racists, racially inflected poverty, black hair politics, and so on. How, then, should these essays be treated by admissions officers wishing to comply with "antipreference" rules that require a color-blind admissions process? As their examples show, the deracialization of personal statements leaves in place writing that, at best, does not reflect the experiences of the author and, at worst, renders their stories comically unintelligible. As Carbado and Harris wryly note: "The fact that an admissions officer understands that she is not supposed to take race into account, does not mean that she is in a cognitive position to comply with that command."[86] Under entirely ordinary circumstances such as these, implementing the color-blind rule may prove to be impossible.

The significance of this thought experiment is profound, and transforms traditional understandings of color-blindness as racially neutral and affirmative action as racially preferential. In practice, the injunction against consideration of race is not an absence of racial consciousness, nor are the burdens of its performance evenly distributed across racial groups. For applicants who consider race to be a significant aspect of their identity or experience, the deracialization of their statements is a burden not borne by applicants for whom race is perceived to be of little or no significance. That whiteness tends to function as an unstated norm—and that white people disproportionately retain the privilege of not having to think about race—ensures that the obligation to translate one's experiences into formally color-blind terms (or have them translated by an admissions officer) will fall overwhelmingly on nonwhite applicants. So-called antipreference laws that prohibit explicit consideration of race turn out to be, in this sense, rewards for "a particular way of relating to and expressing one's racial identity."[87] They are, as Carbado and Harris's title declares, "new racial preferences."

One consequence of this reformulation is to replace rearguard defenses of affirmative action (as justified racial preference) with a direct and unapologetic critique of normative whiteness. Color-blind policies only appear to be racially neutral when we fail to consider the myriad sources of institutionalized white privilege that constitute ordinary politics. Carbado and Harris provide a partial list of this well-studied phenomenon, calling attention to evidence of racially biased standardized tests, the performance-inhibiting effects of stereotype threat, racially unequal patterns of access to quality K-12 education, pervasive exposure to microaggressions by teachers and peers, lack of social capital and ability to navigate the admissions process, credential bias and racially skewed standards of merit, and so on. Taking into account these elements of structural inequality challenges traditional understandings of "preference." Seen this way, affirmative action is not a racial preference at all; it is an effort to achieve race-neutrality by helping to "counteract the structural impediments" to nonwhite applicants operating within an educational system "already stacked in ways that prefer whites and disadvantage blacks."[88]

Notably, this view challenges affirmative action's liberal defenders as much as its conservative critics. Unlike Elizabeth Anderson, who is "disinclined to press this divisive argument"[89]—or Randall Kennedy, who credits himself with a forthright acknowledgment and defense of affirmative action's racial preference ("It *does* discriminate. . . . It *does* favor preferred racial categories")[90]—the argument advanced here strikes at the core of liberal and conservative shared assumptions that color-blindness is an alternative to color-consciousness rather than a form of racial awareness. Framed as covert or subconscious racism, the impossibility of achieving color-blindness appears as a failure to live up to the race-neutral ideal, with race-consciousness as the tainted remainder that persists despite its prohibition. In contrast, I am suggesting a *form* of racial consciousness that is *constituted by its prohibition.*

Just as much as its defense, the rejection race as a basis for legislation ironically works to preserve and intensify racial consciousness by committing the state to ever-diligent enforcement of its erasure. The legal arguments, identities, advocacy groups, and political ideologies that form around this debate will of necessity be products of racial consciousness in one form or another. No organized defense or rejection of color-blindness could proceed without furthering the racial consciousness it claims to transcend. In calling attention to their shared desire for redemption and release from race, and to the stubbornly racializing social processes they enact, I hope to turn discussion away from the false choice between color-blindness and color-consciousness and to reveal the more complex and paradoxical role color-blindness discourse has played in American history, politics, and law. In place of current efforts to "get beyond race" (either now or in a more just future), I seek to open a discussion of race that moves beyond color-blindness and color-consciousness.

The premise of an unrealized yet fully authentic American racial democracy underlies both conservative and liberal formulations of antidiscrimination law. Framed within the boundaries of the American dilemma, or in celebration of "postracial" America, both positions operate upon the shared terrain of competing redemption narratives through which the condemnation of white supremacy is joined to an affirmation of America's more fundamental racial innocence. Normatively and politically these positions would appear to be diametrically opposed: color-blind or color-conscious, the latter defending what the former forbids. And yet, despite their fundamental disagreements, they share an underlying theoretical assumption about the terms of debate. Even in critical race theory's defense of color-consciousness—which tends to regard racism as "ordinary, not aberrational,"[91] and perhaps even a permanent condition of American politics and society[92]—policies such as affirmative action are defended as justifiable departures from strict antidiscrimination principles, either as temporary remedial tools to achieve a more color-blind society in the future (the liberal view), or on the authority of a competing principle of racial equality said to trump that of nondiscrimination (the antisubordination view). Accordingly, even the most ardent supporters of color-consciousness remain in important ways captured by the narrative practices of color-blind conservatism.

In the following chapters, I examine the rise and transformation of color-blind constitutionalism, giving particular attention to the rhetorical and ideological constraints it imposes on American racial discourse in both its legal and its nonlegal settings, and on critics and advocates alike. The theoretical basis for this approach is outlined in chapter 2, which identifies a narrative structure of fall and redemption within which color-blind constitutionalism operates, and against which demands for color-consciousness have been advanced. I argue that critics of color-blind legal doctrine risk being captured by this narrative, when arguments meant to justify color-consciousness implicitly concede the point that recognition of race constitutes a departure from color-blind norms. Rather than engaging debates as to the justness or constitutionality of that alleged departure, my approach challenges the narrative frame within which color-blindness discourse appears as a repudiation of race. Society will not become less conscious of race by barring race-specific legislation—and not only because social goods continue to be distributed in a racially inegalitarian manner. By their nature, I argue, prohibitions against racial classification heighten and preserve racial awareness, in direct contradiction of their stated goals and justification.

In chapter 3, I seek to recover some of the complexity in color-blindness discourse by returning to its origins in the *Plessy* case, which I read less as a textual authority for the antisubordination/anticlassification debate than for its evident concern over racial indeterminacy and the productive power of law as a race-making institution. That complexity is put to use in chapter 4, which examines the slow transformation of color-blind constitutionalism in the post-*Brown* implementation cases. Against popular narratives in which color-blindness supplies the initial and authentic desegregation vision—only to be corrupted by affirmative action's subsequent reintroduction of race-consciousness—this chapter situates color-blind constitutionalism within the coordinated efforts of southern white moderates to resist integration of public schools.

The consequences of this transformation have not been fully appreciated, and are not limited to neoconservative attacks on race-conscious policies such as affirmative action. Chapter 5 identifies two related trends in the Supreme Court's post-*Brown* equal protection decisions. First, in the affirmative action cases, judicial conservatives established a rights-based defense of white political interests that relied upon strong powers of judicial review, typically associated with legal liberalism. Second, while this version of conservative judicial activism necessarily requires a strong recognition of white victims *as a group*, it does not in fact require the state's use of racial classifications to animate its equal protection claims. The pursuit of racial equality, therefore, and not just the use of race-conscious remedies as a means for achieving it, may thus be rendered constitutionally suspect. Taken to its logical conclusion, these developments force us to consider the troubling question: is racial equality unconstitutional?

The Supreme Court has not, as yet, acceded to this ultimate conclusion. Nonetheless, within the terms of the Court's prevailing racial narratives, it is difficult to see how such a conclusion could be avoided. Existing critiques of color-blind constitutionalism demonstrate how such a view deprives policymakers of the tools necessary to achieve a more racially equitable society. However, in justifying color-consciousness as a normatively preferable alternative, these criticisms implicitly accept the underlying racial narratives and constitutional principles of current equal protection doctrine. Consequently, they fail adequately to acknowledge or challenge the transformation of racial equality from an ideal of justice to a constitutionally illegitimate goal. I conclude, in chapter 6, by taking up the question of political possibility within a legal system constituted by racial domination. If I am right that racial equality may not be achievable within the current American constitutional order, then we ought to look elsewhere, for an antiredemptive political vision upon which to found an authentic racial democracy.

CHAPTER 2 | Constitutive Racism, Redemptive Constitutionalism

WHEN THURGOOD MARSHALL DIED in 1993, just two years after retiring from the Supreme Court, his official commemoration provided the occasion for Judge Constance Baker Motley to retell the story of Justice Marshall's "Bible." Judge Motley, who worked with Marshall at the NAACP Legal Defense Fund, recalled how "Marshall had a 'Bible' to which he turned during his most depressed moments. The 'Bible' would be known in the legal community as the first Justice Harlan's dissent in *Plessy v. Ferguson*." Judge Motley's telling of the story adopts a sacrosanct tone wholly appropriate for the occasion: the memorialization of a revered Supreme Court justice, one of the primary architects of the legal strategy to defeat Jim Crow, and the first African American to serve on the Supreme Court:

> I remember the pre-*Brown* days when Marshall's legal staff would gather around him at a table in our small office and discuss possible new legal theories for attacking segregation. Marshall would read aloud passages from Harlan's amazing dissent. I do not believe we ever filed a major brief in the pre-*Brown* days in which a portion of that opinion was not quoted. Marshall's favorite quotation was, "Our Constitution is color-blind." It became our basic legal creed.[1]

In telling this story, on this occasion, the narration of Marshall's devotion to Harlan's text may be understood to perform a kind of double canonization. On its face, the story makes a claim for Marshall's well-deserved inclusion in the judicial pantheon. It situates him in relation to an already established and celebrated figure from the Court's history. Moreover, by invoking his central role in *Brown*, the case that effectively overturned *Plessy*, Marshall becomes the agent of Harlan's vindication and proper inheritor of his legacy. But at the same time, one may plausibly read the association as securing Harlan's place on "the right side of history" in a time when the rightness of the *Brown* decision seemed clearer than the articulation of any specific legal principle for which the opinion stands. In the redemptive language of this memoriam, it may be the case that Harlan sanctifies Marshall rather less than Marshall is made to sanctify the color-blind Constitution.[2]

Seen from this perspective, we may note the story's appearance in a 2007 opinion by Clarence Thomas, who in 1991 filled the seat left vacant by Marshall's retirement. But in this case, the quote is put to a quite different purpose—as evidence to support Justice Thomas's view that race-conscious voluntary integration policies violate the Equal Protection Clause of the Fourteenth Amendment. Writing in a separate opinion, Justice Thomas is not content merely to show the unconstitutionality of the integration plan or the superiority of his own constitutional interpretation; he insists also on laying claim to the legacy of Harlan, Marshall, and *Brown* as supporting his views. Having quoted the above sections of Judge Motley's remarks, Thomas declares: "I am quite comfortable in the company I keep. My view of the Constitution is Justice Harlan's view in *Plessy*: 'Our Constitution is color-blind, and neither knows nor tolerates classes among citizens.' And my view was the rallying cry for the lawyers who litigated *Brown*."[3]

Whether Thomas's view of the Constitution is correct, desirable, or even plausible, it unquestionably was not the view of Thurgood Marshall. Indeed, it is difficult to imagine two views less similar than those held by Justices Thomas and Marshall regarding the constitutional meaning of racial equality.[4] How is it, then, that both men could embrace Justice Harlan's dissent and the figure of a color-blind Constitution as a privileged source of constitutional interpretation? How could judges with such contradictory views each assign near-sacred status to this text? How might the phrase's origins influence our assessment of its current application, and what do their competing claims tell us about the constitutional principle it announces? These differing uses of Harlan's phrase reflect significant differences in the historical periods in which the authors wrote. Unlike Justice Thomas, Justices Harlan and Marshall both used and understood the phrase from within the context of existing state-mandated racial segregation. Justice Thomas's use of the phrase, by contrast, both reflects and contributes to a particular vision of race in the post-civil rights era.

Accordingly, the anecdote raises questions central to contemporary discussions of race, law, and politics.

If the minority rights movements of the 1960s initiated America's second Reconstruction, the period of racial retrenchment that followed marks the beginning of America's second Redemption. The era is marked by profound economic and political realignment: the waning of Keynesian economic policy; domestic deindustrialization and related increases in the quantity and speed of global capital flow; the rise of the new Right and emergence of new and stable electoral majorities for the Republican Party, based for the first time in southern and Sun Belt states. The extent to which Republican electoral majorities were consciously engineered along racial lines has been well documented by scholars of American political development and party systems.[5] This political realignment also had far-reaching consequences for the Supreme Court, in terms of both composition and ideology. Under the influence of ten consecutive Republican appointments (four of them by President Nixon), the Court was converted from a champion of racial equality to an adversary.

However, unlike previous eras of racial reaction—which relied heavily on explicit appeals to biological superiority/inferiority—the post-civil rights retrenchment occurred within a newly established rhetorical frame of color-blind individualism. Because "racial equality had to be acknowledged as a desirable goal," Omi and Winant explain, opponents of civil rights embraced the language of equality but also "*rearticulated* its meaning. Racial reaction repackaged the earlier themes—infusing them with new political meaning and linking them to other key elements of conservative ideology."[6] In this sense, color-blind constitutionalism grew up with, through, and for a constellation of racial interests it openly disavowed. Chapter 1 placed color-blind constitutionalism in the context of post-civil rights racial ideology; in this chapter, I focus on its narrative form, its deployment of redemptive political rhetoric, and the capacity of redemption narratives to obscure the particular form of racial awareness upon which the color-blind principle depends.

American Prophecy, Race, and Redemption

For several reasons, discussions of race in America have been closely linked to the religiously grounded themes of sin, atonement, and redemption.[7] It has been suggested that liberalism itself (with its foundational texts playing and replaying their own origin stories in various states of nature) represents a secularized version of Christianity's epochal transformation of the human spirit, and so also redemption from violence.[8] These themes have particular purchase in the US context, marked as it is by a self-conception of American exceptionalism and being a "chosen people" upon whom the responsibility for bringing liberty and equality into the world especially falls. And it is against this sense of chosenness that the legacy of American slavery is defined as a kind of original sin for which is required a national redemption earned through acts of atonement.[9] In his Second Inaugural Address, Abraham Lincoln gave meaning to the violence of the Civil War by framing it in just these terms. Blood spilled on the battlefield became both righteous punishment and means of redemption. "This terrible war," given by a just God, would wash away the sin of slavery: "every drop of blood drawn with the lash shall be paid by another drawn with the sword."[10]

By linking Civil War suffering not only to punishment but also to atonement, Lincoln underscores the paradoxically restorative potential to create a new nation that is yet more authentically American than the American nation it destroys.[11] In this sense, redemption is always an act of recovery, through which the redeemed object returns to an origin that previously had existed only in compromised or "fallen" form.[12] The gap between American slavery and American freedom (for Myrdal, between segregation and the "American creed") establishes this national need, with the promise of redemption suggesting the completion or perfection of unchanging yet unachieved national ideals. This return to origins need not be a conservative veneration of the actually existing past. Rather, it turns the unfulfilled promise of the past against current injustices in order to restore the founding ideals of freedom and equality. As the poet Langston Hughes wrote: "O, let America be America again— / The land that never has been yet— / And yet must be—the land where *every* man is free."[13]

This mode of criticism adopts the rhetorical form of a jeremiad, which narrates injustice as breach of covenant—and so as corruption, infidelity, or decline. Named for Jeremiah of the Hebrew Bible, it is a prophetic form of address long identified as a central rhetorical tradition within American public culture.[14] By its nature, the jeremiad cuts in more than one direction, fusing condemnation with exoneration, punishment with release. In his masterful account of the prophetic tradition in American political thought, George Shulman positions the jeremiad as a resource for progressive politics in a "left Puritan tradition" that would reject the antinationalist tenor of much of the contemporary academic Left. Seeking "native ground for democratic projects,"[15] Shulman would "recast the political meaning of redemption" in order to save it both from conservative evangelicals (Jerry Falwell, Pat Robertson) and from left critics (Sacvan Bercovitch) who see in it no other political trajectory.[16]

For Bercovitch, the limitations of prophetic speech owe less to the stated conservatism of its principal authors, than to the jeremiad's rhetorical structure, which necessarily grounds critique within the shared values of those it would correct. The result, on his view, is always to contain the criticism it enables. The rightness of American ideals is confirmed in every accusation that America has failed to live up to them. This does not, of course, foreclose criticism of American wrongdoing, either in its treatment of excluded groups within the nation, or as US imperialism. It does, however, condition that criticism upon the promise of redemption and acceptance of a more foundational American virtue. In terms of contemporary racial ideology, as discussed in chapter 1, the jeremiad form may be understood to facilitate a critique of "anomalous" racism within the liberal framework of the American dilemma. However, if Bercovitch is right, it also forecloses a critique of what I am calling *constitutive* racism, by which I mean the kind of racial domination out of which American liberalism grew, through which it was constituted, and which continues to flourish alongside good-faith application of liberal law and social policy.

If the denunciation of racism as "un-American" suggests a more authentic "unracist" America, it worth recalling Malcolm X's admonition, "I am not an American. I am one of the 22 million black people who are the victims of Americanism."[17] Significantly, Malcolm X did not purport to be a victim of *false* Americanism. Had he framed his critique in this way, he would have spoken as a prophet sent to redeem American democracy— as a truer representative of American democracy than the bigots against whom he struggled. But instead, and despite his geographical presence upon "native ground," Malcolm X spoke as an outsider, addressing those he viewed as fellow outsiders who failed in some basic way to recognize themselves as such. Where King's Southern Christian Leadership Conference claimed the motto "To redeem the soul of America," Malcolm X's project instead sought to disrupt the redemptive terms of the American jeremiad. More than this, as Nikhil Singh notes, the elevation of King into "a redemptive national icon" required the twinned suppression of King's criticism of US imperialism (the Vietnam War especially) and his basic agreement with the political diagnosis of black militants (linking US imperialism to racism, poverty, and global economic exploitation).[18] King's hagiography cannot easily be separated from a corresponding demonology of black militancy.[19] Or, as Shulman concedes, "The rhetorics of redemption as deliverance always seem to identify the saved by marking the damned."[20]

Nonetheless, Shulman offers a compelling account for why prophecy has been the dominant mode of address in American antiracist thought, and why redemption in particular so thoroughly structures popular understandings of racism and racial equality. According to Shulman, "To face race in America is to be compelled toward prophecy. For American liberalism is constituted by disavowing its deep connection to racial domination."[21] Inverting Bercovitch, for whom the jeremiad always contains its own criticism, Shulman finds in prophetic speech the resources to "provoke acknowledgment of domination and its disavowal, to depict accountability, to affirm democratic commitments, and to redefine collective purpose."[22] This form of address necessarily is grounded in values held in common with those who it would reform, yet it does not leave those values or the self-understanding of the dominant culture undisturbed. On the contrary, it is the vocation of prophets to "announce truths their audience is invested in denying," not by correcting an error, as with the claim by mid-century liberals that biological races do not exist, but by addressing "a partly willful blindness" and announcing "realities we must acknowledge if we are to flourish."[23] For Shulman, that is, prophetic speech is uniquely well suited to the task of challenging racial domination precisely because white supremacy operates through acts of disavowal and refusal of self-knowledge. Accordingly, successful antiracist challenges depend less upon demonstration of the wrongness of racism than upon revelation of complicity by those who claim to be innocent yet remain deeply invested in that disavowal.[24]

In constitutional terms, the call to prophecy and redemption responds to the fundamental contradiction of slavery's place in the American founding, or what Mark Graber helpfully terms "constitutional evil."[25] The problem is not only that American citizenship has always contained racially inegalitarian traditions that compete with those of liberalism and civic republicanism, as Rogers Smith maintains.[26] Rather, American slavery and freedom were dialectically linked from the beginning. As Edmund Morgan famously demonstrated, slavery not only coexisted with the expansion of democratic freedom, it also made that freedom possible (for some, but categorically unobtainable for others) and so constituted an essential part of the new nation's most basic structure.[27] The necessity of redemption thus echoes back the elevation of slavery to the protected status of constitutional right from the time of the founding. At the same time, it presents something of a puzzle, as the process necessarily relies upon an ideal of

American origins as the basis for rejecting the conditions that the actual founding embraced and protected in the form of federally enforceable constitutional rights.

One possible solution to this puzzle may be found in Jack Balkin's theory of "constitutional redemption."[28] Framing long-standing debates between originalists and living constitutionalists as a problem of democratic legitimacy in the face of doctrinal change, Balkin grounds the authority of evolving constitutional construction upon a fixed framework of rules, standards, and principles that together comprise the Constitution's original meaning.[29] Unlike traditional theories of original intent, the goal of which is to constrain the subjective interpretations of future generations, Balkin finds in the fixed authority of the past an obligation for precisely that sort of constitutional development that renders the Constitution a living document. That this future-oriented process is viewed as a perfection of past ideals and original constitutional meaning is what gives the theory its redemptive quality, as an always flawed or "fallen" Constitution is redeemed and returned to the Constitution it always aspired to be but has yet to achieve.

On this theory of constitutional change, the evolving content of particular constitutional rights and values is set in motion by the past, but not determined by it. What those founding principles may some day come to mean must therefore be contingent upon the outcome of fiercely contested political and legal struggle, popular mobilization, and eventual acceptance by a large enough portion of the citizenry as to secure their democratic legitimacy. Accordingly, redemptive constitutionalism is consistent with Bruce Ackerman's generative account of constitutional revision outside of the formal Article V amendment process, and the crucial role of popular legitimation it describes in moments of constitutional crisis.[30] It is also consistent with Larry Kramer's vigorous defense of popular constitutionalism and the principle that interpretive authority over the Constitution rests ultimately with "the people themselves."[31] On each of these views, the development of constitutional law is necessarily political, and not principally because it is guided by living individuals with their own partialities and personal motivations. Rather, constitutional meaning is the product of a more deeply political process, through which the people exercise the power of popular sovereignty.

But constitutional development, like constitutional debate, is also political in another sense, which outstrips immediate questions of doctrine, rule, or policy, and which at the same time calls our attention to the contested status of "the people." For constitutions are not only the products or expressions of collective will, they are also agents of its creation. As Jason Frank convincingly argues, "The people are a provisional *achievement* of claims-making rather than their pre-existing ground."[32] A perpetually contested and notoriously unstable category, the people are *enacted* through processes of constitutional claim-making, and so cannot provide a prepolitical basis for evaluating rival constitutional interpretations. In these productive spaces, which Frank terms "constituent moments," what is constituted, paradoxically, is precisely the political community upon whose authority constitutional power is exercised. My focus on discourses of constitutional law, in turn, is meant to attend to the heightened symbolic and ideological weight such discourses are thus made to carry. Put slightly differently, racial redemption narratives are both claims for a color-blind rule and enactments of a particularly racialized political community.

This understanding of legal language is consistent with James Boyd White's theorization of law as a species of "constitutive rhetoric" more than a system of rules or set of authoritative commands.[33] Law is both a narrative process and a performative act, White claims. It is "a way of telling a story about what happened in the world and claiming a meaning for it," and at the same time "an art of persuasion that creates the objects of its persuasion, for it constitutes both the community and the culture it commends."[34] Accordingly, the significance of legal argumentation cannot be reduced, instrumentally, to its precedential value or the policy outcomes it compels in a particular line of cases. My reading of Supreme Court cases, therefore, attends carefully to the narrative conventions and rhetorical practices through which legal arguments compete for legitimacy. As Robert Cover observed in "Nomos and Narrative," our normative world is "held together by the force of shared interpretive commitments."[35] This irreducibly narrative quality of law renders it an essentially cultural enterprise, despite being bounded by the specific material conditions and relationships of power in which cultural productions necessarily take form.[36] For this reason, any analysis of color-blind constitutionalism that limits its investigation to the realm of doctrinal rules and policy implications will be incomplete at best.

My purpose in drawing connections between the quintessentially American rhetoric of redemption and the narrative structure of legal discourses concerning race is not to position the Supreme Court as bearer of prophetic speech. Rather, I want to consider what consequences follow from the fact that constitutional law seems almost exclusively to operate within this rhetorical field in regard to race, and to suggest that color-blind constitutionalism derives its authority as much from its narrative structure as from formal legal rules or doctrine. As I argued in chapter 1, liberal and conservative incarnations of the antidiscrimination principle share in this redemptive frame, which has worked in law to facilitate disavowal of inequality rather than to challenge it. In the following sections, I trace narratives of fall and redemption through contemporary arguments both for and against the color-blind Constitution. Redemption narratives on both sides of the debate conceive color-blindness as an absence of (or deliverance from) racial consciousness—as the pursuit of Chesnutt's "next American race"—and so also conceal the race conscious logic of color-blind constitutionalism.

The Fall . . . and the Rise of Color-Blind Constitutionalism

With remarkable consistency, contemporary arguments for color-blind constitutionalism share a common narrative structure. Typically, the story goes somewhat as follows: Long ago, this nation was stained by the sin of slavery, and later by segregation. The laws did not treat individuals with equal dignity and respect, but instead made arbitrary distinctions that treated people differently based solely on their race or color. After great struggle and much sacrifice the nation confronted this sin and, spurred on by the example of great men like Martin Luther King Jr., sought to effect his noble dream by abolishing all racial distinctions in the law. Finally, all citizens would be treated the same—without regard to their race, color, or ethnicity.[37]

As is often the case with redemption narratives, the structure suggests a golden age, the recovery of which holds the key to collective restoration of lost innocence. In this case, the golden age is notably brief, dating to the *Brown* decision of 1954, in which a unanimous Supreme Court struck down segregation, and so vindicated Justice Harlan's celebrated *Plessy* dissent. "Our Constitution is colorblind," the story goes, became part of the nation's basic law upon ratification of the Fourteenth Amendment, received its strongest formulation in Harlan's dissent, was officially confirmed in *Brown v. Board of Education* (1954), and was finally accomplished when the Civil Rights Act of 1964 was signed into law. But the golden age did not last. Soon, for reasons of moral weakness or ignorance or shame or greed, the great principle of antidiscrimination was sacrificed and the nation returned (sometime in the 1970s) to its former ways of discrimination: this time in the form of affirmative action and "special preferences" for minorities.

On this moral and constitutional vision, affirmative action marks a departure from the color-blind principles of the civil rights movement and discriminates on the basis of race. This time its victims are white (and sometimes Asian) rather than black (and sometimes Latino), but there is no principled distinction between the two, and the constitutional violation is precisely equivalent. That the former victims of discrimination would now call for its return merely adds a note of tragic irony: affirmative action betrays the legacy of the civil rights movement; its advocacy by black leadership substitutes clannish self-interest for principled individualism. If slavery represents America's original sin—and *Brown v. Board of Education* its redemption—then affirmative action is narrated as a kind of second fall: from nondiscrimination to special preferences, from equal opportunity to racial quotas, from color-blindness back to color-consciousness, from redemption back to sin.

If this narrative seems overly simplistic, it is all the more surprising how frequently it recurs in the writing of advocates for color-blind constitutionalism. The narrative is historical only in the sense that it orders and periodizes events, mediating our relationship to the past. In this case, the story arc is national as well as temporal, delivering America, as moral agent, from the depths of segregation to the peak of color-blind equality—and back. Andrew Kull's influential legal history *The Color-Blind Constitution*, for example, opens with this sketch of hard-earned national redemption and subsequent fall:

> From the 1840s to the 1960s, the profoundest claim of those who fought the institution of racial segregation was that the government had no business sorting people by the color of their skin, regardless of the equality with which they were treated. By some point in the mid-1960s . . . this once-radical idea had become part of the governing liberal consensus of American political life. But the achievement at long last of "equality before the law" revealed a harsh truth that the long struggle for civil rights had tended to obscure: the fact that guarantees of legal equality would be inadequate to redress the inequality of condition afflicting black Americans as a group. Almost at once, the field of debate shifted; and the older civil rights ideal has since stood as the most widely voiced objection to the race-conscious methods by which, in the post-civil rights era, a fuller measure of equality has generally been sought.[38]

Even while naming the "harsh truth" that formal equality could not deliver on promises of material change, Kull positions resistance to "inequality of condition" as something new and unique, at odds with civil rights rather than its core. Figured this way, Kull fixes the true meaning of civil rights as a moral "achievement," both in the sense of accomplishment and as a recoverable standard of judgment.

On the logic of this strict periodization, America not only begins in a fallen state (the sin of slavery for which Lincoln thought the Civil War served as penance), but also is redeemed from that sin through the accomplishment of civil rights. Several consequences implicitly follow from this staging of the past. First, the full weight of national purpose secures color-blindness as the definitive formulation of racial justice. The achievement of color-blindness is what gives meaning to past suffering (slavery, discrimination) and sacrifice (by the nation, collectively, to secure its innocence). "For approximately 125 years," Kull writes, the color-blind ideal was "the ultimate legal objective of the American civil rights movement."[39] As such, the characterization of integration and affirmative action policies as a fall from freshly achieved innocence also assigns responsibility for contemporary racial inequality—not in the persistence of racial injustice, but in black excess.

This exercise in historical periodization, which amounts also to an assignation of blame, comes out clearly in Robert Bork's *Slouching toward Gomorrah*, in which he condemns affirmative action for, among other things, "destroying what America means."[40] According to Bork, "It is ironic that racism and sexism have been discovered to be the deep, almost ineradicable, sickness of this culture at precisely the time when they have been successfully overcome. If they have not entirely disappeared, they are mere wisps of their former selves, except when it comes to white, heterosexual males."[41] White innocence pairs seamlessly with white victimization. But if 1964 signifies the pivot point around which this reversal of roles takes place, the narration strains to explain why civil rights leadership so quickly abandoned what it fought so hard to achieve. Bork notes as an irony that the fall occurs "at precisely the same time" as the achievement—mirroring Kull's observation that the achievement of color-blindness and its abandonment happened "almost at once." Similarly, with Nathan Glazer's early criticisms of affirmative action:

In the middle of the last decade, we in the United States seemed to have reached a national consensus as to how we should respond to the reality of racial and ethnic-group difference. Almost simultaneously, we began to move away from that consensus into new divisions and a new period of conflict and controversy.[42]

On Glazer's telling, the civil rights movement represents both a commitment to color-blindness and a moment of national "consensus." It is only after black leadership "moved away" from color-blindness that the country was thrown back into "conflict"—a movement he describes as happening "almost simultaneously." The language of national consensus is redemptive, and figures the commitment to civil rights (rather than, say, massive resistance) as authentically American, even as it enacts a backlash against those very rights by equivocating the color-conscious policies of integration and affirmative action to segregation or Jim Crow: "Having placed into law [in 1954] the dissenting opinion of *Plessy v. Ferguson* that our constitution is color-blind, we entered into a period of color- and group-consciousness with a vengeance."[43]

Glazer's rendering of affirmative action as "vengeance" is telling, and helps to explain his reading of minority set-aside admissions plans as "say[ing] in effect, 'no whites or males need apply.' "[44] Conjuring the implausible image of elite colleges and universities turned "blacks only" by reverse Jim Crow, the rhetorical connection between segregation and "racial preferences" narrates affirmative action both as fall from universal principle and as an exercise in equivalent racist practices by racism's former victims.[45] The tone suggests a certain psychological gratification in the reversal of roles, as those who may feel perpetually accused of racism stake a claim now as victims of "the new racism."[46] Thus, in Nino Graglia's succinct formulation, the Constitution, as interpreted by the Supreme Court, "first permitted racial discrimination in public schools in order to separate the races, then prohibited such discrimination, and now often requires such discrimination in order to increase racial mixing."[47]

This rhetorical reversal is authorized, in large part, through the trope of "departure" in color-blind advocacy, which pairs a temporal shift with an asserted shift in moral principle. For Morris Abram, "The Civil Rights movement has *turned away* from its original principled campaign for equal justice under law," replacing the opportunity for a "fair shake" with group-based result-oriented "social engineering."[48] For Thomas Sowell, white supporters of civil rights were "*betrayed* as the original concept of equal individual opportunity evolved toward a concept of equal group results."[49] In both cases—as with the familiar oppositions between equal treatment and preferential treatment, equal opportunity and equal results, or anti-discrimination and affirmative action—advocates of color-blind constitutionalism invest their positions with the moral authority of the civil rights movement, even while reducing the substantive meaning of civil rights to little more than the formal rejection of racial classification. The result is a psychic inversion of existing material hierarchy, by which the current beneficiaries of white privilege appear as victims of racial discrimination morally and legally equivalent to that of Jim Crow.[50]

The narrative of "fall" in color-blind advocacy thus accomplishes what cannot be achieved through argument alone: the appropriation of civil rights discourse, even when the individuals being quoted explicitly endorsed positions impossible to reconcile with those of color-blind conservatism.[51] In the span of just three pages, for example, William Reynolds (assistant attorney general for civil rights under Reagan) manages to quote Thurgood Marshall, Earl Warren, Edmund Muskie, Hubert Humphrey, Roy Wilkins, Jack Greenberg, Martin Luther King Jr., and the first Justice Harlan.[52] There is little room for nuance in such uses of the past. Reynolds cites King's "dream" speech at the Washington Monument, but he ignores King's implicit demand for affirmative action in *Where Do We Go from Here?* He quotes Thurgood Marshall's appeal to the Court in *Brown v. Board*, but ignores Marshall's explicit defense of affirmative action as a member of that Court.[53]

The narrative and rhetorical practices of color-blind constitutionalism assert a deep connection to the civil rights movement that is in sharp contradiction to the policy and doctrinal agenda they serve. In this regard, they exemplify what Omi and Winant have described as a strategy of "rearticulation" characteristic of racial hegemony in the post-civil rights era.[54] Rather than directly confronting the victories of the civil rights movement (seeking to overturn *Brown v. Board*, for example), they would contest their meaning, redirecting the symbolic and ideological resources of past struggle so as to preserve existing racial hierarchy. One measure of their success in this Gramscian "war of position" is the extent to which this narrative frame comes to feel as common sense, and so helps define the terrain upon which legitimate disagreement may be founded. The strategic embrace of "postracialism" in liberal legal arguments and political messaging supplies just one example of how critics of the color-blind become captured by the object of their critique.[55]

In its most familiar form, conservatives invoke the language of postracialism to suggest a completion of the civil rights project, a transcendence of race, or an overcoming of past racial guilt and responsibility.[56] The "post" in postracial emphasizes a sharp break from the past, both to celebrate the achievement of American racial democracy and to reject asserted connections between current inequality and previous eras of explicit state-sanctioned discrimination.[57] The assertion of postracialism thus suggests redemption from a tainted past and deliverance into a more racially just future. For those who describe America as having entered the postracial era, that future has already arrived.

But conservatives are not the only ones to embrace the language and practices of postracialism. Increasingly, liberals have come to adopt a set of political strategies that de-emphasize race in favor of "universal" programs with comparatively broader political support. On this strategy, racial groups stand to benefit from universal programs, and may do so without triggering the racial backlash associated with targeted programs such as affirmative action. This form of postracialism may be understood as a kind of strategic color-blindness. As Ian Haney-Lopez describes it, this "post-racial calculus" is an agreement that "race should not be allowed to become a distraction from non-racial issues ostensibly more amenable to political resolution, and which in any event might do more to budge racial disparities."[58] Despite their differing political goals, then, liberal and conservative messaging often converge around the rejection of race. Mindful of color-blindness's hegemonic status, postracialism fearfully responds by adopting its basic premises. In this sense, liberal postracialism represents both a response to color-blindness and a strategic version of it.

One consequence of this convergence is the systemic erasure of inquiry into the structural causes of racial inequality. Following Daniel Martinez HoSang's crucial work on racial issue-framing in California ballot initiatives, Gary Delgado identifies postracialism as "the standard operating procedure" in various liberal policy fights, ranging from affirmative action and healthcare to criminal justice and immigration reform. "In every circumstance, the advice offered by foundation-supported messaging experts has been the same: 'Don't mention race.'"[59] In part, this strategy follows from research by progressive social scientists such as George Lakoff and Theda Skocpol.[60] But Delgado's larger point is to show how activists and professional media consultants have used this research to prioritize short-term political gains at the expense of long-term ideological engagement. Indeed, the fundamental premise of strategic postracialism is to "*avoid challenging the electorate's beliefs about race and racism*," on the assumption that such a challenge "would be a sure way to trigger White antagonism, and thereby to lose."[61] Short-term political incentives thus encourage the convergence of liberal and conservative rejections of race, leaving discussion of structural racism outside of or beyond racial common sense. Liberal postracialism, that is, plays to color-blind common sense rather than challenging it.

It is not surprising, then, that critiques of color-blindness and postracialism (operationalized by the political imperative, "Don't mention race") so often are framed as demands for racial consciousness, breaking of silence, or recognition of voice.[62] Delgado's critique of postracialism, for example, bears the title "the costs of racial silence."[63] Haney-Lopez makes a similar pitch for race-conscious advocacy that replaces silence with voice: "Silence on race spells defeat for liberalism," he explains. "By staying silent, liberals . . . cede the public square to racial demagogues."[64] In contrast, the path forward requires support for "voices outside the administration willing to raise issues of racial injustice," and "give voice to concerns about racial discrimination."[65] In place of silence, progressive political actors must "put race front and center in voter's consciousness."[66]

Framed as a choice between voice and silence, this call for racial consciousness registers the political urgency of challenging color-blind norms. Moreover, and for precisely the reasons Delgado and Haney-Lopez set forth, such race-conscious advocacy has been the primary vehicle of that critique. But there is good reason to resist this framing of the question, which in fact mirrors the broader impasse between color-blindness and color-consciousness. In both cases, sensory metaphors are used to signify the repression, absence, or lack of racial consciousness (silence implies the absence of voice, blindness the lack of vision), leaving in place the suggestion that color-blindness is a rejection of racial consciousness rather than an assertion of white racial identity.

Viewed this way, however, demands for racial consciousness also confirm the orienting power of the color-blind norm against which they react. Critics of color-blindness who refuse to dissemble—unlike strategic postracialists—are left to argue, again and again, that "race matters" in a society evidently structured by racial hierarchy and domination. And, of course, they are right. But in accepting these terms of debate, the argument against postracialism leaves in place the seemingly nonracial character of arguments "against race." Rather than demonstrating, once more, that America has yet to achieve its postracial dream, my approach suggests we are better served by turning our attention to investigate just what kind of racial consciousness is betrayed by this noisy demand for silence.

Why, for example, should the call for racial nonrecognition be allowed to pass as the rejection of race-consciousness? Arguably, it is those most fiercely opposed to racial classification, affirmative action, and identity politics who have race "front and center" in their minds. And why, we might ask, should the herculean efforts of postracial liberals to avoid talking about race count as evidence that race is *not* in their consciousness? Gary Delgado is right to point out the pervasive nature of postracial strategies, which he notes are "legitimated by academics, supported by philanthropic institutions, and delivered by professional communications organizations to activists engaged in state and local fights all over the country."[67] But we might notice as well, from this list, just how much talk about race is required by the call for racial silence. In both its color-blind and strategically postracial forms, racial "absence" is a product of extensive, racially conscious political work.[68]

Constitutionalizing Redemption

There is little doubt that in recent years the Supreme Court has moved steadily closer to the anticlassification interpretation of the Fourteenth Amendment's Equal Protection Clause. After a period of some doctrinal uncertainty, three elements of emerging consensus have become clear: First, strict scrutiny is the appropriate standard of review in all cases involving racial classifications (whether the purpose of the classification is invidious or benign).[69] Second, student body diversity in higher education is a compelling interest, and therefore justifies appropriately designed affirmative action programs under strict scrutiny analysis.[70] Third, while it is also a compelling state interest to remedy "identified acts of discrimination" by specific individuals or institutions, redress of general racial inequalities or "societal discrimination" is not a compelling state interest and cannot justify race-based remedial policies.[71]

Taken together, these principles install a constitutional presumption of color-blindness from which policies may depart only under extraordinary circumstances. Their significance, however, derives less from doctrinal constraints on policy than from the narrative practices they establish. Indeed, the narrative arc of fall and redemption, so prominent in conservative legal writing, is now equally on display as a controlling metaphor in the Supreme Court's recent equal protection analysis.

In at least two regards, the rhetoric of color-blindness gathers its force through an asserted relationship to the past. First, the claim to a golden age of desegregation distinguishes current material inequalities between races (seen as constitutionally unproblematic) from the older and more explicit forms of racial segregation that it vigorously condemns. In this sense, color-blind rhetoric asserts a sharp historical break that denies any similarity between past and present techniques for the maintenance of white supremacy. But in another sense, framing the injury of segregation principally in terms of racial classification suggests a strong continuity with the past, since it enables the identification of current efforts to minimize racial inequality with a previous era of state-mandated racial segregation.

Critical race theorists have been particularly attentive to the distancing rhetoric in current antidiscrimination law, which labors to deny connections between current racial inequality and past discrimination. Thomas Ross theorizes this denial of past harm in terms of "a rhetoric of innocence" meant to conceal the fact that "white people generally have benefitted from the oppression of people of color."[72] For example, when referring to whites in affirmative action discourse, Supreme Court opinions often substitute the phrase "innocent persons"—as when Justice Powell expresses concern for "innocent persons" forced "to bear the burdens of redressing grievances not of their making,"[73] or disapproves of advantaging "persons perceived as members of relatively victimized groups at the expense of other innocent individuals,"[74] or when Justice Stewart decries "taking detrimental action against innocent people on the basis of the sins of others of their own race."[75]

The sense of innocence used here denies individual culpability for collective wrongs. But it also limits responsibility for racial justice to particular agents of "identifiable" discriminatory acts while, at the same time, denying the link between those acts and current racial inequality. Racial inequality persists under a regime of formal equality, but is reclassified so as to be no longer legally cognizable. For example, in *Richmond v. Croson*,[76] Justice O'Connor acknowledged that only 0.67 percent of Richmond's construction contracts had gone to nonwhites in the previous years, while 50 percent of the population in Richmond was African American. She concluded nonetheless: "none of the evidence presented by the city points to any identified discrimination in the Richmond construction industry."[77] Importantly, the Court does not deny a clear pattern of racial disparity in employment opportunities in *Croson*. Rather, it views racial concentration of wealth and employment opportunities to be wholly consistent with the requirement of a color-blind society. The result is a kind of rearguard action against meaningful social reform, through which persistent racial inequality is dismissed as "amorphous," "de facto," merely "social," or the natural result of "innocent" private choices.

The language of racial redemption accomplishes this double move by exonerating the results of a system denounced, at the same time, as paradigmatically unjust. Sumi Cho has described this conflict as a tension "between the knowledge of white supremacy and the desire to enjoy the fruits of that tainted tree." For Cho, racial redemption entails "repudiation" of previous racial orders (slavery, segregation), "burial" of historical memory about past injustice, and "transformation" of white supremacy into new forms consistent with contemporary antiracist norms: "Such a process reconciles the knowledge/desire tension by denouncing white supremacy while permitting its continued operation."[78] The first two of Cho's categories (repudiation and burial) establish the break from history I have described. Her third (transformation) asserts a continuity with the past, but in rather different terms than I suggest.

On Cho's account, it is white supremacy that remains intact, albeit in different form and according to a different set of strategic operations. Connecting racism's past and present, Cho assigns the name "colorblind fundamentalism" to the peculiar form taken by white supremacy in the post-civil rights era.[79] But more than this, I would emphasize how color-blindness discourse, through the trope of redemption, also asserts a historical *continuity* between past racism and contemporary *anti*racist policies. The accusation of constitutional sin contained within claims to redemption is displayed, for example, in the rhetorical move that figures affirmative action as modern Jim Crow, and the fashioning of a constitutional obligation not to distinguish the two, as when Justice Stewart claims that federal "set-aside" programs for minority businesses are wrong "for the same reason that *Plessy v. Ferguson* was wrong,"[80] or when Justice Thomas declares the " 'moral and constitutional equivalence' between laws designed to subjugate a race and those that distribute benefits on the basis of race."[81] The historical legacy of racial subordination in the United States may be understood to supply the social facts necessary for understanding what distinguishes the two—and it is just this historical legacy that is washed away through constitutional redemption. On this view, the Constitution prohibits rather than requires the Court to take notice of differences between Jim Crow and affirmative action, segregation and integration, or, in Justice Stevens's colorful phrase, "between a 'No Trespassing' sign and a welcome mat."[82]

Within the terms of the controlling redemption narrative, racial consciousness persists chiefly as a holdover from an unjust past—as something the nation must overcome, if it has not done so already. The legality of race-conscious remedies for persistent inequality is thereby construed as a question of how much progress is thought to have been made on questions of race, and how much remains left to be done. Consequently, the resolution of key policy questions turns less upon concern for the injuries of racially subordinated groups than upon the placement of those injuries within national narratives of racial redemption. How this process works can be seen in the 2013 Supreme Court case *Shelby County v. Holder*, which struck down key portions of the Voting Rights Act as irrational and unconstitutional violations of Alabama's right to equal sovereignty.[83]

In *Shelby*, the Court considered a facial challenge to Sections 4 and 5 of the Voting Rights Act of 1965. The Voting Rights Act (VRA) was passed as a response to what Congress acknowledged to be widespread, pervasive, and illegal discrimination in voting, concentrated especially across the southern states. It has since been reauthorized by Congress several times, most recently in 2006.[84] Section 5 of the VRA targeted specific "covered" jurisdictions—those deemed the most egregious violators of voting rights—for whom no changes to voting laws or procedures would be permitted without preapproval from the US attorney general or DC District Court. Section 4 of the VRA specified the formula for determining which states would be subject to this "preclearance" provision. Citing the principle of equal sovereignty, and despite the fact that Alabama would be among the states subjected to preclearance under *any* covering formula, Shelby County challenged the constitutionality of the targeted preclearance requirements, arguing that conditions have substantially changed since 1965 and the requirements are no longer justified.

As neither the massive scale of voting rights violations in 1965 nor the constitutionality of the original Voting Rights Act is open to serious dispute, the outcome of the *Shelby* case turned principally upon the question of racial progress. At the heart of the decision is Chief Justice Roberts's repeated claim, "Things have changed dramatically."[85] That the Court's conservative majority, which in other contexts has been quite keen to point out the judiciary's lack of competency in legislative matters, chose not to defer to the judgment of Congress, is especially striking given the VRA's historic significance, proven effectiveness, and overwhelming bipartisan support.[86] Even more remarkable, in Justice Ginsburg's view, was the majority's willingness to do so without any "genuine attempt" to engage the data from the legislative record.[87] If the *Shelby* majority seems to give less consideration to the evidence than might be expected of a decision to strike down key portions of the nation's principal voting rights legislation (Justice Ginsburg describes it as "hubris"),[88] that might be because the details of the legislative record are of secondary importance to the general progress narrative, which in turn sets the ideological boundaries for a broader conversation about race in America.

Chief Justice Roberts is surprisingly candid in this regard, when he brushes aside rival interpretations of the evidence: "*Regardless of how to look at the record*," he asserts, "no one can fairly say that it shows anything approaching the 'pervasive,' 'flagrant,' 'widespread,' and 'rampant' discrimination that faced Congress in 1965."[89] Roberts is relatively uninterested in the complexities of second-generation barriers to voting, the evidentiary details of multiple studies, or the inadequacy of Section 2 for deterring new discriminatory policies—all of which are subordinate to securing the axiomatic status of a racial break from the past: "Things have changed." In his repeated use of this short declarative phrase, Roberts discloses his investment in racial futurity, which both serves as the overarching theme of the opinion and grounds its consequent refusal to acknowledge the structural nature of persistent racial discrimination.

Throughout the opinion, racism is located exclusively in the past. The continuing legacy of voter suppression is figured not even as injury, but as memory, which must be consigned to the past in order to avoid harming those states upon whom the VRA's preclearance remedy is imposed. The significance of history, in *Shelby*, is not our connection to the past as a privileged source of legal meaning, but only a reminder of how far we have come, as a benchmark of ongoing racial progress. The crucial thing to remember, Roberts instructs, is that "history did not end in 1965."[90] Unlike the past, which remains forever unchanging and serves as a kind of reservoir for national attitudes about racial injustice, the present is forward-looking and connects us to a future no longer weighed down by past racial debt. Reauthorization of the VRA in 2006, Roberts objects, is based upon "decades-old data relevant to decades-old problems, rather than current data reflecting current needs." The Fifteenth Amendment, in contrast, "is not designed to punish for the past; its purpose is to ensure a better future."[91]

On its face, *Shelby v. Holder* may appear to reject the kind of southern exceptionalism that would minimize national responsibility for racism by treating segregation as a problem unique to the South. After all, the core of Roberts's argument is a rejection of the VRA's differential treatment of (mostly southern) covered jurisdictions. This point came out clearly in oral argument, with Roberts's curiously direct question to Solicitor General Donald Verrilli: "is it the government's submission that the citizens in the South are more racist than the citizens in the North?"[92] However, in framing its argument around the theme of change—"things have changed in the South"[93]—the *Shelby* majority reinforces its own version of southern exceptionalism, through which the enormity of past southern wrongs is made to confirm the innocence of current southern practices. The more forceful its denunciation of Alabama circa 1965, the easier it becomes to distinguish from Alabama circa 2013. Indeed, in oral argument Alabama characterized its own racial past as "a disgrace"—precisely in order to deny that the VRA's "current burden" is any longer constitutionally permissible.[94] In *Shelby*, the Court accepted this argument in no uncertain terms when it characterized the basis for the VRA coverage formula as "40-year-old facts having *no logical relation to the present day*."[95] As with other versions of the redemption narrative, this formulation pairs racial condemnation and exoneration by linking the present to an imagined color-blind future while at the same time locating racism stubbornly in the past. In so doing, it also constricts the meaning of racism to the status of anomaly or exception, rather than constitutive of the American racial state.

Indeed, the language of exceptionalism is perhaps the most singular feature of the majority's *Shelby* opinion, which is fairly dominated by the rhetoric of departure, exception, and the extraordinary. In the first paragraph alone, Roberts describes the VRA as an "extraordinary measure," justified only by an "extraordinary problem"; a "dramatic departure" from the principle of equal sovereignty; "a drastic departure" from federalism; and legislation of "an unprecedented nature," justified only by the "exceptional conditions" of the time. In an opinion just twenty-four pages in length, the word "extraordinary" appears no less than eleven times. Additionally, Roberts uses the word "exceptional" four times, "unprecedented" five times, and "uncommon" twice. In its markedly overcommitted rhetorical style, the opinion conveys an anxious need to establish the anomalous nature of racial discrimination—and to confirm the nation's return to a presumptively nonracial (and nonracist) "ordinary" politics. More than any particular point of doctrine, Roberts seems to insist most of all upon a refusal to accept that systematic discrimination in voting, as in other areas of American political life, is anything but an exception.

The Voting Rights Act of 1965 *was* "exceptional"—but not because black disfranchisement was in any way unusual or unprecedented. It was exceptional because it gave Congress, for the first time since Reconstruction, the enforcement powers necessary to secure black access to the ballot. *Shelby* is also extraordinary in this sense, for striking down the very legislation credited with establishing the conditions that are said to prove that "things have changed." Indeed, the majority concedes that dramatic increases in black voter registration and turnout rates are "in large part *because of* the Voting Rights Act."[96] This acknowledged fact leads Justice Ginsburg to quip that striking down preclearance provisions because they have worked is like "throwing away your umbrella in a rainstorm because you are not getting wet."[97]

It is the strength of Ginsburg's argument and not its weakness that ultimately renders it unconvincing to the majority of the Court. For if the achievement of black voting rights depends upon continuing federal oversight, then the problem would appear to be systemic rather than aberrational. And that, in turn, would undermine the presumption that "exceptional" measures such as the VRA can be justified as temporary uses of racial consciousness that lead ultimately to the transcendence of race. Scalia makes this point to Attorney General Verrilli in oral argument: "That will always be true forever into the future. You could always say, oh, there has been improvement, but . . . since the only reason it's improved is because of these procedures, we must continue those procedures in perpetuity."[98] This vision of the future suggests an America that is racially unredeemed, and so falls outside the narrative boundaries of presumptive white innocence that help constitute American racial common sense. Supporters of the VRA thus find themselves in a peculiarly "post-racial" double bind: not only must they prove that racism is still pervasive enough to warrant preclearance provisions in the covered jurisdictions, but they also must make that case without disrupting the narrative assumption that racism is a minor aberration soon to be fixed—that white supremacy is not constitutive of America democracy.

Color-Blindness as Performative Contradiction

Contemporary equal protection law operates within a narrative framework of fall and redemption. The success of color-blind conservatives is registered in the extent to which this narrative also structures the positions of its critics. As we have seen, liberal justifications for race-consciousness share in the redemptive fantasy of transcending race and confirm, in aspirational form, a baseline of putatively race-less neutrality against which color-consciousness is justified on a limited, temporary, remedial basis. A defining feature of critical race theory, in contrast, has been to contest the law's claim to racial neutrality, both epistemologically and in practice.[99] Drawing from the anticolonialism of Malcolm X and Black Power movements in the 1970s, Gary Peller decisively locates the rejection of African American racial consciousness as a basic precondition for civil rights reform and a response to the perceived threat of black militancy.[100]

In one sense, Peller is crucially right to mark the 1960s and early 1970s as a key moment when liberation movements succumbed to the new integrationist civil rights consensus: "The price of national commitment to suppress white supremacists would be the rejection of race consciousness among African Americans."[101] But it would be a mistake to think that color-blind principles or movements represent an absence or suppression of racial consciousness. On the contrary, this "rejection of race consciousness" suggests a more effective installation of the dominant racial perspective, dressed up in the language of neutral principles, objectivity, "merit," and the like. As such, what an effective antiracist theoretical stance turns out to require is not another (or more effective) justification for the reintroduction of racial consciousness, but a more critical awareness of the race-consciousness already performed through the logic of color-blind constitutionalism.

To this end, we might think of color-blind constitutionalism not as a conservative rejection of racial consciousness, but as a kind of *performative contradiction*. To charge color-blind constitutionalism with performative contradiction is to claim a discrepancy between the content of the stated legal principle and the meaning produced through its enactment.[102] As Frank Michelman has observed, whatever else their virtues or vices, laws prohibiting racial classification "make an issue of race" and so "are race-conscious by any definition."[103] Similarly, in the context of voting rights law, Michael K. Brown and coauthors underscore that "paradoxically, the idea that the electoral process should be color-blind is in fact a very *color-conscious* notion."[104] Seen this way, the conflict resides not in the distance between color-blind ideals and color-conscious realities—as with Myrdal's American dilemma—but within the concept of color-blindness itself.

As linguistic acts, performative contradictions may be understood in terms of their propositional content. A performative contradiction arises when the act of stating a claim has the effect of undermining the truth of the claim that is stated. For example, to say, "I can't hear you because I am asleep" might mean that the speaker *was* asleep but no longer is (or is playing a game of some sort, or simply does not wish to talk). But the literal statement is evidently disproved by its articulation, at least to the extent that consciousness is a prerequisite for lucid conversation. There is no contradiction in asking the question, "Are you asleep?"—but an affirmative answer will necessarily be less convincing than no answer at all.

Performative contradictions of this sort often arise in the way that people ordinarily talk about (and around) race in a society keenly attentive to charges of racial insensitivity. Because "racist" is one of the worst things one can be accused of, many whites will take pains to avoid expressing views that could earn them that label. Especially in public, many are reticent to share their thoughts about race, other than to confirm their opposition to racism or, on occasion, spontaneously to announce their unawareness of someone's race. An individual might reasonably reflect upon one's general lack of racial awareness—say, in consideration of covert or subconscious forms of racism. In specific instances, however, the utterance itself contradicts the stated claim. Someone who does not in fact notice race will not be aware of not noticing it. More precisely, one's lack of awareness of race necessarily must end at the moment one becomes conscious of it. This contradiction is felt even more acutely when color-blindness is offered in the form of a legal prohibition. Racial consciousness is a prerequisite for both the enactment and the enforcement of any rule against racial classification.

It is perhaps ironic, then, that color-blind conservatives have objected to affirmative action policies on the grounds that such policies interject racial consideration and are therefore self-defeating by nature. For example, Justice Thomas's critique of affirmative action—that it "makes race relevant"[105]—traces back to William Van Alstyne's 1978 article in the *University of Chicago Law Review.* Against Justice Blackmun's justification for color-consciousness—that "in order to get beyond racism, we must first take account of race"[106]—Van Alstyne retorts:

> One gets beyond racism by getting beyond it now: by a complete, resolute, and credible commitment *never* to tolerate in one's own life—or in the life or practices of one's government—the differential treatment of other human beings by race.[107]

This position has proven especially durable and supplies a central line of attack for color-blind conservatives. With only a slight modification, Van Alstyne's slogan now speaks for a tentative majority of the current Supreme Court and is easily discernible in Chief Justice Roberts's maxim: "The way to stop discrimination on the basis of race is to stop discriminating on the basis of race."[108]

In its various formulations, this argument has been rightly criticized for its equivocation of Jim Crow and race-based affirmative action policies beneath the generic epithet of "racism."[109] But quite aside from this rhetorical sleight of hand, the argument "works" by playing affirmative action's race-conscious methods against its assumed goal of transcending racial consciousness—of "getting beyond" racism. Drawing from Jon Elster's work on rationality and human consciousness, Daniel Sabbagh has attempted to formalize this contradiction as the deliberate effort to achieve a mental state defined by its lack of intentionality. Understood in these terms, race-based affirmative action must fail, or at least "requires a measure of dissimulation to succeed."[110] According to Elster, certain mental states (spontaneity, forgetfulness, sleep, inattention to particular objects or ideas) exist only as "byproducts" of other processes and cannot be achieved through conscious, intentional action. When we "try to forget" something, what we are really doing is intentionally creating the conditions in which forgetting is more likely to result as a byproduct of directing our consciousness elsewhere. For Sabbagh, color-blindness belongs to this category of mental states. An "absence of consciousness of racial distinctions," he argues, "may be the object of a wish, but cannot arise as the product of a specific intention."[111] Like the old saw about telling someone not to think of an elephant, affirmative action is said to raise our consciousness of the very thing we wish to "get beyond." For Sabbagh, as with Van Alstyne, the gap between egalitarian ideals and discriminatory practices thus emerges as a contradiction between ends and means. The goal is to create a society in which race matters less, yet the practice of "racial preferences" requires a greater awareness of race.

While helpful in elucidating the logical premises of anti-affirmative action discourse, this critique fails for several reasons. First, and most obviously, it assumes that affirmative action is justified only as an instrument of "deracialization" and not by more substantive claims for justice or material equality. Additionally, even with regard to liberal defenses of affirmative action that do share these assumptions, race-conscious policies might still be justified, to the extent that actually existing material inequalities in society are comparatively greater contributors to racial consciousness than are formal distinctions written in law. But my interest here is not to defend affirmative action against the color-blind critique. Rather, by attending more carefully to what is meant by "racial consciousness"—and its absence—we might see how formal prohibitions against racial classification *also* require a heightened awareness of the prohibited categories they seek to suppress.

So long as we inhabit a society in which race remains socially significant, it is a mistake to think of race-consciousness chiefly in terms of choice. We may (and do) choose to act in ways that shield ourselves from certain kinds of knowledge, but this suggests the cultivation of a desired relationship toward that knowledge, rather than its absence. As Patricia Williams explains, this denial is not the absence of racial consciousness but, instead, "a profoundly invested disingenuousness, an innocence that amounts to the transgressive refusal to know."[112] For Williams, the crucial thing is to account for the pleasure this innocence affords—the "wistful giftiness with which not-knowing is offered" in the anxious call to color-blindness: *"Would that you would just not know, too."*[113] Racial innocence is always hard won.

And yet debates over the constitutional legitimacy of racial classification continue to be framed in misleadingly voluntaristic terms. For example, Terry Easton claims to "state the obvious" about affirmative action: that it *"makes race and ethnicity salient* by naming the minority groups it ostensibly benefits."[114] As we have seen, champions of color-blind constitutionalism lean heavily upon the idea that racial classifications "make race matter" and therefore undermine the ultimate goal, which is to transcend racial difference itself. Critics of color-blindness, in turn, point to the inequitable results of such a rule. By emphasizing the performative contradiction of the color-blind principle, rather than the unjustness of its results, my approach challenges a presumption shared by both sides of this debate: categorical prohibitions against racial classification are by necessity acutely aware of race—if only in the activity of their denial. Accordingly, what appears as a choice between color-blindness and color-consciousness turns out to be illusory.

The performative contradiction of color-blind constitutionalism can also be seen in the logic and structure of antidiscrimination law, the origins of which explicitly yoked restrictions on race-based legislation to an awareness of their subordinating effects. Under strict scrutiny analysis, the doctrine of "suspect classifications" is both triggered by the use of racial classification and initiates a unique prohibition against the use of race. Taking Justice Stone's explanation in footnote 4 of *Carolene Products* (1938) as illustrative, antidiscrimination claims emerge as arguments about group standing or injury based upon membership in a disadvantaged group. Although not typically treated as such, the same is true of reverse discrimination claims brought by whites.

On Justice Stone's rationale, judicial intervention can be reconciled with the general principle of democratic self-government in cases when (and precisely because) majorities use their legislative powers to curtail the ability of minorities to gain political representation. This process-based argument, developed by Ely into a general theory of judicial review, derives from the predictability of "blockages" or defects in the political process.[115] According to Justice Stone:

[In] the review of statutes directed at particular religious, or national, or racial minorities . . . prejudice against discrete and insular minorities may be a special condition, which tends seriously to curtail the operation of those political processes ordinarily relied upon to protect minorities, and . . . may call for a correspondingly more searching judicial inquiry.[116]

As the underlying basis for strict scrutiny analysis, the argument is explicitly race-conscious in theory and application. "Prejudice against discrete and insular minorities" typifies the "special condition" warranting judicial intervention.[117] The legitimate fear that political processes can be corrupted by racism supplies the need for an exception to the general rule of judicial restraint.

This race-conscious foundation for strict scrutiny analysis is evident in two of the Court's early applications, albeit with dramatically different outcomes. In *Korematsu v. U.S.* (1944), the Court infamously upheld the constitutionality of wartime internment of Americans of Japanese ancestry. In addition to illustrating the perils of excessive deference to military judgment in time of war, the decision establishes a framework that prohibits racial discrimination except in extreme circumstances: "all legal restrictions which curtail the civil rights of a single racial group are immediately suspect" such that "courts must subject them to the most rigid scrutiny."[118] The use of racial classifications for the express purpose of imposing extreme disadvantages on a politically vulnerable minority group, consequently, is just part of the remarkable wrongness of *Korematsu*. More than this, what makes the decision so especially repugnant is the Court's acceptance of the claim that internment of citizens on the basis of ancestry alone nevertheless constituted a *nonracial* basis for these actions. *Korematsu* thus reproduces the worst aspects of the *Plessy* majority, even while denouncing the crude racialist claims for which that case is typically associated.[119]

Indeed, Justice Black's majority opinion takes great pains to emphasize that the exclusion order is constitutional only because it is *not* racially motivated: "Our task would be simple, our duty clear, were this a case involving the imprisonment of a loyal citizen in a concentration camp because of racial prejudice." But, Justice Black implausibly claims, "Korematsu was not excluded from the Military Area because of hostility to him or his race."[120] In retrospect, it is puzzling how anyone could regard even the stated purpose of the exclusion as nonracial in nature—to say nothing of the unstated racial animosities that clearly and evidently motivated the policy,[121] and not just in retrospect, as Justice Murphy's stinging dissent makes clear.[122] But for our purposes, what bears emphasizing in the case is how intuitively all members of the Court, and on both sides of the judgment, associate the heavy presumption against racial classification with an equally acute consciousness of race. Its appalling outcome notwithstanding, *Korematsu* views race as a uniquely prohibited category for policymaking *because* of this heightened racial awareness.

Similarly, in *Loving v. Virginia* (1967), the Court adopted the strict scrutiny framework to invalidate prohibitions against interracial marriage. The legitimacy of racial classifications, the Court held, requires "some permissible state objective, independent of the racial discrimination it was the object of the Fourteenth Amendment to eliminate."[123] *Loving* has come to be viewed as a high point for judicial condemnation of invidious racial discrimination.[124] Nonetheless, the decision's deep mistrust of racial classification is at all times connected to an explicit recognition and condemnation of white supremacy. Writing for the Court, Chief Justice Warren repeatedly reproduces in quotation the most incendiary language from the lower courts and legislative record, including the finding by Virginia's Supreme Court of Appeals that the state's legitimate purposes were " 'to preserve the racial integrity of its citizens,' and to prevent 'the corruption of blood,' 'a mongrel breed of citizens,' and 'the obliteration of racial pride' "—state purposes that Warren characterizes as "obviously an endorsement of the doctrine of White Supremacy."[125] That Virginia prohibited "only interracial marriages involving white persons" but was unconcerned by unions between members of different nonwhite groups, provided further evidence that the measure was "designed to maintain White Supremacy."[126]

The Court's rationale for limiting or curtailing racial classifications in *Korematsu* and *Loving* is unavoidably race-conscious, and is premised in the recognition of asymmetrical power relations between racial groups. The vulnerability of racial minorities is what constitutes them as a suspect class, and what justifies the application of heightened scrutiny. In contrast, the application of strict scrutiny analysis to "reverse discrimination" cases in the 1970s required a rhetorical shift to disavow these race-conscious foundations. Justice Powell's call for a single standard of review in the *Bakke* case is indicative of this move.[127] In what would emerge as the controlling opinion of a fractured Court, Powell justified the application of strict scrutiny to a minority set-aside admissions program at UC Davis Medical School with the universalizing language of color-blind individualism: "The guarantee of equal protection cannot mean one thing when applied to one individual and something else when applied to a person of a different color."[128] If racial classifications by the state are constitutionally suspect, he argued, this must be the case with respect to all racial groups, and without respect to the law's intended purpose. As a consequence, the Court's protection of "suspect classes" (racial or religious minorities) was transformed into a general condemnation of "suspect classifications" (race or religion). The political vulnerability of minorities, which had provided the initial justification for judicial intervention, thus disappears in the Court's categorical prohibition against "all racial classifications" that fail to meet the exacting test of strict scrutiny. On the logic of footnote 4, it is specifically disadvantaged groups that trigger heightened scrutiny. In *Bakke*, it is precisely this recognition of disadvantage that strict scrutiny analysis would prohibit, and which Justice Powell sought to avoid.[129]

Because it employs a single standard of review for all racial groups, the shift from suspect *classes* to suspect *classifications* is generally regarded as a move toward the color-blind ideal. Certainly that is how it is understood by its authors and advocates, for whom racial preferences are regarded as problematic—whether or not they may be constitutionally permissible in some limited set of circumstances. Thus Justice O'Connor's insistence in *Grutter v. Bollinger* (2003) that affirmative action be temporary, with its constitutionality premised upon its diminishing necessity: "the acid test of their justification will be their efficacy in eliminating the need for any racial or ethnic preferences at all."[130] O'Connor's objective thus matches that of the color-blind dissenters in the case, sharing a view of affirmative action as problematic exception to color-blind norms. Their disagreement concerns only whether the racial consciousness "introduced by" affirmative action can ultimately be overcome, and whether the University's interest in student body diversity is sufficiently compelling to warrant this risk.

That the transcendence of race is the ostensible goal of all three positions (the liberal Blackmun, the moderate O'Connor, and the conservative Roberts) underscores both the importance of color-blindness discourse and the extent to which advocates of color-consciousness have been captured by the object of their critique. What makes affirmative action problematic even for its liberal supporters, and what supplies much of color-blindness's appeal, is the belief that government classifications by race will introduce or intensify racial consciousness, thus undermining the redemptive dream of moving "beyond" race. That this understanding seems intuitive for many, that it has become a matter of racial common sense, can be traced to the narrative practices of color-blind conservatism and the vision of racial redemption it affords.

As we have seen, Justice Harlan's dissent in *Plessy v. Ferguson* has come to be understood as the sacred text of color-blind constitutionalism. The next chapter examines *Plessy* in more detail, in an effort to complicate our understanding of what the phrase "Our Constitution is colorblind" might have meant in its historical context—and what it has come to mean as used today. Situating Harlan's words more precisely against the arguments of the now-discredited majority opinion, and as a reflection of arguments advanced by Plessy's legal counsel, Albion Tourgée, I read the case less as a textual authority for the antisubordination/anticlassification debate than for its evident concern over racial indeterminacy and the productive power of law as a race-making institution.

PART II | Color-Blindness against
the Color Line

CHAPTER 3 | The Lessons of *Plessy*

THE LANGUAGE OF COLOR-BLINDNESS enters American constitutional law in dissent. It supplies the rhetorical high-note to Justice John Marshall Harlan's fierce critique of the now-infamous "separate but equal" doctrine embraced in *Plessy v. Ferguson* as constitutional justification for state-sanctioned racial segregation, or the law of Jim Crow.[1] While *Plessy* was, for all practical purposes, overturned by *Brown v. Board of Education* in 1954, its significance is nonetheless of more than historical interest. The case continues to exert considerable influence over constitutional law as a paradigmatic example of what *not* to do, or what equal protection law isn't. In other words, *Plessy*'s power derives from its status as antiprecedent. As such, it continues to shape the constitutional canon as a kind of cautionary tale. As Richard Primus explains, *Plessy* is "not just a dead letter but an anti-canonical text, a negative reference point from which later decisions would have to distance themselves."[2] Accordingly, Harlan's language— "Our Constitution is color-blind"—takes on special significance as the centerpiece of what Primus calls a "redeemed dissent."[3]

We read *Plessy*, then, not (or not only) to condemn past injustices, but for insight into contemporary understandings of constitutional equality. Although Harlan's words have come to be invested with the status of constitutional authority, it is not at all self-evident what his dissent might have meant when it was written, and just how those words ought to be understood today remains a sharply contested matter. In part, this reflects the simple fact that textual meaning inevitably is the product of interpretation. But it is also a consequence of the fact that the meaning of canonical texts emerges through the very activity of their canonization. This may be especially true of dissenting opinions such as Harlan's, the legal authority of which necessarily derives not from the disposition of the case itself, but from the actions of some future Court that overturns the original majority.

"Even more so than with majority opinions," Primus explains, "the substance of a dissent can be the creation not of the dissenting judge but of the redeeming judge, and the critical moment for understanding the substance of dissent is the moment of redemption."[4]

Although *Plessy* ceased to be "good law" when functionally overturned in 1954, the unanimous opinion in *Brown v. Board of Education* made no mention of the case, and its frequent quotation by the Court did not commence until the late 1980s.[5] Harlan's dissent and the phrase "Our Constitution is color-blind" were, then, only elevated to sacred status *after* the doctrine they attacked ("separate but equal") had already been vanquished in law. The canonization of Harlan's dissent thus served "as a memorial, rather than a source, for the demonization of the *Plessy* decision and the racist doctrine it propounded."[6] Which is also to say that the meaning of Harlan's dissent was constructed retrospectively, out the interpretive needs of subsequent majorities seeking to define "the lesson" of past wrongs. It is from these comparatively recent ideological requirements that the phrase has come to symbolize the anticlassification interpretation of equal protection.

This chapter seeks to recover some of the initial complexity in color-blindness discourse by returning to the phrase's origins in the *Plessy* case—which I read less as a textual authority for the antisubordination/anticlassification debate than for its evident concern over racial indeterminacy and the productive power of law as a race-making institution. The meaning of Harlan's dissent derives in part, I argue, from the positions it rejects. The primary object of Harlan's critique is, of course, Justice Brown's majority opinion and the doctrine of "separate but equal." However, Brown supports his position in a number of ways, only one of which centrally relies upon the kind of biological racism or assertion of natural difference against which the anticlassification position effectively contends. On my reading, Harlan's dissent is motivated less by a rejection of racial difference as such than by concern over the majority opinion's posture of legal formalism, by which it disavows the evident meaning of the law it defends. At least in this regard, today's color-blind conservatives more closely resemble the *Plessy* majority than the dissent that they champion.

But Harlan's dissent is also shaped by its relationship to another, less obvious, interlocutor. Like the majority opinion itself, the meaning of Harlan's dissent emerges in response to arguments made by Homer Plessy's legal counsel, Albion Winegar Tourgée, which turn upon questions of racial indeterminacy and the process of legal determination.

While *Plessy v. Ferguson* has become a familiar symbol of legal discrimination against African Americans, most people remain unaware that Homer Plessy himself was, by all appearances, a white man. Born of seven great-grandparents of European descent (an "octaroon" in the parlance of nineteenth-century raciology), Plessy's light skin meant that he was well suited for the test case, which had been arranged by prominent leaders from New Orleans's Creole community. In the language of the Court, Plessy's "one-eighth African blood" was "not discernible in him,"[7] and Tourgée's legal strategy played centrally upon this point. While *Plessy* is ordinarily related as a story about the legal treatment of African Americans, I argue that it is also a story about racial "passing" and how the law is implicated in the production and regulation of racialized identity.[8] My focus on racial ambiguity complicates the simple opposition between race-consciousness and that of color-blindness associated with Justice Harlan's celebrated dissent. Thinking about color-blindness in the context of *Plessy* as "passing" draws our attention to those social structures that make racial identity meaningful, and helps to clarify why there is no contradiction between Justice Harlan's principle of color-blindness and various color-conscious remedies for entrenched racial subordination.

The Segregated Equality of Justice Henry Billings Brown

While deeply engrained in social custom, the formal legislation of segregation did not emerge in America's southern states until decades after the collapse of Reconstruction.[9] This situation reflects the fact that racial hierarchy in the antebellum South was so thoroughly entrenched as to make such laws superfluous. Northern states, in which white supremacy was less explicitly defining of the social order, were for this reason more likely to enact formal rules of segregation.[10] The practice of segregated railway travel also reflected biases of gender and class, as affluent women of color were denied access to the "Ladies Car" and the distinctly nineteenth-century class marker of being recognized as ladies.[11] In the South, the first wave of mandatory Jim Crow laws began around 1890, and focused mainly on railroad travel, with nine states passing such laws between 1887 and 1891. Louisiana's Separate Car Act was signed into law in 1890, requiring "equal, but separate" accommodations on all passenger railways, and mandating that "no person or persons, shall be permitted to occupy seats in coaches, other than the ones, assigned, to them on account of the race they belong to."[12] In *Plessy*, the Court considered whether the Louisiana act ran afoul of the Civil War amendments. In upholding the law, *Plessy* paved the way for sweeping Jim Crow legislation across the South that would prohibit interracial contact in transportation and lodging, drinking fountains, restrooms, graveyards, swimming pools, and other public facilities. *Plessy* drastically restricted the scope of protection that racial minorities could hope to find in the Thirteenth and Fourteenth Amendments, and in so doing gave judicial sanction to the practices of American racial apartheid.

Modern commentary on *Plessy* is nearly uniform in its condemnation of the case. Andrew Kull notes that *Plessy* is "routinely vilified"[13] and directs the reader to Charles Lofgren's "pastiche" of scorn—an assemblage of judgments from various critics that condemn *Plessy* for "reduc[ing] the Fourteenth Amendment to little more than a pious goodwill resolution," for delivering "the ultimate blow to the Civil War Amendments and the equality of Negroes," being "inconsistent" and "irrational," even "slipping into absurdity."[14] Of *Plessy*'s central argument, legal historian Richard Kluger writes: "It would be onerous work to find a more unsupported and insupportable sentence in the annals of American jurisprudence."[15] And while some legal scholars have preferred the understated—Robert McClosky is contented to describe the opinion as "dubious" and John Ely calls it "a mistake"—A. Leon Higginbotham points to the scale of the injustice as "the final and most devastating judicial step in the legitimization of racism under state law" and "one of the most catastrophic racial decisions ever rendered."[16] Justice Brown's majority opinion in *Plessy* has been taken to task for its faulty logic and its misleading citation of precedent, but most of all *Plessy* is criticized simply for its racism. To be sure, the decision is deeply racist, both in its reliance upon racial science and in its constitutional endorsement of white supremacy. But understanding the particular ways that *Plessy* goes wrong is an important project, and one that sheds light on what exactly was meant by Justice Harlan's dissenting claim that "Our Constitution is color-blind."

Reading *Plessy* today is to confront a puzzle: unlike the infamous *Dred Scott* decision, which simply denied that blacks could be citizens (having been no part of "the people of the United States" at the time of the founding and regarded as possessing "no rights that the white man was bound to respect"),[17] Justice Brown's majority opinion readily concedes that the "object of the [Fourteenth] amendment was undoubtedly to enforce the absolute equality of the two races before the law."[18] How, then, could a policy of state-mandated racial segregation be reconciled with the constitutional requirement of *absolute equality*? To this end, Brown adopted two strategies for limiting the scope of the Civil War amendments and justifying the constitutionality of Jim Crow. First, he drew a distinction between the civil and political equality guaranteed by the Fourteenth Amendment, and a social equality which he characterized both as beyond the scope of constitutional protection and incompatible with biologically based natural differences between the races. Second, he advanced a formalistic theory of symmetrical equality, according to which segregation law applied equally to "both races" because whites were separated from blacks just as blacks were separated from whites.[19] Harlan's dissent, as commonly understood, deploys color-blindness against the first of these strategies (biological racism), and so appears to require a categorical rejection of race (anticlassification). Taken as a response to Brown's second argument (symmetrical equality), however, Harlan's dissent actually requires the racial awareness ruled out by the first interpretation.

Brown's first argument, contrasting civil and political equality to social equality, sought to distinguish the *Plessy* case from that of *Strauder v. West Virginia* (1880), in which the Court held that the exclusion of blacks from juries violated the Fourteenth Amendment's guarantee of equal access to the judicial process. This tripartite typology of rights was in fact common to nineteenth-century jurisprudence.[20] Political rights referred specifically to the realm of voting and officeholding, whereas civil rights guaranteed access to the courts, protection of property rights, and enforcement of contracts, as well as protection against the imposition of greater punishments for criminal offenses simply on the basis of race.[21] Social rights, on the other hand, were understood to imply interracial association and social contact, typified by interracial marriage or sexual intimacy. *Strauder* made clear that social rights received no protection under the Fourteenth Amendment.[22]

Brown's majority opinion presented social equality as a radical restructuring of natural and personal preferences that far exceeded the scope of the Fourteenth Amendment:

> [The Fourteenth Amendment was intended to] enforce the absolute equality of the two races before the law, but in the nature of things it could not have been intended to abolish distinctions based upon color, or to enforce social, as distinguished from political equality, or a commingling of the two races upon terms unsatisfactory to either.[23]

Ironically, Brown's argument grants to the social institution of law all the force of nature. The legal enforcement of segregation is said to follow naturally from biological differences ("color" and "race"), which simply exist "in the nature of things." The language of natural difference, sutured to social arrangements based upon those differences, serves to insulate segregation from legal remedy by locating the source of inequality outside of government action. Suggesting the inevitability of racial separation, Brown described race differences as "a distinction which is found in the color of the two races, and which must always exist so long as white men are distinguished from the other race by color."[24] The move is a rhetorical victory regardless of whether one believes in natural racial differences. Because it associates racial segregation with innate biological tendencies, antisegregationists are figured as demanding the impossible from the limited tools of limited government: "Legislation is powerless to eradicate racial instincts or to abolish distinctions based upon physical differences."[25]

But Plessy was not arguing that the Constitution obliged the state to force private businesses to integrate. He claimed only that the Fourteenth Amendment prevented states from *requiring* racial segregation. Indeed, Louisiana's legislative effort to prevent interracial contact was itself an example of social engineering in that it attempted to impose social patterns that might fade absent the coercion of law. Brown's opinion figures segregation laws as preserving rather than imposing racial separation, just as nineteenth-century scientific racism theorized distinct and pure racial types even in the face of an increasingly large mulatto population.[26] And it is against this biologically racialist view that Harlan's dissent is typically understood to support a constitutional rejection of race (the anticlassification principle).

The crucial passage of Harlan's dissent reads as follows:

> The white race deems itself to be the dominant race in this country. And so it is, in prestige, in achievements, in education, in wealth, and in power. So, I doubt not, it will continue to be for all time, if it remains true to its great heritage, and holds fast to the principles of constitutional liberty. But in view of the constitution, in the eye of the law, there is in this country no superior, dominant, ruling class of citizens. There is no caste here. Our Constitution is color-blind and neither knows nor tolerates classes among citizens. In respect of civil rights, all citizens are equal before the law.[27]

To be sure, there are textual resources in Harlan's dissent that seem to support an anticlassification interpretation—and not only in the metaphor of color-blindness itself. There is also Harlan's own formulation of something very close to a rule of racial nonrecognition: "the Constitution of the

United States does not, I think, permit any public authority to know the race of those entitled to be protected in the enjoyment of such rights."[28] Here, Harlan suggests that the state may not "know" an individual's race, or that it must at least act as if it did not know, that it must keep that knowledge from itself. And Harlan denies "that any legislative body or judicial tribunal may have regard to the race of citizens when the civil rights of those citizens are involved."[29] Defenders of a color-blind Constitution maintain that this is the plain meaning of Harlan's dissent and a faithful rendering of the Fourteenth Amendment.

However, this interpretation is misleading. There are several reasons to doubt that Harlan thought the Fourteenth Amendment barred states from ever considering race, and not all of them are flattering to the justice. First, we should not forget that Harlan's dissent is also filled with the language of racial pride (for Anglo-Saxons) and animus (against the Chinese). In the sentences immediately preceding the phrase "Our Constitution is color-blind," Harlan makes clear that the dominance of "the white race" is so great that it will not be challenged if Negroes should be allowed the exercise of constitutionally protected civil rights. In her biography of Harlan, Linda Przybyszewski shows how the justice's racial paternalism (coupled with a religious understanding of the Civil War as fulfillment of national destiny) led him to view a commitment to racial equality as a natural consequence of his Anglo-Saxon racial heritage. "Racial identity was essential . . . because whites expressed their racial identity best by extending civil rights to others regardless of race, and it was irrelevant for the same reason. Harlan declared the Constitution color-blind in the name of his racial heritage."[30]

If Justice Harlan understood the Fourteenth Amendment to reverse *Dred Scott* by guaranteeing the inclusion of Negros into the American political community, he evidently did not feel the same way about the American-born Chinese. In his *Plessy* dissent, Harlan wrote: "There is a race so different from our own that we do not permit those belonging to it to become citizens of the United States. Persons belonging to it are, with few exceptions, absolutely excluded from our country. I allude to the Chinese race. But by the statute in question, a Chinaman can ride in the same passenger coach with white citizens of the United States."[31] Harlan's explicit invocation of racialized nationalism is, at the very least, difficult to reconcile with the absolute rejection of race which his dissent so often is made to represent.[32]

Harlan's coupling of color-blindness with paternalistic racial pride also explains the sentence that bridges the two quotations, above, in which he seemed explicitly to claim that the state may not "know the race" of those seeking protection. "Every true man," Harlan opined, "has pride of race, and under appropriate circumstances, when the rights of others, his equals before the law, are not to be affected, it is his privilege to express such pride and to take such action based upon it as to him seems appropriate."[33] If "pride of race" was compatible with color-blindness, that is because the defining feature of color-blindness is not a self-imposed ignorance of race, but rather the exercise of restraint by the dominant (white) class in regard to Negro exercise of civil rights.[34]

What Justice Harlan Knew

That Justices Brown and Harlan in fact shared similar sensibilities regarding the relative fixity of racial differences in American society casts doubt upon standard interpretations of the phrase "Our Constitution is color-blind." Understood principally as a critique of the majority opinion's formalism, rather than its biological racism, Harlan's phrase takes on a quite different meaning. Where Brown's invocation of natural racial differences sought to justify the injurious effects of segregation upon nonwhite citizens, his second line of argument asserted that segregation placed no additional burdens on Negroes, since the law applied equally to both races and provided identical punishments for whites and for nonwhites who violated it.[35] For this reason, he claimed, racial segregation was perfectly consistent with the Fourteenth Amendment's requirement of "absolute equality" before the law.

Brown's argument severed the connection between the law's formal neutrality and segregation's unmistakable purpose: "Laws permitting, and even requiring, their separation in places where they are liable to be brought into contact do not necessarily imply the inferiority of either race to the other." On this view, racial distinctions need not be abolished but would be treated just like any other legal category, and their constitutional permissibility would therefore be determined by the "reasonableness" of the exercise of state power.[36] The reasonability of racial segregation, moreover, Brown inferred from two judicially sanctioned uses of racial distinctions: segregated schools and prohibitions against interracial marriage and sexual contact.[37]

The basic structure of the argument can be traced back to the unlikely source of Lemuel Shaw, chief justice of the Massachusetts Supreme Judicial Court in the 1850 school segregation case of *Roberts v. City of Boston.*[38] Shaw's opinion in that case upheld the constitutionality of Boston's segregated schools on the grounds that the principle of equality before the law did not imply that all should receive "the same treatment," but rather that all are entitled to equal regard and "paternal consideration."[39] Just as equal protection did not compel the identical treatment of parents and children or women and men, neither did it condemn the separation of students based on differences of age or educational need—or race. Racial distinctions would be prohibited when placed in the service of prejudice and domination, but allowed when, as deemed in this case, "the good of both classes of schools will be promoted, by maintaining the separate primary schools for colored and for white children."[40]

Brown's reliance on *Roberts*, while establishing the structure of his argument, had two obvious drawbacks. First, *Roberts* had been decided before the ratification of the Fourteenth Amendment and so did not speak to the extent of protections that the Equal Protection Clause might afford. And second, it would be difficult to show how the Louisiana Separate Car Act worked to "the good of both classes" of citizens. The Court's treatment of antimiscegenation laws, however, developed the argument in ways that addressed both concerns.

The Court had embraced the idea of symmetrical equality just over a decade before the *Plessy* decision in *Pace v. Alabama.*[41] In *Pace*, Justice Field had insisted on the neutrality of laws prohibiting interracial adultery or fornication on the grounds that "the punishment of each offending person, whether white or black, is the same."[42] Although Justice Brown does not cite *Pace*, the reference may be implied from his assertion that antimiscegenation laws "have been universally recognized as within the police power of the State"[43] and from the structure of the argument.[44] Moreover, the Court in *Pace* had not felt constrained by Shaw's principle that racial distinctions must work for the benefit of both races. Instead, prohibitions against interracial sexual contact were justified as serving the community's interest and general welfare—which the Court nonetheless defined in strikingly racialist terms. As formulated by the Alabama Supreme Court, the expressed purpose of the law was to prevent the "amalgamation of the two races, producing a mongrel population and a degraded civilization, the prevention of which is dictated by a sound public policy affecting the higher interests of society and government."[45]

In similar fashion, Brown's opinion in *Plessy* asserted that segregated railway travel carried with it no implication of inferiority for either race. Ignoring the plain meaning of segregation, Brown blamed the victims of Jim Crow for their recognition of the injury they sustained:

We consider the underlying fallacy of the plaintiff's argument to consist in the assumption that the enforced separation of the two races stamps the colored race with a badge of inferiority. If this be so, it is not by reason of anything found in the act, but solely because the colored race chooses to put that construction upon it.[46]

It was about this last line that Professor Black famously wrote: "the curves of callousness and stupidity intersect at their respective maxima."[47] The literal truth of Brown's claim, that nothing in the statute on its face treats blacks differently than whites, is only intelligible to the extent that it abstracts the law outside of its social context and obvious legislative purpose. It requires one to believe that segregation statutes were intended to keep whites out of "colored cars" rather than to announce with the authority of the state that blacks are degraded, inferior, and unfit for association with whites.

This interpretation was, of course, directly contradicted by the actual practice of segregation. The inferior conditions of the Jim Crow cars,[48] the historical roots of segregation in the regulation of antebellum free blacks,[49] the ideological connection between whiteness and purity or blackness and pollution,[50] and the lack of enforcement of the law against whites (who would often go to the "black cars" to smoke cigarettes or drink alcohol)[51] all testify to the true purpose and function of segregation as an instrument in the maintenance of white supremacy. Brown's suggestion that the degrading social meaning of racial segregation exists "solely because the colored race chooses to put that construction upon it" works a kind of double injury, constitutionalizing the physical segregation of racial minorities while simultaneously disqualifying minority interpretations of their own lived experiences. Justice Brown's argument is disingenuous in its winking disavowal of segregation's degrading intent, but also in its presumption that words can mean whatever one chooses (or mean nothing at all). What disappears in Brown's fantastical linguistic account is just what ought to be at the center of the analysis: the fact of white supremacy.

There is nothing unusual, of course, in a nineteenth-century legal opinion holding to the strict language of the law as an abstraction to be studied independently of social context. Jurisprudence from this era is commonly marked by what modern readers will view as an excessive degree of formalism.[52] That *Plessy* assumes a depoliticized conception of race is not in itself particularly surprising, given the legal conventions of its time. However, when viewed as the target of Justice Harlan's famous "color-blind" dissent, Brown's willingness to disregard the social implications of legislative uses of racial distinctions becomes highly significant. In rejecting "the thin disguise of 'equal' accommodations,"[53] Harlan was criticizing the willful ignorance of Brown's symmetrical equality argument. The phrase was not, as is often suggested, primarily a critique of racial distinctions per se.

It is notable that Harlan's linking of color-blindness and racial pride invokes constitutionally protected "civil rights" rather than the "social rights" of which Justice Brown's majority opinion was so dismissive. The distinction provides another reason to doubt the familiar interpretation of Harlan's "color-blindness" as racial nonrecognition. If that had been Harlan's intent, his prohibition against racial classification would suffice to void the statute, along with all other laws that classified by race. But that position would also have committed Harlan to strike down laws that prohibited interracial marriage and sexual contact. Not only was Harlan not prepared to take such a position, he had recently joined with the majority in upholding just such a law in *Pace*. Consequently, his argument had to explain why the state was justified in outlawing interracial sexual intimacy yet prohibited from barring interracial contact on railway cars or other public accommodations.

This task was accomplished by identifying the right to travel (and the equal use of public accommodations) as a civil, as opposed to social, right. The distinction allowed Harlan to present interracial sexual contact—the quintessential example of "social equality"—as categorically distinct from civil rights and therefore unprotected by the Constitution.[54] In this sense, there is nothing in Harlan's dissent that contradicts Justice Brown's assertion that the Fourteenth Amendment "could not have been intended to abolish distinctions based upon color, or to enforce social, as distinguished from political, equality, or a commingling of the two races on terms unsatisfactory to either."[55] Rather than defending social equality, Harlan shifted the use of public accommodations in travel from a social to a civil right. Harlan's critique of segregated railway travel did not, therefore, commit him to the doctrine of color-blindness in regard to interracial intimacy.

Given Harlan's acquiescence to the holding in *Pace*, it is even more noteworthy that his *Plessy* dissent refuses the underlying logic by which the *Pace* Court reached its conclusion. In neither case can Harlan's decision be explained simply by a "color-blind" rule that prohibits the consideration of race. Harlan's dissent is better understood if proper weight is given to the language that surrounds the phrase "Our Constitution is color-blind," which calls for a more substantive investigation into the law's social meaning and purpose to shore up the boundaries of racial classes or "caste." When Harlan wrote that "in the eye of the law" there is "no caste here,"[56] he meant to enlist the Court against racial hierarchy, not to deny its existence. This much is at least implied by his shift from social to civil rights, since it allowed him to pick up the anticaste language from *Strauder* that Justice Brown had attempted to evade. In *Strauder*, Justice Strong characterized the Fourteenth Amendment as guaranteeing to Negroes "exemption from legal discriminations, implying inferiority in civil society, lessening the security of their enjoyment of rights which others enjoy, and *discriminations which are steps toward reducing them to the condition of a subject race*."[57] This understanding of equal protection, which clearly resonates with contemporary antisubordination theories, was readily available to Justice Harlan, whose invocation of caste drew on a tradition of argument about status hierarchies prevalent in pre–Civil War abolitionist political rhetoric and throughout Reconstruction.[58]

In *Plessy*, Harlan uses the rhetoric of caste to expose the absurdity of Justice Brown's argument from symmetrical equality. Read this way, Harlan's dissent locates the error of the *Plessy* majority not only in its assumption of natural racial difference, but more precisely in the willful ignorance through which Justice Brown claimed segregation laws applied equally to members of both races. The trope of blindness that is the centerpiece of Harlan's dissent is commonly understood to suggest an intentional withholding of knowledge of the racial identity of those on whom the law operates. But it cuts also against Justice Brown's refusal to examine social context and his excessively formalistic interpretation of the law. The Constitution, Harlan wrote, "neither knows *nor tolerates* classes among citizens."[59] If it is the case that "not tolerating" classes (such as racial castes) requires the law to take notice of the practices that keep those classes subordinated, then Harlan's dissent must mean something other than a straightforward rule of racial nonrecognition.

Indeed, Harlan rejects the claim that Louisiana's law was "applicable alike to white and colored citizens" precisely by invoking a shared knowledge of the ordinary meaning of segregation and not by shielding oneself from that knowledge: "*Everyone knows* that the statute in question had its origin in the purpose, not so much to exclude white persons from railroad cars occupied by blacks, as to exclude colored people from coaches occupied by or assigned to white persons."[60] Where color-blindness suggests an act of intentional nonrecognition, Harlan's appeal to common knowledge implies just the opposite: a demand for knowledge of social meaning and a refusal to be misled. Brown's argument is disingenuous because it uses formal legal rules to distort the plain meaning of Jim Crow. It willfully blinds itself to important social facts, foremost among them the fact of white supremacy and the use of Jim Crow as an instrument of domination.

Not only is Harlan's dissent compatible with more expansive conceptions of justice, it also requires judges to discern the legislative purposes and social meanings of specific uses of racial distinctions—which today's color-blind constitutionalists expressly disallow.[61] His rejoinder to Brown's formalism invokes what he takes to be common knowledge about race. The fact of racial subordination, and the purpose of the law in maintaining it, is something that "everyone knows" and (the majority opinion excepted) "all will admit."[62] Harlan similarly rejects the disingenuous claim to equality in separate accommodations, writing that "the thin disguise of 'equal' accommodations for passengers in railroad coaches will not mislead any one."[63] And so it is Harlan's insistence upon knowledge, rather than self-imposed blindness, that reveals the injury in what might otherwise pass as a neutral rule.

When properly understood as a critique of symmetrical equality, Harlan's dissent can be seen as altogether inconsistent with the color-blind approach as it is currently conceived. Contemporary assaults on affirmative action that invoke Harlan's dissent thus distort the meaning of his now-famous phrase. To the extent that Brown's position requires courts to ignore the social significance of specific racial classifications, the Court's contemporary color-blindness more closely resembles the majority in *Plessy* than Harlan's dissent. It is the false neutrality of Justice Brown's willful ignorance (and not just the unequal accommodations) that constitutes "the thin disguise."

The Challenge of Racial Indeterminacy

In the preceding sections, I have tried to show how the meaning of "color-blindness" in Justice Harlan's famous dissent derives in large part from its rejection of specific claims in the majority opinion. Together, this "yoked pair" constitutes one entry in Primus's "dual canon" (as linked canonical and anticanonical texts). But Harlan's dissent is not the only canonical text with which the *Plessy* majority is paired. An overturned precedent may just as easily be yoked to the case that overturns it, which is why Justice Brown's *Plessy* opinion is naturally paired with *Brown v. Board of Education* as well. Harlan's dissent and the unanimous *Brown* decision both take their meaning in relationship to the *Plessy* majority they denounce, and both are cited as such by contemporary courts—despite the fact that "the holding of *Brown* is not the same as the 'holding' of Harlan's *Plessy* dissent."[64] At the same time, however less well recognized, the *Plessy* majority and dissenting opinions are both also marked by their relationship to another text and another set of legal arguments made by Plessy's attorney, Albion Tourgée. While Tourgée's arguments about "passing" and racial indeterminacy remain outside the legal canon, I will argue in this and the following sections that they nonetheless reveal important insights about Brown's opinion and Justice Harlan's dissent. Revisiting Justice Harlan's dissent in the context of Plessy's ambiguous racial status both complicates the binary opposition between color-blindness and color-consciousness, and suggests the need for judicial attention to the social and political forces through which race is made a meaningful social and legal category.

From their inception, Louisiana's segregation laws were marked by the region's strong Creole tradition. As a French colony, both demographic and cultural factors contributed to high rates of interracial sexual contact,[65] and the origins and subsequent development of slavery in antebellum Louisiana provided conditions for a greater hybridity of peoples and cultures than elsewhere in North America.[66] Both French and Spanish law in Louisiana encouraged the growth of sizable free Negro and mulatto communities in possession of legal, social, and economic rights that were denied in the British colonies.[67]

Consequently Louisiana, and particularly New Orleans, became a site in which interracial sex was neither uncommon nor entirely socially condemned. In the early 1800s, New Orleans was known for its quadroon balls—popular dances in which admission was limited to white men and free black women.[68] By the middle of the nineteenth century, the institution of plaçage had developed, in which affluent white men would maintain socially acknowledged long-term extramarital relationships with women of color.[69] The combination of socially recognized interracial relationships with the greater freedoms and economic opportunities that mixed-race people could enjoy fostered New Orleans's thriving community of free people of color (*gens de couleur libre*).

The New Orleans Creole community has been described as "a third race of people neither white nor black and neither slave nor completely free."[70] It would be more precise to say that racial hierarchy in Louisiana followed the three-tiered pattern of the Spanish and French empires and was therefore in tension with the American two-tiered model.[71] Creoles were distinguished by language, culture, and ethnicity rather than color, whereas the American pattern insisted upon racial dichotomy. The "Americanization" of New Orleans after Reconstruction is therefore best understood as a conflict between these two racial systems that comes to a head over the question of segregation: "The imposition of Jim Crow at the dawn of the twentieth century symbolized the ascendance of the new order and accelerated the submergence of ethnicity—both black and white—as a stark racial dualism held uncontested sway."[72] Given Louisiana's Creole heritage, Jim Crow laws helped to create the racial groups that they purported to keep apart. Racial indeterminacy, "passing," and mixed race were all problematic for segregation laws because they unsettled the basic categories upon which such laws relied for their justification and required for their administration.

The Separate Car Act of 1890 was deeply resented by the Negro and Creole citizens of New Orleans alike, but it was especially threatening to the Creole community, who had more to lose from segregation than did their black counterparts.[73] It is not surprising, then, that segregation held a key place in conflicts between the two groups. The conflict reached its peak when the black former Republican governor P. B. S. Pinchback agreed to support the Redeemer Constitution of 1879 in exchange for the creation of a black college, Southern University.[74] As most black leaders adopted this accommodationist strategy, New Orleans's Creoles organized in resistance to the separate car law. Under the leadership of Aristide Mary, Rodolphe Desdunes (founder of the weekly civil rights publication *The Crusader*) and Louis Martinet (the *Crusader*'s editor), the Citizens' Committee to Test the Constitutionality of the Separate Car Law (Comité des Citoyens) was created in order to contest the laws in court. The Comité des Citoyens provided the organizational structure and resources to bring a test case. In addition to raising public interest in the case, it raised the funds to cover the legal expenses that such a case would require, coordinated with railroad companies that also opposed the law,[75] and arranged for Albion Tourgée (the self-proclaimed carpetbagger lawyer, novelist, and outspoken advocate of Negro rights) to handle the legal defense.[76] They also supplied Homer Plessy, who agreed to be arrested on an East Louisiana Railroad train in order to provide a suitable case to test.

Plessy was selected for the job in part because he was a friend of Desdunes, but Tourgée was also explicit in his preference for a light-complexioned defendant with which to test the constitutionality of the Louisiana law. Plessy's complexion was so light, in fact, that a story in The *Crusader* described him as "white as the average white Southerner."[77] This choice may have been a tactical decision meant to appeal to the racist preferences of the judges, but it also served as ironic commentary on the arbitrary nature of racial classifications, given that Plessy's skin color was the same as the judge who presided over the case.[78]

Given the strained relations between black and Creole leaders in New Orleans, and considering the centrality of the segregation issue to that conflict, it is not surprising that the Comité des Citoyens' conscious choice of a light-skinned litigant was met with considerable criticism. In a letter to Tourgée, Martinet relayed concerns from some members of the New Orleans black community that the Citizens' Committee was only representing the interests of "those who were nearly white, or wanted to pass for white."[79] The criticism characterizes passing as an attempt by mulattos to retain the privileges that their light skin had afforded prior to the Americanization of New Orleans and the imposition of a two-tiered racial hierarchy. At stake in this formulation is the meaning of Plessy's light skin and the material benefits it afforded in a society structured by race and color hierarchy. Plessy's ability to pass for white, had he chosen to do so, derives from the inconsistency between his racial appearance and his legal racial status. While critics have charged that Plessy's racial passing represents the ability of light-skinned blacks to appropriate the privileges of whiteness, the *Plessy* case also demonstrates how passing might represent a more radical challenge to white supremacy itself.

In his 1988 law review article "Property Rights in Whiteness: Their Legal Legacy, Their Economic Costs," Derrick Bell illustrates the property-like quality of whiteness by contrasting *Plessy* with *Lochner v. New York* (1905).[80] In *Lochner*, the landmark "substantive due process" case, the Court struck down a maximum-hour worker safety law for bakers on the grounds that it violated the fundamental right to contract. *Lochner* was decided only eight years after *Plessy*, which, Bell notes, upheld racial segregation "even though such segregation must, of necessity, interfere with the liberties of facilities' owners to use their property as they saw fit."[81] If the right to contract prohibited the state of New York from regulating private economic transactions such as work contracts, even in the interest of maintaining safe workplace conditions, why did it allow the state of Louisiana to interfere with the private and voluntary economic transaction between a railway company and passengers of different races who wished to be seated together? Bell argues that the railway's right to contract was trumped by the Court's commitment to maintaining the property interests of whites *as a class*, thus constituting a property interest in their whiteness.

Building on Bell's thesis, Cheryl Harris draws a more direct connection between *Plessy*'s recognition of property rights in whiteness and Plessy's ability to pass. Noting that Plessy's argument "was predicated on more than the Equal Protection Clause of the Fourteenth Amendment," Harris describes Plessy's additional claim that the refusal to seat him on the "white

car" deprived him of property without due process of law: "Because phenotypically Plessy appeared to be white, barring him from the railway car
reserved for whites severely impaired or deprived him of the reputation of
being regarded as white . . . [and] the public and private benefits of white
status."[82] Plessy's claim to injury, in the denial of property without due
process of law, is thus predicated upon his ability to pass for white. Had he
been dark-skinned, he could not reasonably have been regarded as white,
and so could neither possess nor be deprived of such a property.

As Harris observes, *Plessy* explicitly endorsed the general view that
one holds a property right in one's reputation as a white person, yet denied
Plessy's specific claim on the grounds that he was not in fact white—
and therefore had suffered no loss of property. The relevant passage from
Justice Brown's opinion for the Court reads as follows:

> It is claimed by the plaintiff in error that, in any mixed community, the rep-
> utation of belonging to the dominant race, in this instance the white race, is
> *property*, in the same sense that a right of action, or of inheritance, is property.
> Conceding this to be so . . . we are unable to see how this statute deprives him
> of, or in any way affects his right to, such property. If he be a white man and
> assigned to a colored coach, he may have his action for damages against the
> company for being deprived of his so-called property. Upon the other hand, if
> he be a colored man and be so assigned, he has been deprived of no property,
> since he is not lawfully entitled to the reputation of being a white man.[83]

Harris traces the argument to its origins in a brief submitted by Plessy's
lawyer, Albion Tourgée.[84] In that brief, Tourgée asks "how much it would
be *worth* to a young man entering upon a practice of law, to be regarded as
a *white* man rather than a colored one"—and answers that "*the reputation
of being white* . . . is the most valuable sort of property, being the master-
key that unlocks the golden door of opportunity."[85]

For Harris, the passage from the Tourgée brief, like Justice Brown's
appropriation of it, is significant for its clear recognition of the material
advantages that attach to being regarded as a white person in America. It
illustrates what Harris calls "the Court's chronic refusal to dismantle the
structure of white supremacy"—which she identifies as an unstated premise of the Court's current equal protection jurisprudence.[86] Affirmative
action contests the property interest in whiteness, the Court's hostility to
affirmative action preserves it. For Harris and Bell, the *Plessy* doctrine of
"separate but equal" has been rejected, but the *Plessy* principle of property
rights in whiteness has not.

For Tourgée, however, the property-like quality of whiteness is crucial for a somewhat different reason. His formulation of the argument is less concerned with the property value of whiteness, which it assumes, and more concerned with the mechanisms by which whiteness is determined—and the inherent difficulties that racial sorting inevitably encounters. If whiteness is property, and the Fourteenth Amendment prevents the denial of that property without due process of law, then racial classifications might in themselves be unconstitutional if Tourgée could show that the process of classification was arbitrary. The Louisiana law was arbitrary in precisely this way, Tourgée argued, because it required train conductors or other railway employees to make unqualified on-the-spot determinations of a passenger's race and therefore violated the Fourteenth Amendment's prohibition against denying citizens property without due process of law.[87]

In their critique of *Plessy*, Bell and Harris are right to identify the Court's protection of a property right in whiteness implicit in Justice Brown's analysis of passing. But their critique of whiteness as property in the *Plessy* case fails to appreciate Tourgée's subversive use of racial indeterminacy. For Harris, passing is always tied to property rights in whiteness because it is precisely the privileges of whiteness that lead people to pass. In the opening pages of her article, Harris tells the moving story of how her grandmother, part of the great northern migration, found herself living in Chicago with limited economic options and decided to present herself as a white woman in order to secure work in a retail store that refused to hire people of color. Harris describes this decision as "an act of both great daring and self-denial,"[88] not only for the risk of being caught in a racial deception, but also for the risk of losing her true self, of betraying her true identity. Successful "passing" meant better pay and working conditions, but it also posed an existential danger. "Becoming white"[89] violated her grandmother's sense of self just as much as it violated the community norm of racial segregation. Harris describes the dilemma as a trade-off: "the price of her family's well-being was her silence. Accepting the risk of self-annihilation was the only way to survive."[90] The story illustrates how whiteness is property in the most ordinary and practical sense; it is such valuable property that people will endure the emotional strain of living a lie in order to receive its material benefits.

Without detracting from the immense psychological and emotional distress that many "passers" must have experienced, there are still good reasons to resist Harris's implicit joining of the concept of *race* to the language of *truth*. Passing for Harris, as it was for Justice Brown, is an act of deception. Brown characterized the possibility of Plessy's passing as a kind of theft, by which a light-skinned black man falsely laid claim to white identity for the material benefits it entailed. If "passing" is lying, it is only because there exists a truth of race about which one could lie. And it is only because the property value of whiteness is so great that one would choose to endure such a lie.[91] But this formulation of race-as-truth also leads Harris to portray passing as a conservative strategy that bestows the privileges of whiteness on light-skinned mulattos rather than challenging the structure of white supremacy itself:

> Like passing, affirmative action undermines the property interest in whiteness. Unlike passing, which seeks the shelter of an assumed whiteness as a means of extending protection at the margins of racial boundaries, affirmative action de-privileges whiteness and seeks to remove the legal protections of the existing hierarchy spawned by race oppression. What passing attempts to circumvent, affirmative action moves to challenge.[92]

Harris portrays passing as an effort to expand the privileges of whiteness to light-skinned Creoles like Plessy rather than critiquing white supremacy head-on. But this formulation fails to appreciate the more radical threat to whiteness that passing provided in Tourgée's legal strategy. The very concept of whiteness, Tourgée argued, could not be understood independent of the institutional mechanisms through which races were defined:

> The Court will take notice of the fact that, in all parts of the country, race-intermixture has proceeded to such an extent that there are great numbers of citizens in whom the preponderance of blood of one race or another, is impossible of ascertainment, except by careful scrutiny of pedigree. As slavery did not permit the marriage of the slave, in a majority of cases even an approximate determination of the preponderance is an actual impossibility, with the most careful and deliberate weighing of evidence, much less by the casual scrutiny of a busy conductor.[93]

Where Brown's account rests upon the assumption of an underlying racial truth (against which passing is read as deception), Tourgée's argument deploys the idea of passing to call out the inherent instability of those racial categories upon which Brown's argument depends. By shifting the focus from the legal treatment of African Americans as a class to the legal process of determining an individual's race, Tourgée hoped to render the racial classification demanded by segregation both practically and conceptually incoherent.

The racially destabilizing potential inherent in passing is evident in a letter that local attorney Louis Martinet wrote to Tourgée, discussing the choice of a light-skinned plaintiff for the case. Martinet observed that "people of tolerably fair complexion, even if unmistakably colored, enjoy here a large degree of immunity from the accursed prejudice" and therefore might not be arrested.[94] Aside from the obvious complication (that the arrest was necessary to pursue a test case), Martinet's letter to Tourgée is usually quoted to attest to the higher social status of light-skinned over darker-skinned blacks.[95] But while Martinet was alerting Tourgée to the practical problem of finding a suitable test case, he also connected that concern to the notable difficulty in distinguishing whites from blacks in New Orleans. Examined in its entirety, the passage takes on a rather different implication:

> It would be quite difficult to have a lady *too* nearly white refused admission to a "white" car. There are the strangest white people you ever saw here. Walking up and down our principal thoroughfare—Canal Street—you would [be] surprised to have persons pointed out to you, some as white & others as colored, and if you were not informed you would be sure to pick out the white for colored and the colored for white. Besides, people of tolerably fair complexion, even if unmistakably colored, enjoy here a large degree of immunity from the accursed prejudice.[96]

Martinet identifies two different senses in which race and mixed-race find themselves conceptually at odds. In the first lines of the passage he describes a community in which the color line—or at least the precise boundaries of the color line—is thoroughly confounded. This fact does not in itself invalidate racial classification, but it does force Martinet to distinguish these "passers" from another group who remain "unmistakably colored" despite their "tolerably fair complexions." Unlike members of the second group, whose racial identity is "unmistakable," those in the first set remained "colored" *despite their white appearance.* Their "coloredness" derives, then, from some source other than appearance, some source other than color. It is a source that is not named but rather lingers as an implicit if unasked question of racial origins or essence. There is at least a possibility of slippage here, between the problem of correctly categorizing a particular ambiguously raced individual and the broader difficulty of maintaining the salience of those general racial categories under such conditions. Passing, in this latter sense, provides the occasion for pressing these difficult questions that try to remain unasked. This is precisely the strategy that

Tourgée pursues in arguments submitted to the US Supreme Court. It is not an attempt to expand the roster of white privilege but rather to undermine the stability of racial classifications.

The Tourgée brief begins with a seemingly simple question: "Has the State the power under the provisions of the Constitution of the United States, to make a distinction based on color in the enjoyment of chartered privileges within the state?"[97] It is tempting to read this question as concerned primarily with the extent of legitimate state power in treating racial minorities or, conversely, the scope of Fourteenth Amendment protections such minorities could expect. And this would not be incorrect. But one notices also that the question more precisely concerns the legality of state-mandated racial assignments. As Tourgée made clear, "The gist of our case . . . is the unconstitutionality of the assortment: *not* the question of equal accommodation."[98] Tourgée refused to let the question of equal treatment of races come untethered from the logically prior question of how it is determined to what race an individual belongs.

The activity of racial classification is prior to any question of equal treatment because racial classification defines the terms of comparison which later may be judged permissible or not. Before we can discuss the acceptable treatment of blacks, that is, we will have to be able to determine who is black. Tourgée puts the question to the Court:

> Has [the State] the power to require the officers of a railroad to assort its citizens by race, before permitting them to enjoy privileges dependent on public charter?
>
> Is the officer of a railroad competent to decide the question of race?
>
> Is it a question that *can* be determined in the absence of statutory definition and without evidence?[99]

The question that emerged from Martinet's description of "passing" on Canal Street (what does it mean to be "colored" if it is not a question of color?) is thus placed before the Supreme Court in the form of Homer Plessy's own ambiguous racial identity. But where Martinet's description initiated a question of what race *is*, Tourgée's questioning demands an account of how race is *determined*, who makes the determination, and by what criteria it is to be made:

> Has the State the power under the Constitution to authorize any officer of a railroad to put a passenger off the train and refuse to carry him *because*

he happens to differ with the officer as to the race to which he properly belongs?[100]

Before considering the meaning of equal treatment, Tourgée would have us ask what it is that is (or is not) being treated equally. Before considering if Homer Plessy is white, Tourgée asks by what authority a train conductor makes such a determination. On what basis would one know if the conductor was correct in his determination? Questions such as these expose the process by which bodies are raced, and the seeds of skepticism about the process of racial classification come to infect the resulting racial categories. The emphasis on the activity of racial determination in Tourgée's sentence (marked in italics to emphasize the disagreement over classification rather than the legality of removing a passenger from the train) unsettles the status of "properly belonging" to one's race at the sentence's conclusion.

Tourgée continues, but with the status of racial belonging now placed under scare quotes: "Has the State the power under the Constitution, to declare a man guilty of misdemeanor and subject to fine and imprisonment, *because* he may differ with the officer of a railroad as to 'the race to which he belongs?' "[101] The questioning has a certain trajectory, undermining confidence not only in the assessment of Homer Plessy's race, but in the stability of races more generally:

> Is not the question of race, scientifically considered, very often impossible of determination?
>
> Is not the question of race, legally considered, one impossible to be determined, in the absence of statutory definition?[102]

Where the determination of Homer Plessy's race by a train conductor on the East Louisiana Railroad line was too arbitrary to constitute due process of law, Tourgée's argument also suggests that *no* method of racial classification could be sufficiently nonarbitrary as to make segregation constitutionally valid.

Tourgée's argument against racial classification trades heavily upon the practical and logical difficulties of maintaining the boundaries of race in view of a history of race intermixture throughout the country. But the critical force of his claim derives not only from the inherent instability of racial categories, but from his recognition that racial classifications were exercises in power designed to keep blacks a subordinated class. That his deconstruction of racial categories is closely tied to a critique of white supremacy can be seen clearly in the remarkable thought experiment with which he concludes his brief, and which bears quoting at length:

> Suppose a member of this Court, nay, suppose every member of it, by some mysterious dispensation of providence should wake tomorrow with black skin and curly hair—the two obvious and controlling indications of race—and in travelling where the "Jim Crow Car" abounds, should be ordered into it by the conductor. It is easy to imagine what would be the result, the indignation, the protests, the assertion of pure Caucasian ancestry. But the conductor, the autocrat of Caste, armed with the power of the State conferred by this statute, would listen neither to denial or protest . . .
>
> What humiliation, what rage would then fill the judicial mind! How would the resources of language not be taxed in objurgation! Why would this sentiment prevail in your minds? Simply because you would then feel and know that such assortment of the citizens on the line of race was a discrimination intended to humiliate and degrade the former subject and dependent class—an attempt to perpetuate the caste distinctions on which slavery rested—a statute in the words of the Court tending to reduce the colored people of the country to the condition of a subject race.[103]

In imagining the justices of the Supreme Court thus transformed in appearance, Tourgée's thought experiment oddly inverts Plessy's situation. Like Plessy (a white black man), the hypothetical justices (as black white men) would be ordered into the Jim Crow car. Playing on the obvious absurdity of the scene, the hypothetical suggests that Plessy's racial classification is as arbitrary as that of the (phenotypically) black judges.

What decides the question of which race each will be? Tourgée's hypothetical demonstrates the power of law to impose racial subjectivity: it is not simply a matter of properly matching the race of each person to the appropriate train car. Rather, an individual's race may be a *product* of being assigned to a white or a colored car. In this regard Tourgée anticipates W. E. B. Du Bois's quip that the definition of a black man is "a person who must ride Jim Crow in Georgia."[104] The assignment of racial identity in Tourgée's example is arbitrary both in its lack of satisfactory criteria upon which to base the decision, and in the unprincipled and unconstitutional exercise of power. The two elements join in Tourgée's description of the conductor as an "autocrat of Caste." Ultimately, what Tourgée hopes the hypothetical will expose is Jim Crow's true purpose, which is to "humiliate and degrade," to perpetuate racial caste, to reduce colored folks to "the condition of a subject race."

The significance of Homer Plessy's white appearance, and the reason why Tourgée intentionally sought out a light-skinned defendant, is that with such a defendant the normal operation of segregation laws evidently includes the constitutive power to enforce racialized subjectivity. Reading *Plessy* as "passing" makes visible this aspect of the law's operation, drawing our conception of race up from the body and onto the power exercised by the state's assignation of racial categories. From this perspective, the Court may be seen to participate in the creation and maintenance of those very racial categories on whose behalf the law claims to act.

Judicial Responses to Ambiguously Raced Bodies

As we have seen, Harlan's *Plessy* dissent serves as something of a sacred text for color-blind conservatives. On this familiar interpretation, constitutional equality is measured by adherence to the anticlassification principle, the justification for which is demonstrated through its rejection of the majority opinion's evident biological racism. Differences in race and color are natural facts for Brown, just as social relationships organized around race are taken for natural outgrowths of biology and therefore immune to judicial intervention. Yet, despite Brown's assumption of distinct natural races, his opinion is unable to avoid the questions posed by Homer Plessy's racial ambiguity in the Tourgée brief. In contrast to the language of natural difference, Brown is forced to acknowledge the legal process by which courts are called upon to assign races to particular individuals and to issue criteria by which the boundaries of racial categories are defined. Brown's explicit recognition of the legal construction of race appears in the text of his opinion and also can be found in the cases that he cites as precedent.

Brown's decision explicitly addresses the issue of racial classification raised in the Tourgée brief. Despite his earlier claim that race flows naturally from color, Justice Brown notes that the state's authority to segregate based on race will necessitate a legal determination of the boundaries of racial categories:

> The power to assign a particular coach obviously implies *the power to determine to which race the passenger belongs*, as well as the power to determine who, under the laws of the particular State, is to be deemed a white, and who a colored person.[105]

While the logic of the majority decision rests upon the natural distinctions between races, the Court nonetheless recognizes that those boundaries require state definition and regulation. Rather than finding distinct groups in the world, and then regulating their conduct, the Court now appears to describe a scheme of categorization that depends upon legal construction even while acting in the name of those "natural" differences. And because not all states define racial identity according to the same criteria, the Court's reliance upon natural differences runs into the embarrassing fact that someone who is "naturally white" in North Carolina may be "naturally black" in Virginia, or any state with a different legal definition of white or Negro or colored.

Justice Brown is not unaware of this contradiction. The sheer range of racial definitions is problematic for Brown in two senses. First, the diversity of definitions makes the question of *what* one is dependent upon the question of *where* one is. The less consistency with which racial identities are judged, the less natural those judgments will seem. Second, because the diverse standards of racial determination call attention to the legal apparatus by which racial identities are assigned, the seeming naturalness of racial categories is bound to be unsettled by the extensive involvement of social institutions in defining and enforcing racial boundaries.

Justice Brown's solution to this problem is to pass it along to the states to deal with, citing state court rulings that employ various formulae of racial determination:

> It is true that the question of the proportion of colored blood necessary to constitute a colored person, as distinguished from a white person, is one upon which there is a difference of opinion in the different States, some holding that any visible admixture of black blood stamps the person as belonging to the colored race (State v. Chaver, 5 Jones [N.C.] 1, p. 11); others that it depends upon the preponderance of blood (Gray v. State, 4 Ohio 354; Monroe v. Collins, 17 Ohio St. 665); and still others that the predominance of white blood must only be in the proportion of three-fourths (People v. Dean, 4 Michigan 406; Jones v. Commonwealth, 80 Virginia 538). But these are questions to be determined under the laws of each State, and are not properly put in issue in this case.[106]

The passage is remarkable for a number of reasons. Because it is edited out of most legal casebooks that reproduce the opinion, it may be unfamiliar even to those who have carefully read the case. Moreover, it demonstrates an attention to law's constitutive power to impose racial identity that sits uncomfortably with the rest of the opinion. The apparent ease with which Brown dismisses the problem as a matter for state legislatures to decide may be of less significance than the fact that he feels compelled to address the problem at all.

The specific rationales that Brown points to in lower-court rulings are also of interest. Each of the decisions is claimed to make blood quantum the criteria of racial determination, whether it be "any visible admixture of black blood" or a "preponderance of blood" or a "proportion of three-fourths" standard. The "visible admixture" standard, however, while claiming the supposed objectivity of blood, nevertheless remains a visual standard, based on appearance (surface) rather than blood (depth). An assumed connection between surface and depth—which functions here as a rule of racial definition—is an implicit definition of our ordinary race concept: morphological differences thought to constitute distinct racial kinds take their authority from an assumed connection to racial essences that are carried below the skin, in blood (or more recently in the genes). Those physical features that serve as racial markers do so because they are taken as external signs of an internal racial truth. Justice Brown's response to ambiguously raced bodies may thus be understood as an attempt to shore up the solidity of internal racial essences by insulating them from the admittedly variable external criteria which a state may choose as its legal definition. The inherent messiness of racial identity might in this way be dismissed as belonging to the bureaucratic realm of proper administration, or to the legislative realm of adopting agreed-upon criteria for racial definition. Either way, the states are left with the authority to define race by statute, while the contradiction between state recognition of natural difference and the state's construction of those differences is "not properly put in issue in this case."

Brown's attempt to shift the problem to the state level is meant to resolve the difficulty of racial ambiguity. But even a cursory reading of the cases that he cites as precedent reveals the inadequacy of this solution. In each of the five cited cases the court ruled either to dismiss charges or remanded for a new trial because the state had failed to meet its burden of proving the race of the defendant. And in none of the cases does the court resolve the problem in the easy manner that Justice Brown implies. On the contrary, the cases cited in *Plessy*, while meant to show that the questions posed by racial ambiguity are "questions to be determined under the laws of each State," in fact demonstrate just what Albion Tourgée hoped to show—that Jim Crow laws not only constitute unequal treatment of racial minorities, but that they presume the state's authority to impose racial status without justification of the criteria by which such determinations can be made.

In the first case, *State v. Chavers* (1857), which Brown cites as establishing a preponderance-of-blood standard, the Supreme Court of North Carolina set aside the conviction of William Chavers under a statute that prohibited "free negroes" from carrying shotguns. Chavers, who was indicted as a "free person of color," argued "there was no evidence of his being a negro."[107] The court examined statutory and common language usage of the words "white" and "Negro" in order to reach its conclusion that "free negro" and "free person of color" are distinct legal categories, thus raising the possibility that Chavers, as a free person of color, was not subject to the prohibition against free Negroes carrying a shotgun.

In response to his ambiguous racial status, the court allowed various kinds of evidence, not all of which conforms to the visible admixture standard to which Brown refers. As evidence of lineage, the morphology of the defendant's father was introduced via the testimony of a witness who "proved that the defendant's father was a man of dark color and had kinky hair; that he was a shade darker than the defendant himself, and his hair was about as much kinked."[108] The court also allowed evidence of morphology that issued from an invitation by Chavers's counsel for "the jury to inspect him and judge for themselves."[109] But the court also allowed evidence that had nothing to do with physical appearance. Apparently Chavers traveled to his trial aboard a steamboat that charged white passengers a fare of one dollar but carried Negroes for half price. At trial, a Mr. Green testified that Chavers had presented himself as colored and paid only the fifty-cent fare, which was taken as proof of his race by "his own declaration." Presumably it is as important that Chavers was accepted by the steamboat operator as not white as it is that he claimed to be so. But here we find a standard of racial identification that is almost entirely performative. The public display and reception of racial identity is given evidentiary weight equal to that of morphology or lineage. Chavers could well have been "passing" for colored in order to avoid paying the higher fare at the steamboat, but either formulation (white "passing" for black or black "passing" for white) seems arbitrary, as his race was clearly neither black nor white, but rather indeterminate within a classificatory scheme whose purpose was to impose and maintain supposedly "pure" racial types.

In *Gray v. Ohio* (1831), which Brown cites as establishing a preponderance-of-blood standard, the Supreme Court of Ohio set aside the conviction of Polly Gray, who had been found guilty of robbery largely on the basis of testimony by a Negro witness. Under Ohio law, Negroes were deemed incompetent to testify against whites. Gray claimed to be white, thus rendering the testimony invalid. In response to Gray's objection at trial, "the prisoner appeared, upon inspection, and of such opinion was the court, to be of a shade of color between the mulatto and white."[110] Upon review, the Ohio Supreme Court reversed the trial court's judgment, finding that statutory and ordinary language usage recognized only three racial categories (white, Negro, and mulatto), none of which adequately described the defendant.

Far from resolving the problem of racial ambiguity, the court expressed reservations that such resolution could ever be supplied: "We are unable to set out any plain and obvious line or mark between the different races. Color alone is sufficient. We believe a man, of a race nearer white than a mulatto . . . should partake in the privileges of whites."[111] The rationale for the decision makes clear the court's discomfort at the position in which the judges were placed, issuing "partly from the difficulty of defining and of ascertaining the degree of duskiness which renders a person liable to such disabilities."[112] Despite the admittedly arbitrary nature of the rule, and to Polly Gray's great relief, the witness's "degree of duskiness" constituted something just short of white, and so the testimony was disallowed.

Justice Brown also cites two cases involving voting rights, in which ambiguously raced men sought to vote in states that limited the franchise to white males. In both cases the men sought court relief from disenfranchisement on the grounds that they were, in fact, legally white. In *Monroe v. Collins* (1867), the Supreme Court of Ohio struck down an 1868 supplement to the 1841 Act to Preserve the Purity of Elections, which immunized election officials against liability for damages upon denying the vote to those with a "visible admixture of African blood."[113] George Collins sought a ballot and was denied by James Monroe after Collins failed to provide the "proof required" by the 1868 act. That "proof" of whiteness consisted in an elaborate procedure in which the potential voter was asked a series of questions, including questions of lineage ("Had your parents, or either of them, a visible and distinct admixture of African blood?")[114] and questions of association ("In the community in which you live are you classified and recognized as a white or colored person, and do you associate with white or colored persons?").[115] If the vote was not rejected after the initial questioning, the election official was instructed to demand the oaths of "two credible witnesses" testifying that they knew the person challenging, and that they knew the parents of the challenger not to "have a distinct and visible admixture of African blood."[116] The act explicitly rejected evidence "founded merely upon appearance, unless the facts are fully stated as to the parentage of the person challenged."[117] The challenger was then required to take the following oath: "You do solemnly swear (or affirm) that, to the best of your knowledge and belief, you are a white male citizen of the United States, and know the fact to be so from a knowledge of both your parents and your pedigree."[118]

Collins refused to take the oath, and so was ruled ineligible to vote. Moreover, his stated reason for refusing the oath was that his racial classification was indeterminate and so the terms of the questioning precluded an honest response. In an answer that perfectly illustrates Tourgée's strategy, Collins declared: "I know of no established and well defined classification of persons as to color and shades of color, and am, therefore, unable to say how I am classified. I associate with persons white and persons black, when agreeable to all parties."[119] The question "do you associate with white or colored persons?" refuses the possibility of interracial association, making a truthful answer unintelligible.

Justice Brown is not entirely wrong in citing *Monroe v. Collins* for its preponderance-of-blood standard. The court does utilize such a standard in striking down as unconstitutional the Purity of Elections Act. But the facts of the case demonstrate the absurdities that the court encounters when setting out to define racial categories with any degree of precision. The sheer variety of sources of evidence (lineage, appearance, association, affirmation, belief) does little to convince that racial differences are natural facts that seamlessly translate into rules of social organization. Nor can Brown find much support in the court's conclusion that the act imposes an undue burden upon "white citizens of less than half African blood" (688).

The other voting rights case that Brown cites, *State v. Dean* (1866), is similarly ambiguous in its adoption of a clear standard by which to define whiteness. In this case, the Supreme Court of Michigan was asked to consider the conviction of William Dean on charges of "illegal voting,"[120] and took the opportunity to "settle the position of persons of mixed blood under [the Michigan] constitution."[121] As Brown suggests in *Plessy*, the court did settle upon a standard of requiring at least three-fourths white ancestry: "persons are white within the meaning of our constitution, in whom white blood so far preponderates that they have one-fourth of African blood."[122] But the rationale for the decision is less supportive of Brown's goal. The court does not find a natural distinction to guide its decision, but seems instead to accept the responsibility of imposing a uniform standard, arbitrary though it may be:

Rules of suffrage must be presumed uniform as far as possible. It must be admitted, therefore, that we are compelled to discover some mode of classification, and that persons of precisely the same blood must be treated alike, although they may differ in their complexions. There are white men as dark as mulattoes, and there are pure-blooded albino Africans as white as the whitest Saxons. This classification is no doubt a difficult task, and there is room for much disagreement in it, but no rule can be applied without some inconvenience; but that will not justify us, I think, in refusing to assume the duty.[123]

The court does not so much resolve ambiguity as impose an admittedly arbitrary rule of racial definition. The resulting racial categories are at least partly the products of those laws that innate racial differences are supposed to justify. Moreover, the "one-quarter black blood" standard is offered as an alternative to considerations of color that admittedly fail to do the work scientific racism requires of them. Yet, despite having severed the connection between race and color, the court's rationale for the "one-fourth" standard is based precisely upon the significance of appearance: "while quadroons are in most cases easily distinguished as not white, persons having less than one-fourth African blood are often enough white in appearance to render any further classifying difficult."[124] The reasoning of *State v. Dean* is thus quite inconsistent with Brown's interpretation of it. Racial ambiguity motivates the court's imposition of the "one-fourth" standard but does not resolve it.

The final case that Brown cites, *Jones v. Commonwealth* (1885), encounters a similar difficulty. *Jones* was an interracial marriage case that was decided by the Virginia Supreme Court along with *Gray v. Commonwealth*. In this case, Isaac Jones was sentenced to two years and nine months in the state penitentiary for "felonious marriage with Martha Gray, a white woman."[125] As a legal defense, Gray alleged that she had some black blood, while Jones claimed to have some white blood, thus legitimizing the marriage. The court applied a "one quarter black blood" rule, as the Michigan court did in *State v. Dean*, ordering a new trial at which the state would have to show evidence of "the quantum of negro blood in his veins."[126] However, the difficulty of establishing the races of the defendants can be seen in the kinds of evidence that were accepted by the court. As evidence that Martha had some "negro blood in her veins," the court observed that "her mother had given birth to negro children before her birth; that she herself was a bastard, and was accustomed to associate and attend church with negroes; and the colored pastor of the church testified that there were colored persons attending his church whiter than the said Martha."[127] However clear the "one-fourth" standard may seem on paper, the lived experience of race is anything but clear, and remains highly resistant to the kind of tidy classification that Brown assumes in his citation of the case.

In each of the cases that Brown cites as evidence for the claim that racial ambiguity can be easily resolved by state law, a closer reading suggests just the opposite to be true. In none of the cases is a petitioner's contestation of racial classification simply dismissed. In three of the cases convictions were overturned or remanded for a new trial (*State v. Chavers, Gray v. Ohio, Jones v. Commonwealth*), and in one case a state law was ruled unconstitutional (*Monroe v. Collins*). In none of the cases is a blood-quantum rule sufficient to settle an individual's racial status, which ultimately comes to depend on the contingent factors of social performance, presentation, and reception.[128] Brown's attempt to rein in the racially destabilizing implications of passing in Tourgée's argument cannot in the end be considered successful. Rather than resolving racial ambiguity through legal fiat, the cases demonstrate the extent to which racial categories are maintained through the constitutive power of the law.

The *Plessy* doctrine of "separate but equal" no longer carries the force of precedent. Still, the case remains relevant today, not only as an artifact of past racism but also because the case informs contemporary thinking about racialized identity and legal rights. That Justice Harlan's dissent in the case introduced the constitutional language of color-blindness—a concept that remains at the center of contemporary legal struggles concerning race and racism—further secures *Plessy*'s relevance. A proper understanding of the *Plessy* decision is not, therefore, merely a matter of historical curiosity.

Plessy v. Ferguson is best remembered for its infamous doctrine of "separate but equal" and for Justice Harlan's admonition, "Our Constitution is color-blind." In this chapter, I have argued against standard interpretations of the case that take up the discussion only after encountering racial difference, thereby ignoring the constitutive power of law to define, construct, regulate, and maintain racial categories. Focusing on the indeterminacy of Homer Plessy's racial classification reveals the Court's active participation in the construction of race and imposition of racial order—and so also works to undermine the very terms of debate upon which current arguments about color-blindness and color-consciousness are grounded. The *Plessy* case is important not only because it informs our construction of the Fourteenth Amendment and the treatment of racial minorities, but also because it reveals the role of law in generating the orderly racial categories that segregation both depended upon and enforced.

CHAPTER 4 | The Limits of *Brown*

POPULAR MEMORY OF THE civil rights movement is the terrain upon which contemporary racial ideology is contested. Reasonable people may disagree about the extent of the movement's success or its normative implications for current policy, but the wrongness of state-mandated segregation is no longer open to dispute. Rather, competing interests lay claim to the meaning and symbolism of desegregation as a producer of contemporary racial common sense. How we remember past civil rights struggle thus bears serious consequences for contemporary challenges to (or legitimization of) racial inequality. The 1954 Supreme Court case *Brown v. Board of Education* lies at the heart of this racial project. And while the case itself was limited to the specific question of racial segregation in public education, it has since come to represent a broad principle of justice, presumed applicable in almost all circumstances and thought to answer any number of questions not posed to the Court in 1954. *Brown v. Board of Education* speaks not only to what the Constitution permits and forbids, but also to what America is or could be. It is, in this sense, more "constitutional" than perhaps any other Supreme Court decision—more constitutive of political community—and so is asked to carry a cultural load it could not possibly sustain.

In placing *Brown* at the intersection of legal rules and racial formation, this chapter begins with the observation that today's racial common sense is defined largely in reaction against one historically specific form of white supremacist social organization (Jim Crow), and considers what implications this might hold for our ability to confront more contemporary techniques of racial domination. What *Brown* means, and so also what it can and cannot do as a resource in legal decision-making, derives in this sense from the political needs of today and of those in a position to influence how the case is remembered and for what it will stand. As we saw in chapter 1, those political needs are contested within the ideological field of a "new American dilemma" that requires the production of cultural resources capable of condemning racist ideology while simultaneously preserving the material conditions of racial inequality. Chapter 2 explained how broad cultural narratives of fall and redemption manage this contradiction by normalizing the conditions of racial hierarchy, thereby rendering them ordinary, unremarkable, inevitable, and, above all, innocent. *Brown* is thus made symbolically responsible for a particular vision of American democracy. For liberals and conservatives alike, it is a vision that transcends racial division—either in the present or in a more racially equitable future. Both versions of this narrative work within a metaphor of progress and forward movement of the color-blind ideal, from Justice Harlan's dissent in *Plessy* to a unanimous decision in *Brown*, to the current dispute as to whether race-based affirmative action constitutes a departure from that ideal or a method of achieving it.

I have tried to complicate this narrative, in chapter 3, by turning to a rich and, for many, unfamiliar history of the *Plessy* case. Returning *Plessy* to its context of racial indeterminacy (and judicial determination) undermines the popular intuition that Harlan's dissent anticipates *Brown* and that the "original" meaning of color-blindness was simply or self-evidently a matter of prohibiting the state from classifying on the basis of race. Both this chapter and the next, in turn, investigate the slow transformation of color-blind constitutionalism from the post-*Brown* implementation cases to the neoconservative attack on race-based affirmative action and racial equality. Whereas chapter 3 emphasized discontinuities between Harlan's dissent and today's color-blind constitutionalism, this chapter stresses continuities between desegregation and today's explicitly race-conscious efforts to achieve a less racially stratified society.

Familiar narratives of desegregation, as the color-blind ideal from which race-based affirmative action rightly or wrongly diverges, are thus doubly misleading. First, from the outset, the desegregation cases specifically required that school assignments be based in part on the student's race. This was not an historical accident or a failure to live up to an otherwise race-neutral ideal, but followed directly from material conditions in which the desegregation mandate operated. And second, while color-blindness gained legal traction as part of the southern moderates' attack on massive resistance to school desegregation, it was at the same time a reaction against the demands of civil rights activists and a technique for rendering segregation consistent with federal law. Color-blind constitutionalism, that is, was against integration before it was against affirmative action.[1] In contrast to both conservative and liberal redemption narratives, I read the desegregation decisions as demonstrating the paradoxically race-conscious nature of color-blind constitutionalism when applied within a context of existing racial subordination.

The Redemptive Iconography of *Brown v. Board of Education*

The historian Charles Payne has described *Brown v. Board of Education* as "a milestone in search of something to signify."[2] Widely hailed as a symbol of Jim Crow's demise, the case is popularly understood to represent America at its best. For many, *Brown* symbolizes the end of segregation, a national condemnation of racism, a renewed commitment to the ideal of color-blind justice, or some combination of all of these.[3] But *Brown* is equally affirmed in less celebratory narratives, in which it is seen to articulate a constitutional aspiration against which the injustice of current racial practices can be measured. Unlike the celebratory *Brown*, which indulges a fantasy of completion or accomplishment, this aspirational *Brown* marks "an appeal to law to make good on its promises" of equal citizenship and racial democracy, even if that promise remains as yet largely unfulfilled.[4]

In both versions of *Brown*, the cultural significance of the case is chiefly redemptive. According to the legal historian J. Harvie Wilkinson III, "Everyone understands that *Brown v. Board of Education* helped deliver the Negro from over three centuries of legal bondage. But *Brown* acted to emancipate the white South and the Supreme Court as well."[5] Continuing from the redemptive language of emancipation and deliverance, Wilkinson's celebratory account chronicles how "*Brown* lifted from the Court the burden of history."[6] In contrast, Jack Balkin presents the aspirational view of *Brown* as an ideal against which current racial inequalities may be judged. Among legal practitioners, he notes, one does not argue "for" or "against" *Brown*. Rather, equal protection disputes involve rival interpretations of the case's underlying principle, with all sides claiming to be *Brown*'s rightful heir.[7]

That *Brown* figures so centrally in such irreconcilable historical narratives testifies to the case's iconic status. Few would dispute the significance of *Brown*, in part because there is so much disagreement as to what exactly it signifies. This much is implicit in Payne's quip about *Brown* as milestone. But more than this, Payne's comment invites us to reflect upon what social, legal, political, and ideological needs are revealed as a consequence of this contemporary struggle over what the past will mean. We catch sight of *Brown*'s contribution to racial formation, then, by examining what it did *not* do, but what cultural significations have been demanded of it nonetheless. In this sense, Payne's remarks may be understood to comment upon, as well as participate in, a revisionist trend in mapping *Brown*'s meaning.

In recent years, *Brown*'s status among legal scholars has diverged significantly from its popular reception and standing among legal practitioners. Revisionist scholarship has criticized *Brown* on a number of fronts, starting with the obvious: *Brown* did not put an end to segregation, or even to racially segregated schools, as that term is understood by all but the most conservative legal activists.[8] We know this in part because desegregation was never fully achieved, and also because the current trend is, by all measures and in all regions, toward resegregation rather than integration.[9] The revisionist literature thus seeks to explain what went wrong, or why *Brown* failed to achieve the dramatic results that civil rights advocates once anticipated, and for which *Brown* remains at least symbolically responsible.

A number of possibilities have been suggested. For some, the problem lies in a basic misconception about what it is that courts do, and what reasonably can be expected of them. Gerald Rosenberg delivered one of the earliest and most systematic assaults on the mythology of courts as heroic crusaders for justice, by demonstrating how such a view vastly overestimates the judiciary's capacity to effect social change. When southern desegregation did begin, more than a decade after *Brown*, it was due to the involvement of the political branches and the passage of the Civil Rights Act of 1964, not because the High Court decreed it.[10] And, as Mary Dudziak has shown, the impetus for the political branches to act on civil rights derived more from Cold War foreign policy interests than from concern over racial injustice. Moreover, if *Brown* by itself failed to achieve meaningful integration of public schools, Michael Klarman has demonstrated how it succeeded all too well at crystallizing white southern resistance to desegregation, thereby provoking a political backlash that mobilized white anger and undercut moderate civil rights movements indigenous to the South.[11]

This line of criticism raises structural questions about the Court's ability to effect change in the absence of meaningful enforcement power.[12] But for others, *Brown*'s failure can be traced to the decisions of specific actors within the legal sphere. The NAACP lawyers, traditionally cast as heroes in the heroic Court narrative, have come under fire for prioritizing school desegregation over employment discrimination,[13] or for pursuing integration rather than equalization of resources within the separate-but-equal framework.[14] For still others, responsibility lies with the decisions of the Court itself: in *Brown I*, for example, by implicitly adopting proximity to white students as a proxy for quality education;[15] or in *Brown II*, for failing to demand immediate compliance and, instead, leaving white-dominated local school boards and federal district courts to begin implementation "with all deliberate speed";[16] or in the doctrinal shifts ushered in by the Burger and Rehnquist Courts, which relaxed the criteria by which local school districts were declared "unitary" and freed from desegregation orders while dramatically narrowing the scope of available remedies for continuing racial concentration in public schools.[17]

Whether due to lack of capacity or to lack of will, the *Brown* decision did not produce the dramatic reorganization of public education that some had hoped for and others had feared. But the implementation of *Brown*'s initial mandate is also of interest for reasons that go beyond the Court's ability or inability to bring about social change. If *Brown* is "a milestone looking for something to signify," it is not because the case is less important than it is typically thought to be. Rather, it is because the case's significance lies more in its contribution to hegemonic understandings of race and racism (and their relationship to American democracy) than in the creation of enforceable law. To use Omi and Winant's terminology, *Brown* is a powerful producer of "racial common sense."[18] And on Payne's view, that necessarily implies a "mystification of race" that reduces "the systemic character of white supremacy to something called 'segregation.' "[19] It is a double reduction, actually, first in taking segregation for the entirety of white supremacist practices, and again in reducing the meaning of "segregation" to little more than social custom and interpersonal contact rather than "political disenfranchisement, economic exploitation, racial terrorism, and personal degradation."[20] This view has since achieved national ascendency, and has come largely to define a liberal consensus on race, by which overt acts of discrimination, prejudice, and "insensitivity" are roundly condemned while the structural causes of inequality are steadfastly ignored.

If Payne is right that *Brown*'s influence is felt most of all in how Americans *think* about race, then it is not surprising that the case is asked to do a kind of cultural work that pulls in different and often contradictory directions. Perhaps nowhere is this tension expressed more clearly than in the gap between *Brown*'s symbolic value and what the Court actually said in its short, unanimous opinion. In popular representation, *Brown* symbolizes the pivotal moment at which the Court rejected the race-conscious and discriminatory law of "separate but equal" and embraced a constitutional mandate of color-blindness. The case retains this broad cultural appeal despite the fact that Chief Justice Warren's unanimous opinion never uses the phrase "color-blind" and avoids quoting from Justice Harlan's *Plessy* dissent—even while declaring that "in the field of public education, the doctrine of 'separate but equal' has no place."[21]

Moreover, the Court's rationale for viewing segregated schools as "inherently unequal" was intentionally left undertheorized, along with any specification of remedies. Instead, *Brown*'s reasoning emphasized the *consequences* of racial segregation in public schools, and the importance of education in contemporary society.[22] The question of implementation was held over to the following term, pending re-argument by counsel in *Brown II*. Against the advice of petitioners and civil rights amicus briefs (many of which advocated the view that legislators were not permitted to take account of a person's race), *Brown* framed the constitutional question so as to avoid sweeping rejections of racial classification.[23] The "color-blind" position was thus readily available to the Court, both substantively and rhetorically, making all the more conspicuous its absence from the final opinion. It may even be the case that, as legal historian Christopher Schmidt argues, "the *Brown* decision actually reflected a conscious effort by the Justices to *not* accept the general principle of color-blind constitutionalism."[24] How, then, has the case come to symbolize the very principle the Court so labored to avoid?

In part, the construction of *Brown*'s popular meaning is a product of well-funded conservative legal activism and right-wing think tanks. The sheer scope of these knowledge-production networks is remarkable, and surely has not received the scholarly attention it deserves.[25] However, the success of conservative investments in *Brown*'s rearticulation owes also to the broader racial narratives in which the case's meaning is ultimately embedded. Both celebratory and aspirational accounts of *Brown*, that is, reproduce familiar narratives of progress, redemption, and American exceptionalism, through which responsibility for unjust racial practices is distanced from (or defined against) the Constitution's "true" meaning. The redemptive iconography of *Brown v. Board* turns less on its ability to effect social change than on its ability to represent what Jack Balkin calls, candidly, "the Good Constitution"—the Constitution "whose deeper principles and truths were only fitfully and imperfectly realized, rather than the Constitution that protected slavery and Jim Crow. By extension, *Brown* also symbolizes the Good America, rather than the country that slaughtered Native Americans, subordinated women, and enslaved blacks."[26] In representing America at its best, *Brown* provides a constitutional vision that condemns past injustices (genocide, slavery, lynching, Jim Crow) while at the same time positioning those injustices as failures to live up to an enduring American ideal—as aberrational rather than constitutive in nature. On the celebratory account of *Brown*, condemnation of past racial injustices serves to exonerate current racial practices. On the aspirational account, *Brown*'s promise works a critique of current unjust practices in the name of a presumptively innocent Constitution, which the nation then seeks to achieve.

In locating *Brown*'s influence as a resource in the production of racial common sense, I mean to emphasize the centrality of civil rights memory to contemporary racial formation. One reason for *Brown*'s ideological potency, we might say, is the potential for slippage between its symbolization of constitutional equality at the highest level of abstraction and its more proximate condemnation of state-sponsored racial segregation as practiced by the school boards in the consolidated cases. Precisely because of its iconic status, *Brown*'s rejection of a specific form of white supremacist social organization (Jim Crow) has been taken to define the meaning of constitutional equality in itself. Today's racial common sense is defined largely by reaction against Jim Crow, and so also by a corresponding blindness to other, more contemporary techniques of racial subordination.

Sumi Cho describes the logic of racial redemption as comprising three basic elements: repudiation of white supremacy's old regime, burial of historical memories of racial subordination, and transformation of white supremacy into a viable contemporary regime.[27] The appropriation of civil rights discourse by contemporary color-blind conservatives accomplishes these related goals by squarely rejecting the constitutional legitimacy of Jim Crow while transforming the meaning of civil rights struggle into a generic rejection of racial classification rather than a substantive demand for racial democracy. The logic of "burial" may seem to be at cross-purposes with those of "repudiation" and "transformation"—if only because the former suppresses historical memory of events that must be summoned to consciousness for the latter to function. And yet, perhaps ironically, racial progress narratives are as well served by repressing popular memory of systemic injustice as they are by spectacular memorializations of unjust racial practices that affix the contemporary cultural meanings of "equality" and "justice" to their discontinuity from overt acts of racial violence.

Seen this way, *Brown*'s cultural authority is closely tied to its location within broader racial narratives, and so also to the ways in which its condemnation of the past redeems the present. The unquestionable rightness of *Brown*, that is, mirrors the unrecognizable wrongness of Jim Crow—not in the sense that its wrongness is open to dispute, but because it obscures any connection between segregation and the current racial order. *Brown*'s meaning, therefore, is not unaffected by its canonization, which contains responsibility for racial inequality within the broader exculpatory historical framework that Jacqueline Dowd Hall has termed "the short civil rights movement." Despite the best efforts of nearly a decade of civil rights historiography, popular memory of the movement remains predictably limited in ways that contain the location of (and culpability for) white supremacist social relations within each gesture of condemnation:

> By confining the civil rights struggle to the South, to bowdlerized heroes, to a single halcyon decade, and to limited, noneconomic objectives, the master narrative simultaneously elevates and diminishes the movement. It ensures the status of the classical phase as a triumphal moment in a larger American progress narrative, yet it undermines its *gravitas*. It prevents one of the most remarkable mass movements in American history from speaking effectively to the challenges of our time.[28]

The wrongness of white supremacy is thus safely contained in the past, in the South, in crude racial prejudice and the overt acts of Jim Crow segregation vanquished by *Brown*.[29] White racism is not only illegal and unjust; it is *spectacularly* so—and so unjust as to render it unrecognizable in the post-civil rights America of today. Perhaps nowhere is this pairing of condemnation and exoneration more effective than within popular memory of massive resistance to school desegregation.

From Massive Resistance to Minimum Compliance

White southern resistance to *Brown v. Board* was by no means monolithic. While the vast majority of whites in the South were opposed to integration, there was nonetheless considerable variation in the depth of commitment to segregation and in choice of resistance strategies. Images of southern defiance come easily to mind: angry mobs, Confederate flags, the extravagant violence of Birmingham and Selma and of countless other less well publicized scenes of racist repression; federal troops in Little Rock; Governor Wallace at the schoolhouse door promising "segregation now, segregation tomorrow, and segregation forever!" The response of southern moderates, however, is both harder to picture and more representative of the region, which eventually came to reject the disruptions of massive resistance, school closings, and mob violence while nonetheless refusing to accept the civil rights movement's call for racial equality.[30] It is in this context that color-blind constitutionalism's ascendency must be understood. From its inception, the rhetoric of color-blindness served equally as a critique of massive resistance *and* as a defense of segregation, to the greatest extent allowable by law.

The significance of white moderates in the South extends beyond the historical fact of their numbers. Moderates were also crucial politically, and the story of their conversion from passive acceptance of extremism into active challengers of massive resistance is centrally important to current understandings of race, regarding both the timing of change and what kind of changes ultimately would transpire. In part, this is because their (belated) rejection of massive resistance set the terms for an emergent *national* racial compromise reducible neither to the egalitarian demands of the civil rights movement, nor to the preservation of Jim Crow–era racial caste. In both timing and tactics, southern moderates contributed to a new racial common sense that permitted token desegregation along class lines, in accordance with a rearticulated ideology of color-blind individualism. Unlike the spectacular racism of massive resistance, which is framed as both distinctly southern and a relic of the past, this emergent racial understanding is easily recognizable in today's political, legal, and cultural orientations regarding race.

In some regards, the line between moderates and massive resistance was clearly drawn. Moderates overwhelmingly disagreed with the *Brown* decision yet accepted its status as law and thus conceived themselves as duty-bound to bring local school policies gradually into conformity with the US Constitution. Where the forces of massive resistance refused to recognize *Brown*'s legitimacy, moderates sought ways minimally to comply with its ruling while still preserving as much racial separation as possible—an approach rendered all the more reasonable by *Brown*'s separation of right from remedy and *Brown II*'s intentionally vague criteria for implementing its decree. Whereas theories of "interposition" and "nullification" justified massive resistance to school desegregation, moderates sought to minimize conflict through strategies of minimum compliance, gradualism, and delay.

As a popular movement, massive resistance produced highly visible scenes of open defiance and mob violence for which it is best remembered. But it also contained legal and policy dimensions that ought not be overlooked. The theory of interposition, for example, was foremost a claim about legality (that sovereign states retained the right to interpose their authority against an overreaching federal judiciary) even while functioning most effectively as political rhetoric.[31] Massive resistance also contained a range of policy initiatives advanced at both state and local levels. In response to *Brown*, southern states enacted legislation prohibiting the use of state funds for desegregated schools and making it a criminal offense for public officials to assign white and black students to the same school.[32] A number of states repealed compulsory attendance laws and held referendums amending state constitutions to remove language requiring the state to provide public education, thereby setting the stage for public school closings as an alternative to desegregation. In May 1959, Prince Edward County closed its entire public school system rather than accept court-ordered desegregation. The schools remained closed for five years before the Supreme Court ordered them reopened in 1964.[33]

In comparison to the champions of massive resistance, southern moderates were late to organize. And when they did, it was not to defend school desegregation but to oppose the disruptive effects of massive resistance that they correctly identified as a threat to economic development, both in the image of violence and unreconstructed racism it projected to potential sources of capital investment and in the threat to public education upon which the New South economy would depend.[34] So long as the debate was framed as a choice between segregated and integrated schools, the clear preference of nearly all white southerners was for segregation. However, under pressure from civil rights activists and federal courts, it became increasingly likely that school closures would be needed to prevent their desegregation. The prospect of school closures dramatically increased the costs of massive resistance to a level that many whites were unwilling to pay. In turn, moderates were able to reframe the debate as a choice not between segregated and desegregated schools, but between open schools operating with token desegregation and no schools at all.[35] In regard to racial preferences, there was little or no difference between moderates and massive resistance; in regard to public education, there was a tremendous difference. The success of racial moderates therefore depended largely upon their ability to prioritize the demand for public schools over citizens' views on "the race question."[36]

As Lassiter and Lewis point out, "The absence of an effectively organized opposition to massive resistance between 1956 and 1958" should not be taken as "active support for inflexible, hard-line segregationist policies."[37] But neither should the eventual presence of such an opposition be mistaken for support for *Brown*'s desegregation mandate. In rejecting the aggressively defiant position of massive resistance, southern moderates made no secret of the fact that token desegregation was intended to avoid integration—and to do so without sacrificing southern business interests or drawing federal intervention. Virginia's most outspoken moderate, Armistead Boothe, campaigned in 1959 as "a Virginian and a segregationist" on the platform of "public schools segregated to the limit allowed by law"; he boasted that his token desegregation plan would keep schools "99 percent segregated" and could preserve segregation more effectively than would outright defiance.[38]

Moderate evasion schemes (table 4.1) were quite often explicit in their intentions to preserve segregation to the greatest extent possible, and typically emerged from the work of state and local advisory committees tasked with precisely this goal. In Mississippi, the Legal Education Advisory Council anticipated *Brown* by developing pupil placement plans, by which local officials would no longer assign students to schools based solely on their race but instead would rely upon facially neutral criteria closely linked to race. Using socioeconomic status, academic performance, or purported behavioral, health, and hygienic concerns as a proxy, students were assigned to schools on an individual and putatively nonracial basis while still maintaining total or near-total segregation.[39] In Virginia, the Gray Report (named for Garland Gray, the committee's chair) proposed locally administered pupil assignments combined with tuition grants or "vouchers" to facilitate the voluntary transfer of students to segregated private schools. By shifting the point of decision from public officials to private individuals, "school choice" plans sought to insulate segregation from the kind of state action that might trigger federal judicial intervention. Similarly, but in even thinner disguise, Louisiana's Police Power Bill

TABLE 4.1 Moderates versus Massive Resistance

MASSIVE RESISTANCE	MODERATES
Total exclusion	Token integration
Rejection of *Brown*'s legitimacy	Evasion of *Brown*'s implementation
Interposition, nullification	Minimum compliance
School closures	Pupil placement plans
Rural / Black Belt	Urban / metropolitan
Old South	New South
Extralegal violence	Fidelity to law

required segregation in all public schools below the college level, "not on the basis of race, but for the advancement, protection and better education of all children of school age in Louisiana regardless of race."[40]

Perhaps nowhere was the constitutional thinking of minimum compliance more effective and explicitly stated than in North Carolina, where Governor Luther Hodges commissioned a report from the University of North Carolina Institute of Government on the most effective ways to preserve segregation within the constitutional constraints imposed by *Brown* and without abandoning public education. James Paul authored the legal analysis section of the report, which emphasized (in 1954, after *Brown I* but prior to *Brown II*) that the Court had not yet imposed a decree, and so left open the crucial question of "what must be done to comply" with the ruling. The meaning of *Brown* was not yet determined and "might still be interpreted in ways less revolutionary than some reaction might lead one to suspect."[41] Not defiance, the report suggested, but rearticulation (in Omi and Winant's phrase) might prove the most effective method of resistance.

Paul's contribution to the report surveys the constitutional viability of various policy options, including state support for private, segregated schools (either directly or through tuition grants) and a number of assignment plans within public schools. While skeptical that federal courts would allow any of the state-supported "privatization" plans, section 3 of the report counsels North Carolina's attorney general on argumentation for *Brown II*, in hopes of winning the most limited terms for compliance: the longest and least determinate time frames, the highest degree of local discretion and regional variation. Among the factors that local school boards would need to consider the report lists "intensity of racial feeling," "differences is academic backgrounds," and the purported need to "protect the health of individual students" and accommodate "the personality, needs and desires of individual children."[42] These criteria could then be enlisted to justify gradual adjustment policies (described in section 4 of the report) such as pupil placement, school choice, and attendance zones linked to residential segregation.

After *Brown II*, in which the Court elucidated guidelines for compliance with the initial decision, these policies were enacted across the South. Rather than demanding an immediate end to segregation, *Brown II* required only that "defendants make a prompt and reasonable start toward full compliance."[43] The responsibility for implementing *Brown I* thus fell to local school boards who were advised to show "good faith," but also assured that lower courts would allow "additional time [when] necessary to carry out the ruling in an effective manner."[44] By setting no time frames for compliance, asking only that local authorities desegregate "as soon as practicable"[45] and proceed with "all deliberate speed,"[46] the Court severed right from remedy and encouraged local efforts to circumvent the actual process of desegregation. Whatever might have been the Court's understanding of the phrase, local authorities charged with implementing desegregation had other ideas. As the editorial page of the *Richmond News Leader* put it: "There are those of us who would respond that 'as soon as practicable' means never at all."[47]

Numan Bartley explains the bureaucratized and formally deracialized logic by which local pupil placement laws claimed to adhere to *Brown*'s desegregation mandate while failing to bring about any substantial degree of integration:

> Various criteria were listed to guide local agencies in assigning students, and the words "race" and "Negro" found no place on the list. Instead, administrative problems, physical facilities, sociological and psychological factors, and academic background were among the considerations that school boards were required to take into account. Resulting segregation rested not upon an illegal racial classification but nominally upon weighty and responsible concern for individual students.[48]

Pupil placement laws thus supplied the facially neutral basis upon which to ground conventionally segregated outcomes in school assignments. Additionally, most placement laws specified administrative remedies for parents of students unsatisfied with the school board's initial decision. The grievance procedures further insulated discriminatory treatment from constitutional scrutiny for two reasons. First, drawing out the lengthy appeals process meant that it could take years to exhaust local administrative remedies as required to gain a hearing in federal courts. Second, making the process sufficiently daunting discouraged parents from challenging their school assignments. As Michael Klarman explains: "The patent motive behind pupil placement was to frustrate desegregation by inviting surreptitious consideration of race by school boards and then confounding blacks who were dissatisfied with their placements in a maze of administrative appeals."[49]

Perhaps more striking than their effectiveness at thwarting *Brown*'s desegregation mandate is the extent to which advocates adopted color-blind legal rhetoric to pursue consciously anti-integration policies. Indeed, the evasive programs of southern moderates were not only compatible with color-blindness discourse—they required it. As emphasized in the

North Carolina Institute of Government report, gradual adjustment policies would likely prove effective up to the point where courts began to regard them as efforts to retain segregation on a permanent basis. Locating this line—where minimum compliance effectively shaded into a more subtle technique of massive resistance—supplied the very purpose of the report: "to estimate how far the State might go in using them to preserve, permanently, the *status quo* of total separation of the races in the schools."[50] Color-blindness discourse suggested the "good faith" intentions of gradual adjustment plans, and so lent credence to the distinction.

Thinking strategically, southern moderates understood that the purportedly race-neutral character of pupil placement and school choice plans simply lacked plausibility absent repeal of explicitly segregationist laws and state constitutional language. As the North Carolina report advised, federal courts would be more likely to reject plans "if *openly advertised* and employed as a device for insuring total, permanent segregation."[51] To survive constitutional scrutiny, states should "avoid all references" to the hoped-for result—which the report candidly disclosed as that of "maintaining separate schools for the races." The ultimate goal of gradual adjustment, the report counseled, must not be "advertised openly."[52] For this reason, school choice and pupil placement plans typically were accompanied by efforts to remove overt racial classifications from other areas of public law. In Mississippi, this required a constitutional convention to remove Section 207 of the state constitution, which required the state to maintain separate schools. Governor Coleman advocated repeal of Section 207 out of concern that a failure to do so would lead federal courts to view Mississippi's pupil placement plan as an unconstitutional evasion of *Brown*. With the repeal of explicit racial classifications from state law, pupil placement might preserve segregated schools; without it, Coleman observed, the evasion scheme would "come down like a house of cards."[53] The appeal of color-blind constitutionalism, that is, derived from its potential for preserving racially separate schools.

In this regard, the line between massive resistance and minimum compliance is not so clear as at first it may have seemed. Moderates shared with massive resisters a common antipathy to desegregation—and moderate strategies ultimately proved more successful in frustrating the implementation of *Brown* than did open defiance. In North Carolina, which self-consciously avoided the confrontational rhetoric of massive resistance and allowed for the highly visible integration of a handful of black students to white schools, segregation was preserved for more than 98 percent of the state's nonwhite students under an arrangement Governor Hodges termed "voluntary segregation." A full decade after *Brown*, "The number of black children attending schools with white children in states of the former Confederacy rose from zero to two percent."[54]

Nonetheless, it is important to keep in mind ways in which the distinction sheds light on the practices of white supremacy, present as well as past. First, and most obviously, in the political contest between massive resistance and southern moderates, massive resistance lost and the moderates won. Racial moderates became "the primary architects of racial and social policy" in Virginia, and for the nation as well.[55] This simple fact suggests something of an explanation for why a comparatively greater amount of attention has been paid to extreme segregationists and to the civil rights movement with whom they principally were at war. By focusing on the racism of extremists, popular historical narratives invite us to take pleasure in their demise while discouraging identification with the less exotic racism of southern moderates. In emphasizing the central role of moderates, and in contrast to the collapse of massive resistance, we are called upon to recognize techniques of white supremacy that persist to this day. At stake in the distinction, then, is our ability to see how greatly the defeat of massive resistance differs from a victory for civil rights, and to inquire more carefully about what kind of victory the moderates achieved.

Second, the victory of southern moderates over massive resistance is crucially linked to the rise of color-blindness as a central rhetoric of American racial common sense. Accordingly, the distinction between moderates and massive resistance reveals color-blind constitutionalism's rise to hegemonic status as a technique of *resistance* to the civil rights movement rather than its embodiment. In this sense, the emergence of color-blindness may be understood to signify a demand that southern racial practices be brought into conformity with those of the nation as a whole. However, in direct contradiction to liberal narratives of southern exceptionalism, this process facilitated a national convergence around white supremacist racial norms. Such a national convergence, in turn, enabled the rejection of white supremacist ideology while preserving the material conditions of white supremacist rule. As Lassiter explains, the consensus is premised upon (and would be inconceivable without) ostensibly race-neutral mechanisms by which to preserve similar racial outcomes: "The ascendance of color-blind ideology in the metropolitan South, as in the rest of the nation, depended upon the establishment of structural mechanisms of exclusion that did not require individual racism by suburban beneficiaries in order to sustain white class privilege and maintain barriers of disadvantage facing urban minority communities."[56]

On this view, we may accept that Jim Crow segregation was indeed powerfully transformed, while recognizing as well that it was not replaced by racial democracy and inclusion but, rather, by dispersed systems of exclusion "embedded in the built environment" of suburban development patterns and residential segregation.[57] Defenders of massive resistance were thus wrong in thinking that token desegregation would quickly lead to the destruction of white supremacy and a radical reordering of society. As evidenced by the experiences of northern civil rights struggle, racial hierarchy and exclusion find support in an array of formally race-neutral policies, even in the absence of formal segregation. Against the familiar progress narrative of southern conversion to an egalitarian national creed (the American dilemma), the fall of Jim Crow more precisely marks the South's adoption of more suitably *northern* methods for reproducing the material conditions of racial exclusion.

Third, and in evidence of just how extensive was the moderate's victory—a victory as much over civil rights and racial democracy as over massive resistance and Jim Crow—key elements of the legal argument for token desegregation now govern the Supreme Court's current equal protection doctrine. The basic structure of the argument, which reads into *Brown* a sharp distinction between desegregation and integration, originates in the explicit efforts of southern moderates to protect racial segregation by avoiding intervention by federal courts. Judge John Parker's opinion for the Fourth Circuit in *Briggs v. Elliot* (1955) is perhaps the earliest and best-known formulation of this position.[58] Noting that *Brown* had reversed his initial ruling, Parker now resigned himself to the decision, noting that "it is our duty now to accept the law as declared by the Supreme Court." This much set him apart from the interposition and nullification theories of massive resistance. But Parker's interpretation of *Brown* drastically narrowed its scope, drawing a blueprint for judicial evasion that would be adopted by federal courts across the South. The opinion itself is just over a page long and is largely concerned with explaining what the *Brown* decision had *not* required:

> It has not decided that the states must mix persons of different races in the schools or must require them to attend schools or must deprive them of the right of choosing the schools they attend. What it has decided, and all that it has decided, is that a state may not deny to any person on account of race the right to attend any school that it maintains. . . . The Constitution does not require integration. It merely forbids discrimination.[59]

On Parker's interpretation of *Brown*, the constitutional prohibition against segregated schools is satisfied by a transition to facially neutral placement criteria or school choice plans, even when doing so results in school attendance patterns indistinguishable from those under Jim Crow. Racial separation itself need not change, only the stated justification for segregation and the techniques by which it is accomplished.

Like the "separate but equal" accommodations before them, formally nonracial gradual adjustment plans provided another "thin disguise" for racial exclusion. More than a decade after *Brown*, when it became impossible not to recognize them as thinly veiled efforts to avoid implementation of the desegregation mandate, the Court eventually would strike down school choice and pupil placement plans as applied by local school boards.[60] Judge Parker's underlying distinction between desegregation and integration, however, has proven to be far more resilient. Versions of the argument appeared in dissenting opinions in the late 1960s and early 1970s, as Nixon-appointed judges sought to reverse course on desegregation law. By the 1990s, this view would command a narrow but dependable majority of the Court, authorizing a series of "resegregation decisions" and buttressing an increasingly aggressive, rights-based critique of racial equality.

The Color-Blind Retreat from *Brown*

Through the late 1960s, the Supreme Court's desegregation jurisprudence was largely defined by its responses to southern efforts, legal and extralegal, to thwart *Brown*. With the success of southern moderates, this resistance increasingly took a legal form, as legislatures and school boards sought to comply with the letter of the law while nonetheless avoiding actual change to the racial composition of classrooms. Following Judge Parker's lead, the "southern objective" turned away from defiance of *Brown* and now sought to achieve "desegregation with a minimum of integration" by utilizing ostensibly race-neutral measures such as pupil placement schemes, school choice plans, minority-to-majority transfer provisions, expulsion of black students for disciplinary reasons, and manipulation of attendance zones through strategic placement of new "neighborhood schools" in residentially segregated communities. The legal premise of these avoidance strategies was Judge Parker's distinction between desegregation and integration, which may be understood to initiate the mobilization of color-blindness discourse to prevent the achievement of *Brown*'s goal.

After nearly a decade of silence on the issue, the Supreme Court seemed to lose patience with these avoidance strategies and began to demand actual compliance with *Brown*, as measured by tangible integration results. These cases—*Green v. New Kent County* (1968), *Swann v. Charlotte Mecklenburg Board of Education* (1971), and *Keyes v. School District No. 1, Denver Colorado* (1973)—undermine the redemptive narrative of color-blind constitutionalism in two important ways. First, they shed light on the nature of the harm that *Brown* sought to correct. Despite *Brown*'s narrative positioning as the ultimate achievement of color-blindness, the Court fully understood that its rejection of segregation created a constitutional requirement for various race-conscious remedies. Accordingly, the early desegregation decisions simply do not support the anticlassification reading against which affirmative action policies are so often described as "special privileges" or "reverse discrimination." Second, the cases illustrate a clear connection between color-blind constitutionalism and white political interests—a connection that predates the supposed "backlash" against judicial overreach and affirmative action. The Court's current embrace of color-blindness may thus be understood to descend more from resistance to desegregation than from *Brown* or the civil rights movement itself. Seen this way, color-blind constitutionalism emerges not as an ideal of race neutrality, but as an institutional mechanism through which white interests could be rearticulated in the form of legal rights.

In *Green v. New Kent County*, the Court rejected a "freedom of choice" plan in a small, non-residentially segregated Virginia school system, under which the district's only two schools remained largely defined by race. Not one white student attended the formerly "black school." In *Green*, the Court pointedly rejected the view that, absent any actual change in student school assignments, adoption of formally race-neutral procedures was sufficient to demonstrate compliance with *Brown*. Writing for a unanimous Court, Justice Brennan explained that New Kent County's acceptance of some black students into the formerly "white" school "merely begins, not ends, our inquiry whether the Board has taken steps adequate to abolish its dual, segregated system." Rather, school boards that formerly had operated segregated "dual systems" were charged with "an *affirmative duty* to take whatever steps might be necessary to convert to a unitary system in which racial discrimination would be eliminated root and branch."[61] Brennan's language was plainly a response to a decade of *Brown*'s circumvention. His message to southern school boards and lower courts was that the constitutional requirement of desegregation is not met when the material conditions of racial separation remain in place.

Green is thus an important rebuke to Judge Parker's interpretation of *Brown*, which would evaluate compliance with desegregation by examining the neutrality of assignment methods rather than the resulting racial composition of schools. Brennan states as much, defining the burden of school boards to "come forward with a plan that promises realistically to work, and promises realistically to work *now*."[62] But the conclusion also follows logically from his understanding of the constitutional evil that *Brown* identified; equal protection of the law is not measured by the presence or absence of racial classifications, but by "the pattern of segregation" they enforced.[63] Therefore, compliance with the Fourteenth Amendment requires an active transformation of segregated patterns of school attendance—and by implication, the rest of society as well.

As critics of desegregation were quick to point out, Brennan's measure of success evaluated facially neutral policies by the extent to which they achieved racial mixing of students, and so were not "color-blind" in the sense of racial nonrecognition. A student's race was in fact highly relevant to school attendance decisions. Contrary to conventional "overshoot" or "departure" narratives, school desegregation from the outset required race-consciousness, and did so in much the same way as affirmative action policies that later would be charged with betraying *Brown*'s original commitment to racial nonrecognition.

Indeed, several of affirmative action's more vocal critics identify *Green* as the critical moment of departure from color-blindness. Thomas Sowell sees in *Green* "a substitution of a very different process—one in which children were to be assigned to schools by race instead of *without regard to race*."[64] And Nathan Glazer characterizes the Court's post-Brown desegregation cases as the transformation of "a legitimate, moral, and constitutional effort to eliminate the unconstitutional separation of the races" into "something else—an intrusive, costly, painful, and futile effort to stabilize proportions of races in the schools."[65] The connection is telling: antidiscrimination and desegregation may announce color-blind ideals, but their implementation, by nature, requires race-conscious affirmative measures.

In *Green*, the Court dealt with a rural school district with a history of explicit, de jure racial segregation. The requirement of a "plan that works"—to say nothing of one that works "*now*"—proved more complicated in the contexts of large southern cities where school segregation was reinforced by residential segregation, and northern school districts, which typically lacked any history of de jure segregation. Dealing with these contexts in *Swann* and *Keyes*, respectively, brought to the fore the tension between passive desegregation plans that focused on neutral criteria for school assignments and the sweeping mandate of Brennan's call for affirm-ative integration measures. Taken to its logical conclusion, Judge Parker's invocation of color-blindness as a limit to the scope of court-imposed rem-edies ensured both that school desegregation was constitutionally required and, at the same time, that the methods necessary to achieve it would be constitutionally prohibited. If this paradoxical result suggests a failure of constitutional interpretation, it nonetheless proved a remarkable political success in satisfying the ideological needs of the new American dilemma and contributing to an emergent post-civil rights racial common sense.

In *Swann v. Charlotte Mecklenburg Board of Education*, the Court approved a district court-ordered desegregation plan involving gerryman-dered school districts and the remedial use of busing in residentially seg-regated Charlotte, North Carolina. At conference, Chief Justice Burger initially had indicated he would side with the Charlotte school board, but changed his position in order to preserve a unanimous opinion—and to prevent the more liberal Justice Douglas from assigning the writing of the opinion, as would be the case should the chief justice end up in the minor-ity. Burger assigned the opinion to himself and was thus in a position to deliver a unanimous but much weaker opinion than would otherwise be the case. The opinion both affirms and contains *Brown I* as it turns away from "large constitutional principles" to take up "the flinty, intractable realities of day-to-day implementation of those constitutional commands."[66] The result is a somewhat uneven opinion that justifies and upholds the lower court's aggressive desegregation plan while emphasizing the temporally and geographically limited context in which such remedies would be given free rein.

To begin, *Swann* reiterates the constitutional requirement actively to effect the dismantling of former Jim Crow school systems, as well as the broad scope of the courts' equitable powers in fashioning a remedy when local authorities fail to meet their constitutional obligations: "The objec-tive today remains to eliminate from the public schools all vestiges of state-imposed segregation. . . If school authorities fail in their affirmative obligations under these holdings, judicial authority may be invoked."[67] This expansive authority, however, is framed by the narrow context of southern intransigence (the "dilatory tactics" of local officials that initially provoked *Green*'s "root and branch" formulation) in an apparent effort to insulate other, purportedly less clear-cut instances of segregation from its reach.

In confirming what *Brown* does do, Burger seizes an opportunity also to say what it does not. If aggressive race-conscious enforcement measures are warranted to combat de jure segregation, Burger suggests, it is because official policies and deliberate acts of segregation are "what *Brown v. Board of Education* was all about."[68] By implication, *Brown* is not "about" de facto segregation—those often-extreme levels of racial exclusion not easily traceable to specific, identifiable acts of state officials. Neither would the Court consider the constitutional implications of school segregation resulting from "other types of state action" than that of local school authorities—either in specific federal or state policies contributing to residential segregation, or from "the myriad factors of human existence which can cause discrimination in a multitude of ways."[69] Nor would it require "any particular degree of racial balance or mixing" of the student populations. On this last point Burger is especially clear, noting that if this had been the view of the lower court, "it would be disapproved and we would be obliged to reverse."[70] Consequently, and in light of Charlotte's extensive residential segregation, the Court allowed that some single-race schools could exist within a unitary school system, so long as they are "not the result of present or past discriminatory action on their part."[71] Of what they *were* a result, the Court did not say.

Despite these efforts on the part of the chief justice to contain *Brown*'s transformative potential, the process of dismantling "dual systems" under *Swann* nonetheless would require that pupil assignments be highly dependent upon race in three specific ways. First, the Court upheld the remedial plan's use of "racial goals" as a measure of compliance with desegregation. According to Chief Justice Burger, "awareness of racial composition of the whole school system is likely to be a useful starting point in shaping a remedy to correct past constitutional violations," including the limited use of "mathematical ratios" as a starting point in fashioning an equitable remedy.[72] This acknowledgment does not imply a "substantive constitutional right" to "any particular degree of racial balance or mixing"—but neither does it rule out consideration of a remedial plan's actual effects, measured in terms of quantifiable achievement of more integrated schools.[73] Second, the Court encouraged racial gerrymandering of district lines, including oddly shaped and noncontiguous school zones, as a necessary step in offsetting the discriminatory nature of existing districting and school locations. Not only was "affirmative action in the form of remedial altering of attendance zones" permissible, it was constitutionally *required*, since " 'racially neutral' assignment plans proposed by school authorities . . . may be inadequate."[74] Third, and most controversially, the Court upheld the use of busing as "one tool of desegregation."[75]

Swann's unequivocally "results-oriented" approach to desegregation illustrates the contradictory nature of color-blind constitutionalism in a society structured by race. While making clear that "racial balance" is not in itself a constitutionally required goal, it also acknowledges that some quantifiable measure of "actual desegregation" would be needed, given the relative ease with which near-total separation can be achieved within a formally race-neutral legal framework. Unwilling to accept this predictable result, and unable clearly to distinguish "actual desegregation" from "racial balance," the Court settled for the ambiguous language of mathematical ratios as a "goal" or "starting point."

This ambivalence over how to measure compliance with desegregation should not be taken as evidence that *Swann* endorsed an anticlassification view of equal protection. To the contrary, it rejected that view in no uncertain terms. In *Davis v. Board of Commissioners of Mobile County*, one of the companion cases to *Swann*, the Court emphasized that a return to "neighborhood schools" does not in itself demonstrate that desegregation has been achieved, especially when those neighborhood schools remain predominantly single-race. Formal race neutrality does not constitute "actual desegregation." Rather, "the measure of any desegregation plan is its effectiveness."[76]

Another of the companion cases, in which the Court struck down North Carolina's antibusing law, went so far as to suggest that *Brown*'s mandate in certain circumstances actually *prohibited* legislative requirements of color-blindness. The intent of the antibusing law quite clearly had been to thwart the court-ordered desegregation plan and expressly prohibited just the sorts of race-conscious desegregation remedies under consideration in the consolidated *Swann* decision.[77] Notably, the text of the North Carolina statute simply required fidelity to the anticlassification principle, which it defined as incompatible with intentional racial-balancing. According to the statute: "No student shall be assigned or compelled to attend any school on account of race, creed, color or national origin, or for the purpose of creating a balance or ratio of race, religion or national origins."[78] The Court rejected this gambit as well:

> The statute exploits an apparently neutral form to control school assignment plans by directing that they be "color blind"; that requirement, against a background of segregation, would render illusory the promise of *Brown v. Board of Education*. Just as the race of students must be considered in determining whether a constitutional violation has occurred, so also must race be considered in formulating a remedy. To forbid, at this stage, all

assignments made on the basis of race would deprive school authorities of
the one tool absolutely essential to fulfillment of their constitutional obligation to eliminate existing dual school systems.[79]

As late as 1971, then, it was the Court's unanimous view that *Brown* not
only permitted but at times also *required* explicit consideration of race in
order affirmatively to transform social patterns previously established by
the legacy of segregation.[80]

In one sense, *Swann* seems straightforwardly to support the antisubordination view of equal protection.[81] It roundly criticizes the various
"color-blind" techniques for resisting desegregation, emphasizing instead
the law's substantive effects and the importance of acknowledging certain
social facts about the culture in which law operates. Burger's argument
recognizes, explicitly, that contemporary prohibitions against racial classification may work to preserve past exercises of discriminatory state power.
For this reason, strict adherence to "nonracial" placement criteria will be
racially neutral neither in outcomes nor intentions. But the argument cuts in
another direction as well. While affording explicit recognition to the broad
social forces through which racial segregation might be maintained—
even in the absence of overt racial classifications of students—the Court
was nonetheless careful to condition judicial remedies upon findings of a
specific constitutional violation: "Absent a constitutional violation there
would be no basis for judicially ordering assignment of students on a racial
basis."[82] In this sense, while apparently conceding the systemic nature of
concentrated racial privilege, the opinion nonetheless retains an ideal of
a nonracialized society to which we might return, ironically, through the
aggressive deployment of explicitly race-conscious remedial measures.

Moreover, the opinion concludes by looking forward to a time, not too
far in the future, when judicial oversight would no longer be needed or
justified: "At some point, these school authorities and others like them
should have achieved full compliance with this Court's decision in *Brown
I*. The systems would then be 'unitary' in the sense required by our decisions in *Green* and *Alexander*." Local communities would at that point
no longer be burdened by the historical legacy of racial exclusion, Burger
suggests, and so any subsequent return of racially identifiable schools need
not imply any constitutional violation:

> It does not follow that the communities served by such systems will remain
> demographically stable, for, in a growing, mobile society, few will do so.
> Neither school authorities nor district courts are constitutionally required to

make year-by-year adjustments of the racial composition of student bodies once the affirmative duty to desegregate has been accomplished and racial discrimination through official action is eliminated from the system.[83]

While *Swann*'s rejection of "race neutral" resistance strategies openly acknowledges that segregation may be maintained without ever classifying students by race, it also anticipates a return to racial separation—which it regards nonetheless as presumptively innocent. This vision of equal protection is a redemptive vision. It preserves a more fundamental American racial innocence even as it names and condemns segregation as a departure from constitutional norms. The transformative potential of *Brown* is thus contained by its own critique of segregation, which it defines narrowly and in ways tied temporally to the past and geographically to the South.

Typically, the story of *Brown v. Board of Education* unfolds in a language of heroes and villains. From our post-civil rights vantage, there is little doubt as to who plays which role in the pre-1968 cases. Those who defended segregation against *Brown*'s call for "simple justice" (in Richard Kluger's famous phrase) ultimately would find themselves on the wrong side of history. However, and despite the sense of inevitability this familiar progress narrative conveys, the unanimity of the early Supreme Court decisions was intended to suppress real and serious conflicts over the meaning, pace, and scope of the desegregation mandate. By all accounts, members of the Court understood that unanimous opinions would be crucial for winning popular support and enforcement of its decisions—even if that unanimity came with a price.[84] However, as the Court was pushed from its principled rejection of Jim Crow to more practical questions concerning implementation of the ruling, those divisions would become impossible to contain. By 1972, with Nixon's appointments of William Rehnquist and Lewis Powell to the Court, they emerged openly as dissenting opinions that later would come to define contemporary "liberal" and "conservative" positions on issues of race.

Breaking a line of unanimous decisions, Justices Rehnquist and Powell each wrote dissenting opinions in *Keyes v. School District No. 1, Denver Colorado*, the Court's first major desegregation case to involve northern schools. Although state law had not formally required segregation in Denver's schools, the district court found evidence that attendance zones and selection of school sites had been manipulated in order to keep schools in the Park Hill area of the city all or virtually all white. Other areas of the city were as segregated as Park Hill, but no judicial inquiry or findings of cause were properly before the Court. The question, then, was whether a remedy ought to include just Park Hill or incorporate the entire city. At stake in this seemingly legalistic distinction were a number of crucial questions: What was the relationship between school segregation and residential segregation? Between explicitly mandated de jure segregation and so-called de facto segregation (segregation in practice, which resulted from more diffuse and complex causes)? Did the *Brown* desegregation mandate authorize more aggressive remedies (such as busing) that would be needed to combat segregation in the racially concentrated yet more fluid and mobile housing markets of the urban North? And would racial separation in the North be viewed as analogous to southern segregation, or treated as constitutionally inapposite, and so held to standards different from those articulated in *Green* and *Swann*?

In large part, Justice Brennan sought to avoid these questions when he could. His majority opinion does not call for desegregation remedies in cases of purely de facto segregation, but neither does it surrender judicial authority to confront residentially based urban segregation throughout the Denver school district. Instead, Brennan reasoned that the existence of intentional discriminatory policies in some parts of the district (Park Hill) shifted the burden of proof onto the school board to demonstrate that de facto segregation elsewhere in the city was not also "motivated by segregative intent."[85] Unable to show that Denver's racially concentrated schools did *not* result from intentional discrimination, the district would be required to desegregate the entire city. If de facto segregation was not in itself unconstitutional, it nonetheless provided strong evidence of constitutionally prohibited discriminatory intent. The case is less interesting for the legal rule it established than for what it reveals about the Court's broader vision of racial equality in a context where segregation had never depended upon official racial classifications or an explicit legal requirement of separate schools—and for the dissenting opinions, which provided a constitutional foothold to the color-blind critique of desegregation that *Green* and *Swann* had rejected.

Justice Rehnquist's dissent is notable for its effort to revive the desegregation/integration distinction outlined by Judge Parker in *Briggs v. Elliott*, which it grafted onto the distinction between de jure and de facto segregation, with predictably similar results. In the context of Judge Parker's initial ruling in favor of state-mandated segregation in public schools, that distinction struck many as a thinly veiled effort to circumvent *Brown*. In the context of *Keyes*, however, it suggested an uncomfortable similarity between the techniques of segregation in the North and those backed by southern moderates. How the Court responded to northern segregation would therefore be crucial in tracing the limits of how far it would go in requiring the actual transformation of racially divided conditions throughout the nation.

Characterizing the affirmative obligations of *Green* as a departure from *Brown*, Rehnquist tried to rein in the scope of *Green*'s duty to dismantle segregation:

> To require a genuinely "dual" system to be disestablished, in the sense that the assignment of a child to a particular school is not made to depend on his race, is one thing. To require that school boards affirmatively undertake to achieve racial mixing in schools is quite obviously something else.[86]

In reviving the distinction between desegregation (which the opinion calls "disestablishment") and integration (referred to as "racial mixing"), Rehnquist leans heavily on a rhetorical strategy of natural color-blindness and artificial racial management that recalls the biological determinism in the *Plessy* majority.[87] But where *Plessy* had turned scientific racism to a defense of Jim Crow, Rehnquist's dissent privatizes racial preferences as beyond the legitimate concern of a color-blind state. Within this narrative of redemption and fall, *Green*'s affirmative obligation to desegregate betrays a color-blind indifference to "racial balance" said to be represented by *Brown*. Efforts to address racialized housing and education patterns are thus figured as impermissible interjections of race into an otherwise neutral arrangement. As a consequence, the material conditions of racial exclusion—because not easily traceable to particular acts of intentional discrimination—would be insulated from judicial scrutiny, while efforts to remedy that exclusion could be seen as unconstitutional acts of discrimination. On this view, school boards could not constitutionally require segregation by race, but neither could they seek to achieve racial compositions that resist entrenched social patterns of racial concentration.

Justice Powell's dissent goes even further in criticizing *Green* and *Swann* as departures from the "original meaning" of desegregation in *Brown*, counseling a wholesale retreat from the requirement of "affirmative state action to desegregate school systems" and attacking what it refers to as "forced busing" with particular ferocity.[88] For Rehnquist, desegregation was foremost concerned with the neutrality of student assignment plans, while integration implied an actual change in a school's racial composition. In contrast, Justice Powell allowed that segregated schools could be consistent with *integration* as well: "I would hold, quite simply, that where segregated public schools exist within a school district to a substantial degree," the burden lies on school boards to "demonstrate they nevertheless are operating a genuinely integrated school system."[89]

If Powell's dissent seems to strain at the limits of language, we might recall that his invocation of segregated schools operating within "integrated" districts largely reproduces the ideal of token desegregation that southern moderates had hoped would ward off further federal intervention during the struggle over massive resistance. Nor could Powell's position come as much of a surprise, given his involvement in the school crisis prior to joining the Court. Powell was deeply involved in local politics in his hometown of Richmond, Virginia, and from 1952 to 1961 served as chairman of the Richmond School Board. Of Richmond's twenty-three thousand black children, only *two* attended schools with whites at the time of Powell's departure (to assume a position on the state board of education).[90] The partners at his law firm represented Prince Edward County in one of the cases consolidated with *Brown v. Board of Education* in 1954, which he thought wrongly decided as a matter of both law and policy. When Prince Edward County shut down its schools rather than comply with desegregation, he helped mount a defense of public schools against the extremism of massive resistance. And yet, when the Supreme Court ordered the public schools reopened, Powell voted to resume payments for tuition grants that sent children to private, segregated schools.[91] Like other Virginia moderates, he managed to be a committed enemy of massive resistance without surrendering his opposition to integration and civil rights.

Rehnquist's and Powell's dissents are keenly aware of the race-conscious nature of successful desegregation strategies, and each finds this fact to be deeply constitutionally problematic. Both dissents are also keenly *un*aware, or willfully ignorant, of connections between current racial disparities and present or past state action. Powell's curious redefinition of integration to include segregated educational facilities, for example, requires judges not to see such connections:

[A]n integrated school system does not mean—and indeed could not mean in view of the residential patterns of most of our major metropolitan areas— that every school must in fact be an integrated unit. A school which *happens to be* all or predominantly white or all or predominantly black is not a "segregated" school in an unconstitutional sense if the system itself is a genuinely integrated one.[92]

What makes some incidents of segregation constitutionally permissible, then, is that they are not products of identifiable discriminatory action. On this purportedly color-blind view, the fact of existing residential segregation is transformed into an unexplained and constitutionally off-limits phenomenon that "does not depend" on race. The causes of such discrimination remain mysterious: it just "happens to be." Denver's pervasive residential and educational segregation is thus figured as unrelated to discrimination; attempts to remedy segregation, on the other hand, "introduce" race as the basis of decision-making, and so may be prohibited by the Equal Protection Clause of the Fourteenth Amendment.

It would not take long for Rehnquist's and Powell's views to command a majority of the Court. In 1974, *Milliken v. Bradley* struck down interdistrict busing between Detroit's inner-city and suburban schools, inaugurating a new era of resegregation. *Milliken*, like the series of decisions to follow in the 1990s, was principally concerned with limiting the scope of relief from federal courts rather than combating southern attempts at "getting around *Brown*."[93] This dramatic reversal is framed within a redemption narrative that simultaneously *praises* desegregation as the price paid to be freed from past sins, and *condemns* it as judicial overreach and violation of white rights. In both regards, white innocence requires a paradoxical relationship to race, the significance of which is figured as so minor as to render race-conscious remedial programs unnecessary, yet so great as to render them presumptively unconstitutional.

Like *Keyes*, *Milliken* concerned busing in a northern, metropolitan context. Unlike *Keyes*, the busing at issue in *Milliken* crossed district lines in order to draw in predominantly white students from suburban schools that, the Court noted, had not initially been party to the lawsuit. Chief Justice Burger wrote the majority opinion. In it, he acknowledges both the fact of large-scale segregation in Detroit's schools and that state action of various kinds (manipulation of attendance zones and school construction sites, school choice plans, and busing of black students away from nearby white schools) was responsible for creating and maintaining that segregation. However, he argued, because the evidence spoke only to segregation within Detroit's schools and not to the actions of the surrounding suburban school boards, interdistrict remedies were not justified: "To approve the remedy ordered by the court would impose on the outlying districts, not shown to have committed any constitutional violation, a wholly impermissible remedy based on a standard not hinted at in *Brown*."[94]

As framed by the Court, the issue pitted a constitutionally suspect goal of "racial balance" against the "deeply rooted" tradition of "local control over the operation of schools."[95] But it could just as well be framed as a question of whether successful efforts to secure residential segregation could be used as a shield against the constitutional requirement to desegregate public schools. Despite evidence that a Detroit-only plan would fail to achieve meaningful desegregation results, the Court by a five-to-four vote rejected interdistrict busing as a remedy for segregated schools in urban Detroit. By ruling out metropolitan-wide desegregation plans, *Milliken* virtually foreclosed the possibility of urban school desegregation, particularly in the North and West, where patterns of white suburbanization left many districts with too few white students to create meaningfully multiracial schools.[96] As Justice Marshall predicted in his dissent, the overwhelming response to a "Detroit-only decree" was the rapid acceleration of white flight, which quickly turned Detroit's public schools into "virtually all-black institutions."[97]

Locating *Milliken* within the narrative structure and ideological demands of a new American dilemma helps explain how it is that *Brown*'s categorical rejection of racial segregation in education could so handily be transformed into a tool for preserving separate and unequal public schools. Whereas Jim Crow segregation had once been defended through a mythology of black inferiority, northern segregation would be defended through a mythology of white innocence. Whereas southern moderates had adapted a rhetoric of color-blind constitutionalism to critique massive resistance while preserving the material conditions of segregation, the Court's labeling of those material conditions as "de facto" now rendered them constitutionally benign. At first, this meant simply that there was no constitutional requirement to remedy segregation when so named; eventually it would supply the basis for a constitutional prohibition against state efforts to remedy entrenched racial inequality. In either case, from this point forward the way to avoid integration was to deny the link between state action and residential segregation while assigning students on the purportedly color-blind basis of racially segregated neighborhood schools.

Remarkably, anti-integrationists weren't even required to do this much. Rather than investigating the historical evidence of state involvement in the creation of segregated neighborhoods and suburbs, to which student school assignments could be "innocently" attached, critics of desegregation could simply assert that the causes of residential segregation were sufficiently complex as to prevent tracing their origins to any particular actions. Without providing any justification for segregation, that is, the cultivation of ignorance as to its causes would ensure immunity from otherwise binding constitutional obligations. In this sense, *Milliken* typifies the ideological structure of racism in the post-civil rights era. Borrowing techniques from southern moderates, the case illustrates how condemnation of racism can service the exoneration of white privilege. Just as southern guilt was made to confirm national innocence—and the backward wrongness of massive resistance helped position moderates as pioneers of a color-blind, postsegregation future—*Milliken* pairs Detroit's culpability for racial segregation with, in Gary Orfield's phrase, "a theory of suburban innocence."[98]

Framed within the redemption narrative of an originally color-blind *Brown*, followed by color-conscious judicial overreach and subsequent white backlash, it is easy to miss the connection between southern moderate evasion strategies and color-blind defenses of segregation in the North. But these connections were not lost on the Second Circuit, whose support for interdistrict remedies *Milliken* overturned. In language clearly meant to invoke southern resistance, the circuit court opinion condemned all actions "*interposed* to delay, obstruct, or *nullify* steps lawfully taken for the purpose of protecting rights guaranteed by the Fourteenth Amendment."[99] Nor did the lower courts have any difficulty discerning extensive government involvement in developing the overwhelmingly white suburbs that ringed Detroit's increasingly black inner city. At trial, the district court determined:

> Governmental actions and inaction at all levels, federal, state and local, have combined, with those of private organizations, such as loaning institutions and real estate associations and brokerage firms, to establish and to maintain the pattern of residential segregation throughout the Detroit metropolitan area.[100]

The story of how government action facilitated residential segregation is by now quite well known. Unlike the Supreme Court, whose treatment of residential segregation emphasizes private preferences, market forces, and natural demographic trends, historians have long been aware of the policy choices and resource investments that link residential segregation to employment and educational opportunities. An extensive literature now documents the history of explicit racial zoning laws, state enforcement of restrictive covenants in housing contracts, racially targeted FHA and VA mortgage financing, the location and placement of federally funded housing developments and highway construction projects, so-called urban renewal programs that gutted low-income housing to make way for white-owned business development, and extensive discriminatory practices of the state-certified real estate profession.[101]

None of this did the Court so much as attempt to dispute. Rather, and to the evident dismay of the dissenting justices, the majority opinion focused almost exclusively on the innocence of suburban school officials and the priorities of local decision-making and administrative efficiency. In this regard, *Milliken* is noteworthy foremost for what it allows itself to *not* know about the development of urban segregation. Justice White, in dissent, professed to be "mystified" by the Court's ignoring the actions of federal and state officials outside the limited sphere of local suburban schools.[102] But the resegregation decisions clearly require such ignorance. Once it is conceded that current patterns of distribution in educational, housing, employment, and other measures of life opportunity are themselves structured by the legacy of racial subordination, the distinction between de jure and de facto segregation is critically weakened. Indeed, the distinction between color-blindness and color-consciousness is itself undermined, deprived, as it were, of any race-neutral social location against which departure or "overshoot" could be meaningfully assessed. Still, ignorance of this magnitude is hard won and requires hard work to maintain. As Justice Douglass pointedly observed in his dissent, to reach its conclusion required the Court to believe "that ghettos develop on their own without any hint of state action."[103]

More precisely, it required the Court to know nothing at all, but only to exercise that great privilege of ignorance so well captured by Justice Stewart's memorable phrase when he characterized the causes of residential segregation in Detroit as "unknown and perhaps unknowable."[104] George Lipsitz has described this "stupefyingly innocent assertion" in terms of possessive investment in whiteness.[105] His language of investment recalls the *Plessy* Court's frank recognition of property rights in whiteness and is meant to suggest certain continuities between nineteenth-century segregation and our own. But *Plessy*'s defense of whiteness as property relied upon a language of biological racism no longer available to the Court in *Milliken*. In its place, the resegregation cases substituted rights without remedies and a willful ignorance as to the actual practices of racial exclusion.[106] At just the historical moment when segregation was becoming indefensible, its legality would no longer require a defense.

The resegregation cases of the 1990s continued this trend by formalizing the legal rules through which local school districts would be released from court-ordered desegregation plans. These cases leverage *Brown*'s condemnation of segregated "dual" systems (in which districts maintained separate schools for white and nonwhite students) to define "unitary status" at the moment compliance was reached. Being declared "unitary" marks the end both of judicial oversight and of responsibility for past discrimination. Unitary status offers a clean slate, release from the burdens of the past, or, as Gary Orfield describes it, "judicial absolution."[107]

In *Board of Education of Oklahoma City v. Dowell* (1991), the Court established two general guidelines for this process: in determining whether to dissolve a desegregation order, courts were to consider "whether the Board had complied in good faith with the desegregation decree since it was entered, and whether, in light of every facet of school operations, the vestiges of past *de jure* segregation had been eliminated to the extent practicable."[108] In theory, the two factors could be evaluated independently of one another. Faithfulness of compliance efforts speaks to the school board's intent, while elimination of "vestiges" of de jure segregation concerns the tangible success of those efforts. In practice, the de jure / de facto distinction tended to collapse the two, making it nearly impossible to prove that continuing racial concentration resulted from past intentional segregation rather than constitutionally "innocent" demographic trends beyond the school board's control. Indeed, *Dowell* seems singularly concerned with the elimination of judicial oversight and a return to local control of public schools. "As to the scope or meaning of 'vestiges,'" Justice Marshall observed in dissent, "the majority says very little."[109]

Nor was the majority particularly concerned that the school board's Student Reassignment Plan (SRP), at issue in the case, resulted in a dramatic return to single-race schools. Under the SRP, 44 percent of all African American children in the district were assigned to schools ranging from 96.9 to 99.7 percent African American, and more than half of the elementary schools in the district had student bodies with at least 90 percent students of a single race.[110] Under the *Dowell* guidelines, this demonstrable return to racially separate schools was not evidence of constitutional injury. Rather, compliance with the court-imposed desegregation plan for "a reasonable period of time" in itself would establish good faith on the part of local school boards—who were then free to implement school assignment plans that restored levels of segregation previously understood to be indicative of intentional segregation.[111]

Rehnquist's opinion thus neatly inverts Brennan's logic from the *Keyes* majority, which viewed existing racial imbalance as suggestive of discriminatory intent. In *Dowell*, it is the absence of evidence of discriminatory intent that is taken to indicate that racial imbalance is not a "vestige" of unlawful segregation, but merely a product of demographic shifts and private choices in the market. On this view, it is not constitutionally troubling that schools might remain permanently separated by race. What *is* constitutionally troubling, in *Dowell*, is the prospect of permanent judicial oversight of local schools. As Rehnquist was quick to remind, this was not what the Court initially had signed on for in *Brown*: "From the very first, federal supervision of local school systems was intended as a temporary measure to remedy past discrimination."[112] To demand a more rigorous test of compliance, he felt, would ensure the "Draconian result" of "condemning school districts once governed by a board which intentionally discriminated, to judicial tutelage for the indefinite future."[113] This, the Court was flatly unwilling to do, even when failure to do so ensured the resegregation of public schools.

Dowell is a disturbing decision for civil rights leaders and advocates of desegregation, for whom Rehnquist's opinion evinces a casual disregard over the return to separate and unequal education while nonetheless claiming fidelity to *Brown v. Board*. For this reason, the case has been criticized as a betrayal of the Constitution and *Brown*. After all, desegregation had in many ways been working prior to the Court's withdrawal of judicially imposed remedies.[114] But perhaps even more troubling is the possibility that Rehnquist may have been right in suggesting that *Brown* never envisioned (and did not authorize) the kind of remedies that would in fact be necessary to ensure "actual desegregation" of public schools. If this is so, it is not because current "de facto" segregation is any less stigmatizing, less damaging, or less a product of intentional state action, as Rehnquist would have it. On the contrary, it is because racial subordination and exclusion are more deeply embedded in the American social structure than cases like *Brown* could allow. Like other liberal redemption projects, *Brown* indulged the fantasy that racism was a temporary aberration from an otherwise egalitarian national creed. In criticizing racial discrimination as unconstitutional (and thus un-American), *Brown* implicitly named the Constitution (and America) as racially innocent, and so promised a *return* to the more truly American principles of the so-called liberal consensus. When racial subordination proved more intractable than this narrative suggests, the Court was forced to confront a more difficult choice than it initially had been willing to face. Resegregation cases like *Dowell* attempted to avoid this confrontation by laying claim to *Brown's* initial liberalism, turned now to the task of delegitimizing the sorts of remedies necessary to confront racial domination in its more systemic and institutionalized forms.

According to dominant narratives of equal protection, *Brown* was "the turning point in America's willingness to face the consequences of centuries of racial discrimination."[115] For liberals and conservatives alike, that moment of self-knowledge was critically tied to a color-blind vision of American democracy. For liberals, the aspiration to racelessness remains an unfulfilled goal. In contrast, conservatives tell a story of its achievement, soon followed by a period of racial "overshoot" that reintroduces race through policies of racial balance, quotas, and affirmative action—which in turn provoke a white backlash against excessive judicial solicitude, special preferences, and Black Power.[116] In both popular opinion and legal doctrine, the conservative version of this story has largely won out. But liberal redemption narratives are in some ways equally bound by the structure of this story, albeit with different normative commitments. On both accounts, that is, courts are said to offer special protections to nonwhites, just as on both accounts this judicial solicitude is said to conflict with democratic principles of local control and electoral accountability. What distinguishes the two views is not a disagreement about whether color-conscious remedies constitute a break from color-blind norms, but whether that break is justified in light of past discrimination. Recognizing the race conscious logic of color-blind constitutionalism allows us to see the resegregation decisions in a quite different light.

Initially, the resegregation cases do seem to conform to this standard interpretation. Where *Green* and *Swann* openly acknowledged the necessity of judicially mandated color-conscious remedies, *Milliken* and *Dowell* each limited the extent of judicial authority and the scope of available remedies. *Freeman v. Pitts* (1992) lowered the bar still further by allowing school districts to be declared unitary even before full compliance had been established. And *Missouri v. Jenkins* (1995) cut off many of the equalization remedies that *Milliken II* previously had offered in lieu of actual integration across district lines. However, minimizing the link between current inequality and "vestiges" of past discrimination was just one prong of the judicial retreat from desegregation. Just as the Court made it more difficult for the victims of Jim Crow to prove a constitutionally recognizable injury, it was becoming much easier to prove injuries for *whites*, as victims of precisely those desegregation remedies the Court now held unconstitutional.[117] Ironically, the rhetoric of color-blind constitutionalism facilitated both prongs of this attack on racial equality. The resegregation decisions thus did not make it harder to prove discrimination, as is commonly supposed. Rather, in the name of color-blindness, they made it harder for *nonwhites* to prove discrimination while making it substantially easier for whites to do so.

Color-blind constitutionalism typically is associated with the "conservative" virtues of judicial restraint and local decision-making. Justice Scalia sounds this theme in *Freeman v. Pitts*, as he laments the slow pace of federal courts to dissolve desegregation decrees: "though our cases continue to profess that judicial oversight of school operations is a temporary expedient, democratic processes remain suspended, with no prospect of restoration, 38 years after *Brown* v. *Board of Education*."[118] But the color-blind constitution served equally well as a foundation for aggressive rights-based activism by conservative critics of civil rights. As we will see in chapter 5—in the contexts of voluntary school desegregation, affirmative action, and workplace discrimination—the Court increasingly would come to void democratically enacted legislation not only when it employed racial classifications, but when racial egalitarianism served as the primary motivation for the law. With the rise of conservative judicial activism, and in the name of transcending racial consciousness, color-blindness discourse effectively articulated white political interests as enforceable legal rights.

PART III | Color-Blindness after
the Color Line

CHAPTER 5 | Defending White Rights

EMERGING AS IT DID in formal opposition to Jim Crow, yet also as a key element in the legal strategy against integration, color-blind constitutionalism bears an uneasy relationship to both segregation and civil rights. To its supporters, the color-blind Constitution represents a fulfillment of the ideals of the civil rights movement and the very definition of democratic equality. For critics, it represents a co-optation of civil rights memory in order to limit judicial protection for racial minorities and preserve unjust advantages derived from past discrimination. Against both of these views, my argument emphasizes the race-conscious logic of color-blind constitutionalism, and so calls attention to a more fundamental level of agreement between them, conceptually and in regard to the narrative practices within which their arguments are framed.

For a number of reasons, the shared terms of this debate often have turned on the question of how much protection the Supreme Court ought to extend to racial minorities. Echoing positions put in place in reaction to *Brown v. Board of Education*, judicial conservatives tend to speak of color-blindness as a check against excessive interference by activist judges in local democratic processes, with judicial liberals countering that past and continuing discrimination justify heightened judicial protection for subordinated racial groups. Both sides, that is, have largely accepted the narrative frame of "judicial solicitude," with critics of color-blindness seeking to justify rather than contest this basic orientation toward racial equality.

The argument of Circuit Court Judge J. Skelly Wright, in a now-classic 1979 *University of Chicago Law Review* article, well captures this familiar perspective. "Genuine equality," Wright notes, "requires, as a matter of common sense, special treatment for the victims of past discrimination."[1] Mirroring the doctrine of suspect classes from *Carolene Products*' footnote 4, which linked heightened judicial scrutiny to conditions of political disadvantage, Wright's argument justifies the departure from color-blind principles on the grounds that "one race and not the other needs such help." Wright explains:

> Minority groups have been given special consideration for their interests, and special protections against the majoritarian political process, because of the reality that otherwise they will continue to be oppressed by an unsympathetic and often hostile majority. They require *greater assistance* to receive *equal protection*.[2]

On its face, and as it is commonly understood, this quote provides a counterargument to the anticlassification interpretation of color-blind constitutionalism. It justifies race-consciousness for remedial purposes, and so distinguishes policies such as affirmative action from the invidious discrimination of Jim Crow. The crucial point for Wright, and for other proponents of this liberal view, is to position color-consciousness as a requirement of justice rather than its violation, and to link this justification to the social-political condition of nonwhite groups: equal protection both allows and requires "special consideration" and "greater assistance" from the Court because of the subordinated position of the groups that would receive it.

Judge Wright's quotation, and the broader argument it represents, is foremost a claim about the status of subordinated racial groups. But it also suggests an implicit claim about courts themselves, namely that the judiciary is uniquely positioned to defend the rights of racial minorities, and therefore justified in supplying this "special consideration." In this regard, the argument both answers to and concedes a long-standing legal narrative about equal protection and racial favoritism, infamously put by Justice Bradley in the *Civil Rights Cases* of 1883.[3] After explaining why the Civil Rights Act of 1875—which, among other things, prohibited racial segregation in hotels, theaters, public conveyances, and the like—overstepped congressional authority in violation of the Tenth Amendment, Justice Bradley added this characterization of the recently freed slave population:

> When a man has emerged from slavery, and, by the aid of beneficent legislation, has shaken off the inseparable concomitants of that state, there must be some stage in the progress of his elevation when he takes the rank of a mere citizen and ceases to be *the special favorite of the laws*, and when his rights as a citizen or a man are to be protected in the ordinary modes by which other men's rights are protected.[4]

In a misleadingly literal sense, Justice Bradley is correct in his characterization of the antidiscrimination requirement as creating a "special favorite of the law"—if only because whites (presented here as the universal,
racially unmarked "mere citizen") evidently would not require judicial
protection from politically disenfranchised racial groups. White citizens,
as a class, would have no difficulty protecting their rights "in the ordinary
modes" of democratic politics. Justice Bradley is right, in other words, to
see racial consciousness in even the most "color-blind" application of antidiscrimination law, even if he is laughably wrong to portray the victims of
slavery and segregation as "special favorites."[5]

What may seem perfectly obvious in the context of the *Civil Rights
Cases*—that simple equality will appear under conditions of white
supremacy as a demand for "special rights"—is curiously overlooked in
the context of affirmative action in the post-civil rights era. The position
of Judge Wright, and the judicial liberalism of which it is representative,
holds affirmative action to be justified on the grounds that such "special
protections" continue to be necessary in a racially inequitable society such
as our own. While supplying a powerful and useful response to the color-
blind critique of affirmative action, this position nonetheless concedes
Justice Bradley's underlying narrative of "special favorites" and "mere citizens"—yet fails to point out that reverse-discrimination claims denounce
racial consciousness precisely through demands for heightened judicial
solicitude for whites.

If color-blind constitutionalism once served as a rearguard defense
against liberal activism by the Warren Court, as resistance to desegregation, it was soon transformed into a powerful conservative rights-based
attack on legislative efforts to minimize racial inequality. The consequences of this transformation have not been fully appreciated, and extend
well beyond the question of affirmative action in college admissions.
Starting with the color-blind critique of affirmative action and extending
through more recent school desegregation and employment discrimination
cases, this chapter argues that current equal protection doctrine calls into
question whether the pursuit of racial equality itself is a constitutionally
permissible legislative goal. Although framed as a rejection of race, the
Court's current trajectory and theory of equal protection enshrines existing racial disparity as a constitutionally enforceable right. In chapter 4 we
saw color-blind constitutionalism used principally to reduce the scope of
recognizable racial injury for those hoping to use the courts to challenge
entrenched racial hierarchy. In this chapter, color-blind constitutionalism increasing comes to support a judicially active, rights-based strategy,

the logical conclusion of which is to render the pursuit of racial equality unconstitutional.

The Affirmative Action Consensus

Since it first took up the issue in the late 1970s, the Supreme Court has struggled to establish clear or decisive doctrinal rules regarding race-based affirmative action. In 2003, the Court considered equal protection challenges to admissions policies at the University of Michigan Law School and College of Literature, Science, and the Arts (LSA). By upholding the constitutionality of the Law School's use of race in its admission process (*Grutter v. Bollinger*),[6] but striking down those employed by the LSA (*Gratz v. Bollinger*),[7] the Court extended its previous logic of compromise on race-based affirmative action for colleges and universities as articulated in the 1978 case *Regents of University of California v. Bakke*.[8] That compromise, and the "diversity" rationale on which it is premised, steers an uneasy path between the Court's normative commitment to color-blind jurisprudence and its grudging recognition that American society continues to be structured by race in many important regards. As doctrine, the diversity compromise commands a narrow majority of the current Supreme Court and was recently reaffirmed in *Fisher v. Texas*, upholding a similar admissions policy at the University of Texas.[9]

In the Michigan cases, as it did in *Bakke*, the Court labored to reconcile what are commonly regarded as two competing values emanating from the Equal Protection Clause of the Fourteenth Amendment. Invoking *Brown v. Board of Education*, Justice O'Connor observed that "the Court has long recognized" the link between education and citizenship that makes educational and civic inclusion a core value of the Constitution: "Effective participation by members of all racial and ethnic groups in the civic life of our nation is essential if the dream of one Nation, indivisible, is to be realized."[10] At the same time, however, the Court underscored that the Equal Protection Clause applies to individuals rather than groups, thus rendering inherently suspect all government action based on race. It is this competing principle of antidiscrimination that triggers the Court's application of strict scrutiny for all legislation that explicitly classifies by race.[11]

As it is commonly understood, the evolution of equal protection law is characterized by a steady progression toward the color-blind view and corresponding rejection of racial-consciousness, with only a few narrowly defined (and rapidly shrinking) exceptions for redress of past acts of intentional discrimination, national security, or the pursuit of diversity in higher education. In terms of doctrine, the turning point was a fractured *Bakke* decision that (by a five-to-four vote) applied strict scrutiny to all racial classifications, including those meant to benefit rather than burden the traditional victims of invidious discrimination: the "discrete and insular minorities" from footnote 4. Joining four conservative justices, for whom all forms of affirmative action are constitutionally prohibited, Justice Powell's swing vote emphasized the individualistic nature of personal rights to equal protection, as opposed to "the artificial line of a 'two-class theory' of the Fourteenth Amendment."[12] In language that eerily reproduces Justice Bradley's characterization of newly freed slaves as "special favorites of the law," Powell justified the application of strict scrutiny to affirmative action policies as a refusal to permit "the recognition of *special wards* entitled to a degree of protection greater than that accorded others,"[13] and an inability to determine "which groups would merit 'heightened judicial solicitude' and which would not."[14]

On this view, the uniform application of strict scrutiny to all racial classifications is necessary to protect whites—to whom Justice Powell refers simply as "innocent persons"—from being made to "suffer [the] otherwise impermissible burdens" of racial preference in order to "enhance the societal standing" of ethnic groups.[15] Joining with Justices Stevens, Stewart, and Rehnquist and Chief Justice Burger, Powell's application of strict scrutiny held unconstitutional the University of California–Davis Medical School's minority set-aside affirmative action program. Unlike the four conservative justices, however, Powell's application of strict scrutiny would allow other affirmative action programs, such as that used at Harvard, provided that each candidate received individualized consideration and was eligible to compete for all available spots, and so long as each candidate's race figured as just one factor among many.

Additionally, because strict scrutiny requires that policies be narrowly tailored to achieve a compelling state interest, Powell was pushed to articulate the precise interest affirmative action serves. In so doing, he further narrowed the scope of constitutional permissibility for the state's use of racial classifications. First, Powell rejected the pursuit of racial quotas for their own sake, "not as insubstantial, but as facially invalid." Figuring race as an abstraction, disconnected from the historical circumstances that make racial distinctions socially meaningful, Powell assures that preference may never be given to members of a group "merely because of its race or ethnic origin" or "for no reason other than race."[16] Race is not in itself meaningful, Powell suggests, and its use may in limited instances be justified only when it serves as a proxy for some other, constitutionally permissible, goal or condition. Indeed, strict scrutiny analysis is meant to test the tightness of fit between race and whatever that more substantive goal is said to be. Second, while it is constitutionally permissible to redress "the disabling effects of *identified* discrimination," Powell distinguished these specific acts (for which there has been "judicial, legislative, or administrative findings of constitutional or statutory violations") from the more general effects of "societal discrimination."[17] Specific individuals, that is, may have suffered from specific acts of discrimination, but policies of racial preference are constitutionally problematic when not sufficiently tied to those identified acts. Absent findings of particular violations, the Constitution prohibits all classifications that aid "persons perceived as members of relatively victimized groups at the expense of other innocent individuals."[18]

If Powell's *Bakke* opinion calls into doubt the constitutional legitimacy of efforts to achieve a more racially egalitarian society, it nonetheless preserves the interests of educational institutions that would use race to attain a more diverse student body. Further decoupling race from questions of power or subordination, the diversity rational makes no claim in the interest of racial equality, serving instead as a counterbalance against the constitutional presumption for color-blindness. As Powell explains, the interest in diversity is retained by the educational institutions rather than the students who may be admitted through affirmative action programs, and so falls under the broader rubric of academic freedom. Accordingly, diversity supplies "a countervailing constitutional interest" rooted in the First Amendment.[19] Not justice, but utility, is at stake, as the selection of a diverse student body constitutes "a goal that is of paramount importance" to the university.[20] As victims of mere "societal discrimination," minority candidates are not bearers of rights to inclusion or equality on this rationale but simply "exhibit qualities more likely to promote beneficial educational pluralism," no different in principle from being a skilled musician or athlete, having traveled abroad or grown up on a farm, or any other diversity-promoting personal characteristic.[21]

Framed in terms of competing values, the legal significance of race is subsumed under a general interest in diversity, which the Court understands as cutting *against* the constitutional value of antidiscrimination, not in favor. That African American, Native American, and Latino/a students remain significantly underrepresented in colleges and universities is, on this view, perfectly consistent with the ideals of equal protection, while efforts to achieve a more racially equitable distribution of social goods is constitutionally problematic. Justice Powell does not offer the diversity rationale as a competing conception of equality, but rather as an educational interest of sufficient importance as to justify departing from the ordinary standards of racial equality.

It is not surprising, then, that the Court's embrace of diversity as the sole justification for race-based affirmative action has fallen under heavy criticism from both sides of the political-legal spectrum. Critics of affirmative action fail to see why diversity is of such importance as to justify a departure from the constitutional requirement of color-blindness.[22] Proponents of race-based affirmative action fail to see why noninvidious racial classifications such as affirmative action should be held to the same constitutional standard as overtly racist policies such as segregation, or why the state's interest in combating "societal discrimination" does not constitute a compelling state interest when the pursuit of diversity does.[23] That the *Bakke* decision upheld the constitutionality of certain limited forms of race-based affirmative action is, in the end, far less significant than the "competing values" framework it imposed and the shared narrative commitments within which both sides articulated their positions.

In the aftermath of *Bakke*, Justice O'Connor emerged as the decisive vote in a series of cases that solidified the Court's anticlassification interpretation of equal protection, held unconstitutional affirmative action employment provisions at both the state and federal levels, and pushed liberal defenders of affirmative action to justify their positions as temporary departures from an otherwise implicitly race-neutral norm. In *Richmond v. J.A. Croson* (1989), the Court invalidated the Richmond City Council's Minority Business Utilization Plan, which required recipients of city construction contracts to reserve, as a goal, 30 percent of each job to be subcontracted to minority business enterprises, or MBEs. The plan had been adopted, in part, in response to a study that revealed minority businesses to have received less than 1 percent of all city construction contracts, and that many or most of Richmond's contractor associations "had virtually no minority businesses within their membership."[24] In 1989, African Americans constituted over 50 percent of Richmond's population. Nonetheless, Justice O'Connor, writing for the Court, denied that the 30 percent set-aside could "in any realistic sense be tied to any injury suffered by anyone."[25] While conceding that a "sorry history of both private and public discrimination" had "contributed to a lack of opportunities for black entrepreneurs," O'Connor nonetheless denied that the plan ought properly be understood as remedial, since a general history of societal discrimination does not rise to the level of "identified discrimination" for which a remedy is warranted.[26]

In separate concurring opinions, Justices Kennedy and Scalia each wrote to emphasize the crucial importance of "racial neutrality," which Kennedy described as "the driving force of the Equal Protection Clause."[27] Unlike Justice Powell—for whom the strict scrutiny bar had not been set so high as to exclude affirmative action plans such as that in place at Harvard—Justice Kennedy took pains to emphasize that strict scrutiny must be applied so as to "forbid the use even of narrowly drawn racial classifications except as a last resort."[28] Justice Scalia was even more emphatic in his rejection of racial classifications, which he viewed as unconstitutional even when used to redress the effects of past discrimination. Where the Court was unable to discern any constitutionally relevant injury in the near total exclusion of nonwhites from government building contracts, it had no difficulty in framing remedies to that condition as the more egregious offense. Justice Scalia's concurring opinion offers a vivid picture of the severity of the purported harm:

> The difficulty of overcoming the effects of past discrimination is as nothing compared with the difficulty of eradicating from our society the source of those effects, which is the tendency—fatal to a nation such as ours—to classify and judge men and women on the basis of their country of origin or the color of their skin.[29]

If by "the effects of past discrimination" Scalia means the legacy of slavery and Jim Crow, it is quite remarkable (and especially so given the statistical evidence of persistent racial inequalities) to think that the difficulty in their overcoming could be "as nothing" compared to the harm of a 30 percent minority set-aside program. The former, for Scalia, is easily overcome; the latter is "fatal" to the nation.[30] By framing color-blindness as "racially neutral," the rejection of affirmative action is invested with the same urgency and moral authority as that with which we would oppose slavery or Jim Crow.

In the 1995 case of *Adarand v. Pena*, which extended to the federal level *Croson*'s prohibition against affirmative action in the distribution of state and local contracts, Justice O'Connor reiterated that "all racial classifications, imposed by whatever federal, state, or local governmental actor," must be reviewed under strict scrutiny.[31] For O'Connor, who announced the judgment of the Court, this need not disqualify all racial classifications, since redress for specific acts of discrimination could in limited circumstances qualify as a state interest sufficiently compelling as to justify a narrowly tailored race-based remedy. "Strict in theory," for O'Connor, need not mean "fatal in fact."[32] No doubt recognizing this understanding of strict scrutiny to hold open the possibility of a compromise such as that offered by Powell in *Bakke*, Justice Scalia wrote separately to emphasize his belief that the government "can *never* have a 'compelling interest' in discriminating on the basis of race in order to 'make up' for past racial discrimination in the opposite direction."[33]

For Scalia, the principle of race-neutrality maps seamlessly to the principle of individualism and unconstitutionality of class legislation:

> To pursue the concept of racial entitlement—even for the most admirable and benign purposes—is to reinforce and preserve for future mischief the way of thinking that produced race slavery, race privilege and race hatred. In the eyes of government, we are just one race here. It is American.[34]

But this quote is also perhaps more revealing than Scalia intends, and helps to explain his earlier claim from *Croson*, comparing affirmative action to slavery. Despite his implication, Justice Scalia obviously does not believe that affirmative action is worse than slavery. Rather, he understands affirmative action as betraying an underlying premise of racial nonneutrality that is, in his view, racism's root cause—if not its very definition. In *Croson* it was described as a fatal "tendency"—in *Adarand* it becomes a "way of thinking." And because Scalia takes color-blindness for an absence of racial consciousness, that "way of thinking" remains disconnected from any theorization of white supremacy or the material interests that in fact "produced" chattel slavery and segregation. Consequently, Scalia finds no credible way to distinguish the underlying motives behind racial classifications that enforce racial caste and those that seek to dismantle it. Efforts to combat racial hierarchy, rather than racial hierarchy itself, appear as "racial entitlement." Or, as Justice Thomas would have it, "there is a moral and constitutional equivalence between laws designed to subjugate a race and those that distribute benefits on the basis of race in order to foster some current notion of equality."[35]

Unfortunately, liberal defenses of affirmative action tend to reinforce rather than challenge this narrative. Framed in terms of competing values, color-blind conservatives are free to declare the injury of racial classification in increasingly hyperbolic terms while affirmative action's advocates are left to defend the policy on primarily utilitarian grounds, as an interest sufficiently compelling to excuse an otherwise constitutionally impermissible departure from race-neutrality. These competing values assume various forms and may be instrumental or substantive, individual or group based, compensatory for past harms or integrative and future oriented. Justice Powell's diversity rationale illustrates the instrumental justification, since it values an applicant's race for its contribution to classroom diversity rather than a marker of past injury for which compensation would be justified. By limiting remedial uses of affirmative action to specific acts of identified discrimination, the Court has significantly undermined traditional compensatory rationales. Consequently, when affirmative action is defended (by anyone hoping to prevail in court), it is increasingly justified "not as a remedy to historical discrimination and inequality, but as an instrumentally rational strategy used to achieve the positive effects of racial and gender diversity in modern society."[36]

Affirmative action may also be defended as a necessary means of integration, even without reference to past discriminatory acts.[37] When focused on present barriers to full social inclusion, affirmative action may be viewed as necessary to ensure that individuals will not be disadvantaged, de facto, on the basis of their race.[38] Advocates of this view will find validation in the references to participation and inclusion in Justice O'Connor's reformulation of Powell's diversity rationale. And while this conception of fairness remains decidedly individualistic, similar arguments might emphasize fair treatment of groups rather than integration of individuals by invoking competing values such as antisubordination, anti-caste, or Fiss's group-disadvantaging principle. Competing substantive values such as these are not always well specified, but generally advocate for a more extensive redistribution of social goods than do the principles of anticlassification or racial nonrecognition. And while there exist meaningful differences between such various competing values, they all aim to justify a departure from color-blindness on the grounds of some more compelling value. Thus Glenn Loury's prioritization of "racial justice" over color-blindness, or Amy Gutmann's insistence that color-blindness is not a fundamental principle of justice: "Fairness is a fundamental principle of justice, and . . . it is a principle that does not always call for color blindness."[39] If recognition of race is at times necessary to treat groups or individuals fairly, as these authors suggest, color-consciousness need not violate the principle of equal treatment even when it does violate the principle of racial neutrality.

This surprising level of agreement between critics and supporters of affirmative action is one measure of the success that color-blind conservatives have had in establishing the narrative boundaries under which race is commonly discussed and legally contested. For even the staunchest critics of color-blindness, affirmative action policies are defended as justifiable departures from the ordinary operation of antidiscrimination law—either as a necessary means to achieve a more color-blind society in the future, or on the authority of a competing principle of racial equality said to trump that of nondiscrimination. Indeed, even when *permitting* affirmative action programs such as those at Harvard (*Bakke*) or the University of Michigan Law School (*Grutter*), the Court has agreed with color-blind conservatives that such policies are fundamentally in tension with the principle of non-discrimination at the core of the Equal Protection Clause.[40] Accordingly, race-based affirmative action policies must "have a logical end point" and are subject to "periodic reviews to determine whether racial preferences are still necessary."[41] Writing for the Court in *Grutter*, Justice O'Connor repeatedly emphasized that affirmative action can only be justified as a temporary measure, and that requiring "all race-conscious admissions programs [to] have a termination point" confirms an underlying commitment to color-blindness.[42]

For Justice O'Connor, and for the liberal-integrationist position more broadly, affirmative action can only be justified as a temporary aberration because racism itself is assumed to be an anomaly within an otherwise egalitarian sociolegal order. However, the Court's manifest anxiety over affirmative action's persistence—that it threatens always to become an ongoing de facto racial quota—also discloses an underlying concern that racism itself might turn out to be a permanent condition rather than a temporary anomaly. Based on no particular evidence, and without so much as a citation, O'Connor conjectures that "25 years from now, the use of racial preferences will no longer be necessary."[43] Concerned that critics of affirmative action might seize upon this language as an implicit sunset provision, Justice Ginsburg reframes O'Connor's optimism as a "hope," but not a "forecast."[44]

Significantly, this is not a dispute between racial optimists and pessimists. The disagreement between Justices O'Connor and Ginsburg turns neither on how hopeful we ought to be, nor on how much racial progress the nation might reasonably be expected to make by 2028 (twenty-five years after *Grutter*). Rather, what would seem to be a minor semantic distinction between a "hope" and a "forecast" in fact marks a more fundamental disagreement over what exactly would have to change in the world before it is possible to say that programs like affirmative action are "no longer necessary." It is, in other words, a dispute over what vision of equality the Constitution demands—and what level of racial stratification may be tolerated within America's self-conception as committed to, or perhaps already having achieved, the transcendence of race. In this sense, Justice O'Connor's compromise position reveals an unwillingness to concede that racial exclusion is in some fundamental way constitutive of American liberalism, while *also* denying (contra Justices Scalia and Thomas) that persistent material inequalities by race are of little or no constitutional concern. It is not an empirical judgment, then, but a narrative commitment that makes O'Connor construe racial inequality (of the scale that makes affirmative action "necessary") as a temporary phenomenon in the United States.

In reading Justice O'Connor's twenty-five-year time frame as a narrative commitment, I aim to redirect criticism of the Court's equal protection doctrine in ways that challenge the shared assumptions of affirmative action's critics and those of its liberal defenders. For O'Connor, the "durational requirement" of constitutionally permissible affirmative action programs is necessary in order to confirm that any "deviation from the norm of equal treatment of all racial and ethnic groups is a temporary matter."[45] Within the constraints of American liberalism's racial common sense, this doctrinal requirement responds to the perceived contradiction between affirmative action's means (which require classification of individuals by race) and its ultimate goal of deracialization.[46] But the real force of the argument should be understood to derive less from O'Connor's advocacy of a specific durational requirement than from her implicit premise: that color-blindness supplies a race-neutral "norm" against which affirmative action constitutes a "deviation."

Arguments that justify a supposed departure from racial neutrality may be those most likely to win in court. However, even when successful, such victories are won at the cost of foreclosing a more fundamental challenge to the neutrality of the anticlassification rule itself. In *Grutter*, that foreclosed perspective took the form of an organized group of student interveners—a grassroots, student-based civil rights movement associated with the BAMN coalition[47]—who entered the case and filed a supporting amicus brief for the express purpose of raising a rights-based defense of affirmative action not offered by the University or any of the military and business elites who supported the admissions policy. While the *Grutter* majority did uphold the constitutionality of Michigan's affirmative action program, it did so entirely for utilitarian reasons, emphasizing the importance of diversity for military and business effectiveness in an increasingly globalized world.[48] In contrast, student interveners challenged the neutrality of the Law School's "ordinary" admissions process itself. Grounding their arguments in a theory of "credential bias" rather than diversity, the student intervenors cast affirmative action "as a remedy for the University's reliance on discriminatory admissions criteria"—an argument left wholly unaddressed by the Court.[49]

This missing challenge to "ordinary" racial privilege underscores the dangers of what I described in chapter 2 as a liberal redemption narrative. As we saw in the school desegregation cases, it is a narrative capable of condemning racist ideology while simultaneously preserving material conditions of racial stratification. Indeed, it is in part *because* of this condemnation of older and more explicit forms of white racial consciousness that the connection between past racial subordination and current forms of exclusion are, for some, difficult to discern. Kimberlé Crenshaw has suggested the language of "white norms" to explain this continuity between these contemporary forms and the old racial order.[50] Accordingly, an effective theorization of racial discrimination today necessarily must attend to those dispersed forms of racial privilege named by color-blind ideology simply as "race neutral."

Conservative appeals to color-blind constitutionalism serve to conceal such institutionalized forms of racial disadvantage. More critically, the same will be true of liberal redemption narratives that would allow race-conscious policies as a temporary measure to facilitate a return to otherwise presumptively race-neutral norms. Both positions, that is, take shape around a racial imaginary of America's future innocence. Both share a fantasy of America *after race*, in which ordinary politics and social policy might function as if outside of or beyond all racial logic. If we pose the question in this way, it is not the failure of a particular policy or plan to achieve "nonracial" status that is at issue. Rather, we ought to inquire in what sense an absence of racial classification (or more than this, a *prohibition* against racial classification) could be race neutral. In recognizing the race-conscious logic of color-blind constitutionalism, that is, we are well placed to challenge the assumption of a race-neutral reference point against which racial consciousness is marked as an extraordinary departure.

Defending White Rights

Critical race theory's groundbreaking analysis of post-civil rights racism was intended, in part, to push back against the evident success that neoconservative think tanks and political appointees (most notably within the Reagan Justice Department) had experienced in rearticulating hostility to the civil rights legacy as a return to first principles of equal treatment and fair play.[51] To this end, critical race theorists braced their critique against an understanding of racism as relations between dominant and subordinate social groups and identified specific institutional mechanisms through which color-blind ideology ascended to the status of racial common sense. More than just differing constitutional or moral ideals, appeals to color-blindness and color-consciousness represent a clash between highly polarized political coalitions, which political scientists Desmond King and Rogers Smith analyze as competing "racial policy alliances."[52]

Writing in the late 1980s and early 1990s, CRT scholars brought a justifiable sense of urgency in the face of what was, in retrospect, a period of full-scale ideological realignment. Kimberlé Crenshaw recognized before others a fundamental ambiguity in antidiscrimination discourse that rendered it susceptible to conservative rearticulation: "Because antidiscrimination law contains both the *expansive* and the *restrictive* view, equality of opportunity can refer to either. This uncertainty means that the societal adoption of racial equality rhetoric does not itself entail a commitment to end racial inequality."[53] By "restrictive," Crenshaw means a "formalistic, color-blind view" of equal protection that accommodates levels of racial inequality that the more "expansive" antisubordination view would not. In one sense, Crenshaw is surely right that color-blind constitutionalism restricted what would count as a legally cognizable injury, and so made it increasingly difficult for victims of white supremacy to succeed in court. However, in another important sense, the rise of color-blindness represents a dramatically *expansive* view of equal protection, making it increasingly less difficult for white people to claim constitutional injury on the basis of race. Indeed, color-blind constitutionalism signaled the emergence of an aggressive rights-based movement to enlist the power of the courts against racially egalitarian social policy. Conservative political rhetoric routinely denounced the evils of an "activist" Court for rewarding groups rather than individuals, but in mobilizing judicial protection against "reverse discrimination," the color-blind movement successfully harnessed the power of an activist Court in defense of white victims as a group.

For critics and supporters alike, color-blind constitutionalism is commonly evaluated in terms of the prohibition against racial classification it demands. But color-blindness is not the absence of racial consciousness. In practice, legal prohibitions against racial classification have the effect of placing special emphasis on injuries said to be suffered on the basis of race. In this sense, all claims of discrimination invoke group membership. As Kenneth Karst and Harold Horowitz point out, "To complain against a classification scheme is not merely to say 'I am wronged,' but to say 'We are wronged.' Every lawsuit based on a claim to equal protection is, in spirit, a class action."[54] The centrality of group membership to claims of discrimination is no less on display in the cases of reverse discrimination, which are in fact claims of injury *as members of a racial group*. This point is easily overlooked, in part because of the close rhetorical connection between reverse discrimination and color-blind individualism, but also because the racial group claiming injury (whites, as a class) is characteristically thought of as unmarked by racial difference—the unstated norm against which racial difference is measured.

Nonetheless, the effectiveness of the anti-affirmative action movement can largely be attributed to its simultaneous mobilization of white identity politics and categorical rejection of "race" as a legitimate category of law or public policy.[55] Conservative legal advocates have pursued both of these goals by vigorously defending a color-blind interpretation of the Fourteenth Amendment's Equal Protection Clause while, at the same time, organizing litigation strategies to defend the rights of white "victims" of affirmative action. As Thomas Keck has observed, the Supreme Court's receptivity to color-blind principles created strong incentives for conservative legal groups to organize "white individuals as aggrieved rights-bearers, treated unfairly by powerful liberal institutions and ready to seek their day in court."[56] As with other "cause lawyer" organizations, the activities of groups such as the Center for Individual Rights extend beyond legal argument and representation to include public relations media work, advertising to and active solicitation of clients, and other social movement activities.[57] Keck emphasizes the dynamic relationship between interest groups and an activist conservative Court to explain the general growth of conservative rights consciousness. In regard to the anti-affirmative action movement, color-blind rights discourse also produces a heightened *racial* consciousness: "The Court's decisions fostered both a white racial consciousness among ordinary citizens and a set of organized groups committed to representing those citizens."[58]

Both on and off the Court, arguments for color-blind constitutionalism take their justification from a perceived contradiction between the practical effects of classifying individuals by race, and the enduring national dream of racial transcendence. However laudable as an ideal, a more candid acknowledgment of the race-conscious logic of color-blind constitutionalism suggests that prohibitions against racial classification do anything but "transcend" race. As suggested by Justice Scalia's line of questioning in *Grutter*, reverse-discrimination claims necessarily incorporate white racial consciousness into their construction of legal injury. Scalia goes out of his way to emphasize that the grounds upon which an applicant for college admission may permissibly be rejected is nearly limitless. No constitutional injury results when admission is denied because of preferences given to a "less qualified" student whose oboe playing fills a need in the orchestra or whose parents contribute large sums of money to the alumni fund, or various other nonracial criteria. Indeed, judging by grades and scores alone, for example, Allan Bakke was indeed "more qualified" than many of the students admitted ahead of him—many of whom were white.[59] Yet it is only the nonwhite students whose admission is construed as "taking his spot" and that raises a constitutional challenge. Allan Bakke and Jennifer Gratz have no legal basis on which to object to "less qualified" white students who were admitted ahead of them. Their injuries are only legally cognizable when the "less qualified" students admitted are black or Latino—that is, when they are denied admission *as whites*.

In this manner, and in the name of color-blindness, organized opposition to affirmative action might therefore be understood to crystallize white interests and mobilize social movements in their defense. As Glen Loury observes, when "anti-preference activists form institutions, amass funds, solicit plaintiffs, and rally troops to make America a 'race-free zone,' they necessarily help to construct a racial—that is to say 'white'—interest."[60] Strict adherence to principles of antidiscrimination and color-blindness cannot bring about the "getting past race" that provides their justification. Instead, these principles logically require a special sensitivity to race that heightens racial awareness and serves as a focal point in mobilizing white social movements.

Like "racial preferences," the language of "special rights" plays a central role in the success of conservative legal activism. As a strategy of rearticulation, the disparagement of "special rights" allows critics to claim moral authority as defenders of "equal rights" while, at the same time, mobilizing against the achievements of traditional civil rights groups. Echoing Michael Rogin's theorization of political demonology, Jeffrey Dudas documents how conservative rights-talk generates a sense of group identity through acts of social exclusion. Rather than mobilizing against racial, ethnic, or sexual minorities, conservative rights-claims are presented as a defense of an embattled American way of life—and so function also to "deflect popular scrutiny from unresponsive political and economic institutions," thereby displacing the blame onto marginalized groups.[61]

In emphasizing this element of displacement, Dudas helpfully calls attention to the constraining nature of conservative rights-based grievances. The rhetoric of racial demonization and "special rights," that is, evades discussion of the actual causes of white working-class resentment, which derive from broader economic structures of neoliberal globalization. From this perspective, the rhetoric of special rights functions as "an engine of resentment" that in fact undermines the class interests of those it claims to protect. But the assertion of universality in appeals to "equal rights, not special rights" might also be understood to produce the racialized identities they purport to denounce. Seen this way, as racial identities forged from attacks on race, it becomes clear that Dudas concedes too much when he describes conservative rights-talk as regarding "any consciousness of race and gender in public policy morally noxious and socially destructive."[62] In fact, conservative rights claims do *not* reject "any consciousness of race and gender"—even if they claim to do so—since the mobilization of that stated rejection requires an intensification of white racial identity. What they do, rather, is rearticulate white resentment in the idiom of equal rights, encouraging political mobilization to secure white privilege through "race neutral" means. Advocates for color-blindness may identify themselves as against race-awareness, but this identification is itself an exercise in racial identity.

As a principle of political organization and legal advocacy, the transformation of racial resentment into political identities forged from the rejection of race has proven a remarkably successful strategy. And no one has employed it more successfully, in the legal arena, than Edward Blum, the former stockbroker turned conservative legal activist who became the director of the Project On Fair Representation (POFR).[63] Blum's organizations were instrumental in advancing both *Shelby v. Holder* and *Fisher v. TX* to the Supreme Court. Two more high-profile affirmative action cases, involving Harvard and the University of North Carolina, are currently on the dockets in US district courts.[64]

On its website, POFR advertises its mission as a legal defense foundation "designed to support litigation that challenges racial and ethnic classifications and preferences" in voting, education, and government contracting, as well as "representing individuals who have been victims of racial discrimination in hiring, firing, and promotion." Adopting race-neutral language and the rhetoric of civil rights, the presentation simultaneously condemns race as a corrupting influence on the democratic process and organizes its supporters along racial lines: against minority groups deemed to receive racial preferences. Both elements of the appeal are required to make sense of POFR's claim to fight against workplace discrimination. Most directly, the organization evinces no concern for black and Latino victims of employment discrimination, and brings no lawsuits on their behalf. The implicit racial identity of POFR's "victims" is revealed in its exclusive focus on so-called reverse-discrimination cases. Nor is this fact incidental to the political force of the project, as the lawsuits (and social organizing necessary to sustain them) trade precisely upon a perceived sense of group injury defined necessarily along racial lines.

The double nature of this appeal is even more explicit on the Students for Fair Admissions (SFA) website, which greets viewers with an explanation of the group's collective goals as well as an invitation to join in its legal advocacy. Not surprisingly, SFA defines itself as a nonprofit membership group opposed to racial "preferences" in college admissions. Invoking a golden age of color-blind equality, SFA's mission is to "restore the original principles of our nation's civil rights movement: A student's race and ethnicity should not be factors that either harm or help that student to gain admission to a competitive university."[65] And yet, in pursuit of this nominally color-blind goal, SFA solicits new plaintiffs in a manner seemingly calculated to maximize the racial identification of its membership. On the site's opening page, beneath a headline announcing the Harvard and UNC lawsuits as efforts to "challenge racial admissions policies," is an online form, in which readers are asked, "Were You Denied Admission to College? *It may be because you're the wrong race.* Students for Fair Admissions would like to hear from you." Along with name and contact information, the form includes a field for "year you applied" and "schools that rejected you."[66]

The SFA website is perhaps more candid than most, but its enactment of white victimhood out of a professed rejection of race is in fact common to reverse-discrimination claims. Here unsuccessful candidates are encouraged to attribute their rejections to a racial injustice (spots allegedly going to undeserving minority applicants) above all other factors, to identify themselves principally as members of a racial group ("the wrong race"), and to join a political organization on the basis of that shared racial identity (for a $10 fee). Of all the various reasons why an applicant might not be accepted to a competitive school, race stands alone as "the reason" for being denied admission. In the name of color-blind equality, unsuccessful applicants are transformed into injured parties, and conservative advocacy groups into champions of white rights.

The rhetoric of color-blind constitutionalism tends to obscure the racial consciousness inherent in unique prohibitions against racial classification; nonetheless, color-blind arguments simply cannot work in its absence. Justice Scalia's critique of affirmative action in *Grutter v. Bollinger* is especially telling in this regard. In *Grutter*, the University of Michigan

Law School defended its admissions policies as compliant with the *Bakke* decision on the grounds that race was treated simply as one aspect of diversity that it sought to promote, while each candidate in the admissions process was treated as an individual. In this context, the permissibility of affirmative action rests on the fact that race is treated no differently than other relevant criteria in selecting a diverse student body: geographical representation, musical ability, international travel, and so on.[67] Yet, as Scalia's line of questioning makes clear, the suspect classification doctrine insists on just the opposite:

> QUESTION: Does the Constitution prohibit discrimination against— against oboe players as opposed to flute players?
> MS. MAHONEY: No, Your Honor.
> QUESTION: Does it prohibit discrimination on the basis of alumna status?
> MS. MAHONEY: No, Your Honor.
> QUESTION: But it does prohibit discrimination on the basis of race?[68]

The Equal Protection Clause provides no remedy for discrimination on grounds other than race or similarly prohibited categories such as sex, nationality, or religion—and what qualifies these other categories for anti-discrimination protection arguably is their similarity to race. Race is special in this regard. And yet the diversity rationale for affirmative action has at times been criticized by conservatives as a disingenuous cover for otherwise impermissible racial quotas.[69] Scalia's candor is therefore all the more remarkable. While defenders of affirmative action strain to show how race is simply one of many relevant qualities in an applicant, Scalia's point is that it is *unconstitutional* to treat race in the same manner as other traits.

It is a testimony to the effectiveness and longevity of antiblack post-Reconstruction narratives—such as that of Justice Curtis in the *Civil Rights Cases* of 1883—that the language of African Americans as "special wards" and the denunciation of excessive "judicial solicitude" could carry through to today's conservative rights-based attack on affirmative action while at the same time securing what can only be called "special rights" for whites as the recipients of heightened judicial scrutiny. Seen this way, Justice Marshall's scathing dissent in *Croson* is clearly warranted, yet oddly too optimistic in criticizing the Court for failing to recognize "the tragic and indelible fact that the discrimination against blacks and other racial minorities in this Nation has pervaded our Nation's history and continues to scar our society."[70] This criticism, of the majority's refusal to see constitutional injury in "societal" rather than "identified" acts of discrimination, is well placed. But it fails to appreciate the greater import of *Croson* and *Adarand*, which is not to *limit* judicial solicitude but to heighten it—for whites. Obviously, the two elements are linked. Yet they are not the same: the former inhibits the Court from acting aggressively to protect racial minorities against white supremacy; the latter deploys the Court as an active agent in white supremacy's defense, calling into question the permissibility of racial equality as a legislative goal. A series of rulings by the Roberts Court shed light on the possible implications of this trend. In the next section, I focus on two particularly relevant cases— *Parents Involved in Community Schools v. Seattle School District No. 1* (2007) and *Ricci v. DeStefano* (2009)—in order to gauge the extent of this new judicial solicitude.

The New Judicial Solicitude

The 2007 *Parents Involved* case involved a voluntary desegregation plan in Seattle in which race was among the factors considered in determining student school assignments. According to this plan, incoming ninth graders were allowed to choose their preferred high schools, ranking in order of preference as many schools as they desired. In the event that more students selected a particular school than that school was able to accommodate, admissions to the oversubscribed school were determined on the basis of several "tie-breaker" criteria. Primary consideration was given to students with siblings currently enrolled at the preferred school. After that, students were admitted based upon geographical proximity and consideration of the school's racial composition. Oversubscribed schools with racial compositions not within ten percentage points of the district's overall racial balance were thus able to enroll students whose race would "serve to bring the school into balance."[71]

At issue in the case, as framed in Chief Justice Roberts's plurality opinion, was whether a school that had not previously been segregated by law (or had since been declared "unitary") was constitutionally permitted "to classify students by race and rely upon that classification in making school assignments."[72] By a five-to-four vote the Court ruled that it is not. Writing for the Court, the chief justice emphasized that previous cases recognized only two state interests as sufficiently compelling to warrant the use of racial classifications under strict scrutiny analysis: remedying the effects of past intentional discrimination and diversity in higher education.

Because Seattle had never maintained intentionally segregated schools, and because the diversity rational applies only in the context of higher education, Roberts concluded, neither interest applied.

But *Parents Involved* also raises two additional questions, the answers to which hold serious implications for our understanding of what the Roberts Court's commitment to color-blind constitutionalism is likely to entail. First, while previous decisions established that the Fourteenth Amendment's obligation to desegregate schools did not require "racial balance," those cases concerned court-ordered desegregation plans.[73] Because Seattle had voluntarily adopted its plan, the issue at hand was not whether racial balance in public schools was constitutionally *required*, but whether efforts to address racial isolation were constitutionally *permitted*. And second, if the Seattle plan was unconstitutional, it remained to be determined whether that violation reflected an impermissible *goal* or if the plan, by classifying individuals by race, was simply an inappropriate *means* to achieve an otherwise legitimate state interest—and so failed to meet the narrow-tailoring requirement. This second question split Justice Kennedy from the other four members of the plurality, and so remains unsettled. But the stakes here are especially high, with the potential to strike down in the future even "race neutral" policies (those that do not classify individuals by race) intended to achieve the "race conscious" goal of minimizing racial isolation. At stake then is whether, on the color-blind view, efforts to pursue integration and racial equality will turn out to be unconstitutional.[74]

Notably, the portion of Roberts's opinion that Kennedy declined to join is that which, like Justice Thomas's concurring opinion, pushes the logic of color-blind constitutionalism closer to openly denouncing racial equality as a permissible goal and bitterly contests the robust definition of a government interest in "integration" offered by Justice Breyer in dissent.[75] To this end, Roberts insistently characterized the Seattle plan as "directed only to racial balance, pure and simple, an objective this Court has repeatedly condemned as illegitimate."[76] Seizing upon a basic weakness of the Powell-O'Connor compromise, Roberts in effect uses the Court's definitive condemnation of racial balancing to trump its stated (if increasingly tenuous) commitment to competing values such as diversity:

> Racial balance is not transformed from "patently unconstitutional" to a compelling state interest simply by relabeling it "racial diversity." While the school districts use various verbal formulations to describe the interest they seek to promote—racial diversity, avoidance of racial isolation, racial

integration—they offer no definition of the interest that suggests it differs from racial balance.[77]

If diversity and integration turn out to be indistinguishable from racial balance, for five members of the Court, then even currently acknowledged exceptions would become vulnerable to an ever-expanding color-blind rule.

Moreover, in turning the language of equal protection against the goal of integration, both Justice Thomas and Chief Justice Roberts rely heavily upon a rhetorical appropriation of *Brown v. Board of Education*. Insisting (somewhat ambiguously) that "history will be heard," Roberts recalls that "before *Brown*, schoolchildren were told where they could or could not go to school based on the color of their skin"—and cautioning that the school districts challenged in *Parents Involved* would "allow this once again."[78] Justice Thomas is even more explicit in equating today's integrationists to the segregationists of 1954.The moral authority for this equivocation is drawn from Harlan's *Plessy* dissent, *Brown v. Board*, and a string of uncontextualized quotations from leaders of the civil rights movement:

> I am quite comfortable in the company I keep. My view of the Constitution is Justice Harlan's view in *Plessy:* "Our Constitution is color-blind, and neither knows nor tolerates classes among citizens." And my view was the rallying cry for the lawyers who litigated *Brown*. ("That the Constitution is color blind is our dedicated belief"), ("The Fourteenth Amendment precludes a state from imposing distinctions or classifications based upon race and color alone"), ("Marshall had a 'Bible' to which he turned during his most depressed moments. The 'Bible' would be known in the legal community as the first Mr. Justice Harlan's dissent in *Plessy* v. *Ferguson*. I do not know of any opinion which buoyed Marshall more in his pre-*Brown* days . . .").[79]

In addition to the near-religious standing conferred upon Harlan's dissent (Justice Marshall's "Bible"), it is worth noting that Thomas's claim on the past asserts more than a similarity between his own views and those of the civil rights leaders he selectively quotes. For their refusal to invalidate the Seattle and Louisville voluntary integration plans, Thomas also accuses the Court's four dissenters of Jim Crowism.[80] Dismissing the distinction between racial inclusion and racial exclusion as a "faddish social theory," Thomas concludes: "What was wrong in 1954 cannot be right today."[81]

Recalling Judge Parker's construction of *Brown* to require desegregation without integration, Justice Thomas notes that "it is important to define segregation clearly and to distinguish it from racial imbalance." In the context of public schooling, "segregation is the deliberate operation of a school system to 'carry out a governmental policy to separate pupils in schools solely on the basis of race'"—while "racial imbalance" is simply "the failure of a school district's individual schools to match or approximate the demographic makeup of the student population at large. Racial imbalance is not segregation."[82] What segregation means—and all that it means—is the deliberate and intentional separation of students on the basis of race. Because Seattle schools never practiced de jure segregation, there is no constitutional requirement to desegregate public schools that, on Thomas's argument, remain "racially imbalanced" but not "segregated."

Armed with this precise definition of segregation, Thomas affirms a radically limited scope of constitutionally cognizable injury for nonwhite students in de facto segregated schools. Despite the fact of overwhelming racial imbalance, Thomas finds "no danger of resegregation" since "no one contends that Seattle has established or that Louisville has reestablished a dual school system that separates students on the basis of race."[83] And yet, in another sense, the scope of constitutional injury is greatly expanded— for white students and their parents—to the extent that even *voluntary* integration measures become constitutionally prohibited. This conclusion is all the more puzzling, given Thomas's precise definitions. Even if racial imbalance fails to meet this definition of segregation, surely no one would contend that race-conscious policies of voluntary *integration* establish "a dual school system that separates students on the basis of race." And yet, this is precisely what Thomas claims, explicitly, in analogizing Seattle's integrationists to "the segregationists in *Brown*."[84] Just as Judge Parker had hoped decades earlier, the rejection of racial segregation has been stripped of any corresponding obligation to integrate schools. *Parents Involved* extends Parker's antidiscrimination logic a step further: not only is mandatory integration not required, voluntary integration is constitutionally prohibited.[85]

In this regard, *Parents Involved* demonstrates the role of color-blind redemption narratives in structuring current equal protection doctrine— and how they invert the meaning of early desegregation cases like *Brown*, *Green*, and *Swann*. In *Swann*, for example, the Court could not have been clearer that local school boards retained broad discretion to adopt the kinds of policies held unconstitutional in *Parents Involved*:

School authorities are traditionally charged with broad power to formulate and implement educational policy, and might well conclude, for example, that, in order to prepare students to live in a pluralistic society, each school should have a prescribed ratio of Negro to white students reflecting the proportion for the district as a whole. To do this as an educational policy is within the broad discretionary powers of school authorities; absent a finding of a constitutional violation, however, that would not be within the authority of a federal court.[86]

The distinction in *Swann*—between the authority of federal courts and that of local authorities—is meant to underscore that school boards may voluntarily adopt integration measures beyond those imposed by the courts as a constitutional obligation.[87] Thus understood, the elision of this crucial difference in *Parents Involved* illustrates the new judicial solicitude, which appropriates the language of desegregation in order to prohibit integration and protect white rights.

Parents Involved all but finalizes the Court's steady drift toward color-blind conservatism, tempered only by Justice Kennedy's hesitance to embrace an absolutist interpretation of that rule: "as an aspiration, Justice Harlan's axiom must command our assent. In the real world, it is regrettable to say, it cannot be a universal constitutional principle."[88] It does so in part by declaring anticlassification as the controlling principle of the Equal Protection Clause. Less explicit (but perhaps more distressing) is the decision's open embrace of those rhetorical strategies cultivated by color-blind advocates over the past thirty or more years, the implications of which are likely to be quite far-reaching.

Much like the compromise positions of Justices Powell and O'Connor, Justice Kennedy writes separately in *Parents Involved* both to affirm the goal of racial inclusion and to condemn policies that classify individuals by race as a means to achieving that end. Like the color-blind conservatives he joins in part, this perceived contradiction between means and ends supplies his primary objection to policies that classify individuals by race: "to make race matter now so that it might not matter later may entrench the very prejudices we seek to overcome."[89] However, in contrast to the plurality, Kennedy acknowledges that such an "absolute" color-blindness would have the perverse effect of rendering racial equality a constitutionally impermissible goal, which he is evidently unwilling to do: "To the extent the plurality opinion suggests the Constitution mandates that state and local authorities must accept the status quo of racial isolation in schools, it is, in my view, profoundly mistaken."[90]

Instead, Justice Kennedy would allow legislators to consider the likely overall effects of their policies upon racial demographics—and so to be "race conscious" in this limited regard—so long as they refrain from classifying *individuals* by race. Kennedy's compromise is thus hostile to affirmative action programs such as those approved by Justices Powell and O'Connor.[91] However, on Kennedy's view, school authorities remain "free to devise race-conscious measures to address the problem in a general way, and without treating each student in a different fashion solely on the basis of a systematic, individual typing by race."[92] For example, districts could draw attendance zones or select locations for new school construction based upon recognition of neighborhood racial demographics. Targeted recruitment efforts or funding for special programs might be used, as could statistical tracking of enrollments or performance by race. "These mechanisms are race-conscious," he admits, "but do not lead to different treatment" based on an individual's racial classification.[93]

Offered as a reasonable middle ground, the Kennedy compromise is vulnerable to critique from both sides. From the left, his extreme anticlassification views are open to all of the criticisms of traditional color-blind conservatism while at the same time raising questions as to why "openly using race as a criterion" is less constitutionally sound than "concealing it through some clumsy or proxy device."[94] From the right, it remains unclear why Justice Kennedy's preferred "race-neutral means" of pursuing explicitly race-conscious ends do not trip the same constitutional concerns as the affirmative action policies he rejects—all the more so, given Kennedy's unequivocal statements as to the impermissibility of "racial balancing." In other words, if the Constitution forbids policies that classify individuals by race, why does it permit the state to pursue policies intentionally designed to alter the racial composition of a workforce or school?

Kennedy defends this position by locating the injury of racial classification in strictly individualist terms. Where the plurality is inclined to speak broadly against "racial reasoning," "forbidden classifications," or the need for "nonracial" decision-making, Justice Kennedy is drawn again and again to the phrase "individual racial classifications." Because they do not force individuals "to live under a state-mandated racial label," he writes, "race-conscious measures that do not rely on differential treatment based on individual classifications present these problems to a lesser degree."[95] As doctrine, it remains to be seen whether the Kennedy compromise will be any more effective than was the Powell-O'Connor compromise in its attempt to reconcile competing ideals of racial inclusion and what the Court takes for "racial neutrality." However, like Justice O'Connor's, Justice Kennedy's position is better explained by its narrative commitments than its doctrinal logic. Kennedy is compelled to break from the

Parents Involved plurality because he recognizes and refuses to accept the hostility to racial equality it implies. He wants racial equality, he claims, but wants also to achieve that equality without resorting to racial classifications or "racial balancing." His belief in the reconcilability of the two follows not from any constitutional demand, but from his vision of a racially redeemed or imminently redeemable America.

The power of this narrative can be seen in the distance between Justice Kennedy's *Parents Involved* opinion and his opinion, writing for the Court, in *Ricci v. DeStefano*.[96] In *Ricci*, the Court considered a workplace discrimination claim brought under Title VII of the 1964 Civil Rights Act, arising from the actions of the City of New Haven regarding its handling of a conflict over the promotion of municipal firefighters to the rank of officer. Over one hundred firefighters took the promotion examination, which included both written and oral components. Based on the results of this exam, twenty candidates would qualify for promotion to officer. Nineteen of those candidates were white; one was Latino. Set against what Justice Ginsburg described as "a backdrop of entrenched inequality,"[97] and unwilling to believe that no African American firefighters were qualified to be officers, the city was hesitant to certify the results of the exam. After a round of highly contentious public hearings, it decided against certification and, in Justice Kennedy's phrase, "threw out the examinations."[98] In doing so, the Court ruled by a five-to-four vote, it illegally discriminated against the white firefighters.

In part, the racially skewed results raised concerns about the fairness of the exam process itself. But the city's concerns were also informed by a history of employment discrimination litigation. In the 1970s, for example, African Americans and Hispanics had comprised 30 percent of New Haven's population, but only 3.6 percent of the city's firefighters; of the Fire Department's 107 officers, 106 were white.[99] Predictably, these massive disparities prompted litigation, which resulted in a settlement agreement designed to increase minority representation among officers and entry-level firefighters. These litigation-driven efforts to open employment opportunities for members of all races were relatively successful among entry-level firefighters, but less so in regard to supervisory positions. In 2003, roughly 40 percent of the city's residents were African American and more than 20 percent were Hispanic—while just 9 percent of the senior officer ranks were African Americans and 9 percent were Hispanic. In light of this history, New Haven claimed that decertification of the test results was in fact required under Title VII's "disparate impact" provision. In response, some of the firefighters who expected promotions based on their exam scores filed suit for racial discrimination under Title VII's prohibition against "disparate treatment" by race.

In contrast to affirmative action cases, which seek to increase minority representation through use of express racial classifications, the actions under consideration in *Ricci* neither relied upon individual racial classifications nor took their justification from the desire to create a more diverse workforce. Rather, New Haven's decision not to certify the exams reflected a judgment that to do so would be to engage in discriminatory conduct, since the test itself was racially biased. This understanding of "disparate impact" discrimination emerged out of the 1971 Supreme Court case, *Griggs v. Duke Power*, which grounded its analysis in a reading of Title VII's general prohibition against employment practices that detrimentally "limit, segregate, or classify" employees "because of such individual's race."[100] In a unanimous decision, *Griggs* interpreted Title VII to prohibit facially neutral practices with discriminatory effects, unless justified as a business necessity. As the facts of *Griggs* made clear, discriminatory practices need not require express racial classifications to be effective. In this case, the Duke Power Company sought to retain its all-white workforce in certain higher-status positions and was able to do so without classifying any individuals by race. Instead, the company adopted new employment requirements that, while not significantly related to job performance, predictably disqualified minority applicants at a substantially higher rate than whites.[101] Although racially neutral in form, these and similar practices, the Court unanimously held, constituted illegal acts of racial discrimination under Title VII of the Civil Rights Act.

Just five years later, however, the Court dramatically reversed course. In *Washington v. Davis*, a case concerning the use of standardized testing as an employment criterion for police officers in the District of Columbia, the Court radically limited its understanding of discrimination to instances where it could be proven that racially disproportionate results were the intended purpose of the action.[102] This requirement of intentionality—what Alan David Freeman named as the "perpetrator perspective"—has the effect of insulating facially neutral standards that systematically disadvantage minority groups, and so works to reconcile antidiscrimination law with the material conditions of racial subordination.[103]

While *Davis* restricted the scope of constitutional relief for victims of racial discrimination, Congress sought to restore *Griggs* by giving disparate impact analysis a legislative foundation. Congress in 1991 amended the Civil Rights Act to include language, modeled on *Griggs*, making public and private employers liable for the use of facially neutral practices that adversely impacted a protected group.[104] Until *Ricci*, both sections of the act were regarded as equally binding. Recognizing that there is more than one way to discriminate, Congress outlawed both. *Ricci*'s turn against disparate impact is thus especially troubling. By characterizing voluntary compliance efforts as impermissibly "race based," *Ricci* uses Title VII's guarantee of protection from intentional discrimination to undermine its guarantee of protection from facially neutral discriminatory acts. Unlike *Davis*, which shrunk the scope of equal protection by making it more difficult to prove claims of discrimination, *Ricci* expands one area of antidiscrimination law at the expense of another. While racial minorities face heightened evidentiary burdens to establish the connection between observed racial disparities and intentionally discriminatory acts, white plaintiffs are not even required to prove discriminatory intent, which is simply inferred by the characterization of voluntary compliance as a discriminatory purpose.[105]

Ricci's contribution to the new judicial solicitude is thus measured in the distance traveled from *Griggs*: while the Court once viewed state action creating disparate impacts as illegal, it now sees state action to *prevent* disparate impacts as the greater concern and likely constitutional injury.[106] *Ricci* was decided on statutory grounds, and so did not reach the constitutional question of whether New Haven's actions also violated the Equal Protection Clause. Nonetheless, as Justice Scalia's dissent noted with evident glee, the Court's resolution "merely postpones the evil day" when it will have no choice but to confront "the war between disparate impact and equal protection."[107]

The possibility of conflict between disparate impact and equal protection (or between the disparate impact and disparate treatment provisions of the Civil Rights Act) illustrates more than just how far the Court has moved to the right in recent years. Additionally, it reveals how tenuous is the ideal of race-neutrality that underwrites current equal protection law. Departing somewhat from his position in *Parents Involved*, Kennedy's *Ricci* opinion repeatedly denounces "color-consciousness" as such. It does so, however, while assuming the racial neutrality of policies that tend to benefit whites—in this case a racially biased exam—and reading efforts to mitigate inequality as racially conscious. And while he studiously avoids using the phrase "color-blindness," Kennedy nonetheless pushes that view even farther than the anticlassification position articulated in *Parents Involved*. In *Parents Involved*, Kennedy held off the implication that racial isolation could not constitutionally be addressed (an implication Justice Scalia seemed intentionally to court) by distinguishing "individual racial classifications" from a more general concern over "racial consciousness." In *Ricci*, however, he denounces New Haven's actions in unusually stark terms: "Whatever the City's ultimate aim," Kennedy wrote, New Haven "rejected the test results *solely because the higher scoring candidates were white*."[108] Thus, the decision illegally violated Title VII's prohibition against disparate treatment.

Starting from this premise, the only question is whether New Haven's interest in avoiding disparate impact litigation provided a "valid defense" for the violation. Absent a "strong basis in evidence" that the city would lose such a suit, Kennedy concluded, it did not. Significantly, the attention to racial demographics that Kennedy allowed in *Parents Involved*—as a way to avoid the plurality's seeming requirement of indifference to racial isolation—serves in *Ricci* to establish a presumption of discriminatory intent:

> All the evidence demonstrates that the City chose not to certify the examination results *because of the statistical disparity based on race*—i.e., how minority candidates had performed when compared to white candidates ... Without some other justification, this *express, race-based decision-making* violates Title VII's command that employers cannot take adverse employment actions because of an individual's race.[109]

There is no question that New Haven acted "because of statistical disparities based on race." But prior to *Ricci*, and in light of Kennedy's *Parents Involved* concurrence, one might have thought such attention was required by law, or at least constituted a compelling state interest. If "it is permissible to consider the racial makeup of schools and to adopt general policies to encourage a diverse student body,"[110] as Kennedy stated in *Parents Involved*, why is it not also permissible to consider the racial makeup of a fire department, and to adopt general policies to ensure that "all groups have a fair opportunity to apply for promotions"[111] under a process by which they are not disproportionately disadvantaged? To put the question slightly differently: if consideration of "statistical disparities based on race" in itself now constitutes illegal "express race-based decision-making," why isn't the legality of *all* policies intended to reduce racial inequality now put into doubt?

To be sure, Justice Kennedy does not explicitly adopt such a rule—any more than Justice Scalia announces an intention to make racial equality unconstitutional. Nor is my aim to predict the Court's actions in future employment discrimination or affirmative action cases or beyond.

Nonetheless, *Ricci* marks a significant shift in the Court's understanding of equal protection and reveals the distressing extent to which Kennedy's core premise leads him ever closer to a conclusion that, in *Parents Involved*, he took pains to renounce almost as a reductio ad absurdum.[112] Moreover, in *Ricci* he seems to have relinquished the sharp distinction between "individual racial classifications" and more generally race-conscious motives, upon which his efforts to avoid that conclusion had so heavily relied. In its place, Kennedy is left with an increasingly untenable distinction between ends and means, which claims to preserve the city's goal of avoiding litigation (as opposed to pursuing an integrated officer corps) while condemning "the City's conduct in the name of reaching that objective."[113] Yet his opinion is unclear on how to accomplish this task while holding to such a rigid standard of racial-neutrality, since *any* action taken for the express purpose of combating racial exclusion or achieving integration will by definition be "because of race."

Typically, this tension is characterized as a conflict over the limits of color-blindness, and the extent to which race-consciousness is justified by historical inequality. As framed by political scientists Desmond King and Rogers Smith, for example, the Court's color-blind position supplants a position of moderate color-consciousness urged by the Obama administration (and defended in Justice Ginsburg's dissent):

> To Ginsburg and the Obama Justice Department, it was legally appropriate, if not mandatory, for cities to use "race-neutral" tests that focused on merit, but also to look, in unavoidably "race-conscious" fashion, for tests that could identify the merits of long-excluded groups, as well as whites, better than past alternatives. To the majority, such race-conscious selection between putatively race-neutral tests threatened constitutional commitments to judge applicants in color-blind fashion.[114]

This framing is understandable, given its wide acceptance by jurists, legal commentators, and the public alike. Indeed, as pure description of political discourse, King and Smith are right to conclude that "race-conscious" and "color-blind" are the "competing mantras of America's contemporary racial alliances."[115] Even so, the ubiquity of the characterization does not alter the fact that it encourages a false understanding of disparate impact analysis as a departure from racial neutrality, as well as a false understanding of color-blindness as the absence of racial consciousness. This framing characterizes color-blindness as a failed strategy to eliminate racial inequality rather than an apology for racial hierarchy.

As it is typically framed, *Ricci* represents the latest battle in an ongoing war between color-blind and color-conscious understandings of equality. Within these terms, *Ricci*'s critics lament the Court's willingness to strip policymakers of color-conscious policies needed to address persistent racial inequality. As with *Parents Involved*, popular and legal commentary speculate over whether it will be possible to close the racial gap using race-neutral means (class-based affirmative action, 10 percent plans) or calling once more for a return to color-consciousness. However, the full extent of the Court's rightward drift is measured not by its rejection of color-consciousness, but by its mobilization of judicial power to protect white interests. And while it is impossible to know whether future decisions will follow through with this trajectory, recent equal protection doctrine threatens to undermine more than just race-conscious remedial policies such as affirmative action. Even when pursued by race-neutral means, efforts to pursue racial equality may themselves be at risk of being ruled constitutionally impermissible.

CHAPTER 6 | Is Racial Equality Unconstitutional?

THIS BOOK STARTED with a puzzle: how to reconcile the persistence of racial subordination in the United States with a near-universal condemnation of white supremacist ideology in American political discourse and legal thought. In our current political moment, with a new administration more openly associated with white nationalism than many had thought possible in the post-civil rights era, even this nominal commitment to official antiracism seems stretched overly thin. Nonetheless, if it is disturbing to contemplate the real depths of popular bigotry, all the more noteworthy is the extent to which all but the most extreme elements of this political bloc identify in explicitly antiracist terms.[1] Even amidst a new era of racial retrenchment, it would seem, and while putting in place an array of social and economic policies that will ensure the continued subordination of racially defined groups, American self-identity is tightly bound to the *idea* of racial equality.

This puzzle will be familiar to many academics and students of the American racial state. It is not, however, a puzzle that typically structures the thinking of most social scientists or legal scholars—to say nothing of mass-media representations or American popular attitudes and beliefs. With few notable exceptions, American legal thought tends to focus on quite different sets of concerns when taking up questions of race: does the US Constitution permit elected governments to enact race-conscious remedies for past discrimination? To what extent ought privately held racial preferences or beliefs be insulated from government regulation? Is affirmative action legally or morally justifiable? These questions are not unrelated to the puzzle that initially motivated this book. But they also differ in important respects. By approaching legal discourse from the more theoretical and explicitly ideological perspective of racial formation, I have attempted to reframe the question of color-blindness in less voluntaristic terms. In place of an assumed choice between color-blindness, on the one hand, and color-consciousness, on the other, I have sought to understand the peculiar racial consciousness that is enacted through appeals to a color-blind norm.

Following this course of thinking, which identifies color-blindness discourse as an assertion of white racial interest and identity, the book arrives at two related but slightly different puzzles than that with which it started. First, if the Court's current understanding of equal protection logically propels it toward a conclusion that cannot openly be accepted—namely, that the pursuit of racial equality itself, and not just the use of racial classification, is a constitutionally suspect goal—how then will it fend off this untenable conclusion without giving up the underlying ideology that it has helped elevate to the status of racial common sense? How will it respond when confronted by cases that seek ever further to press white institutional advantage into enforceable constitutional rights? Framed this way, constitutional law is encountered both in its limited sense of doctrine or rule and as a contested site of racial formation. Without speculating as to the outcome of future Supreme Court decisions, the question nonetheless tests the ideological capacities of color-blind constitutionalist discourse. But, as we have seen, constitutionalism functions also in the broader sense of constituting the nation or people in whose name its authority is exercised. Framed this way, my critique of redemption narratives raises more troubling questions, and may indeed lead to logical conclusions that few would wish to embrace. What does it mean, precisely, to consider that racial equality could be unconstitutional in this second, performative, sense of the term? What follows from an acknowledgment that America is founded upon and remains constituted by the exercise of racial domination? What substantive commitments are implied by an antiredemptive politics of race? These questions I take up in this concluding chapter, in hopes of signaling a way toward a more productive discourse that could emerge beyond the current boundaries of color-blindness and color-consciousness.

In framing the unconstitutionality of racial equality as a question of antiredemptive racial politics, I break from a rhetorical convention that obligates critical presentations to conclude on a hopeful or upbeat note and to identify practical solutions that follow from the theoretical insights argued in the book. To accept this obligation would reproduce precisely the redemptive imperative I mean to challenge. To be clear, this is not because I regard white supremacy as an existentially fixed condition of the American polity. Rather, mine is a thoroughly political claim, upon a recognition of what I take to be the actual conditions of possibility for

American race politics. The conventional demand for practical solutions is illustrative in this regard, for within its redemptive frame the requirement of solutions that "actually work" effectively freezes in place precisely those conditions that most need to be challenged. In place of the potentially revolutionary question, "What is to be done?" a more candid statement of the question reveals something far less grand: What realistically can be done, without speaking in a way that will alienate those you criticize or seek to convince, and without requiring people to do things that they will not in fact do? What can be done to achieve racial equality that will not disrupt the ordinary citizens' sense of themselves as basically good people or make them feel unfairly accused? What can be done to solve this urgent problem, but without asking me to surrender the advantages that I currently enjoy?

Rejecting this convention, I call instead for a rethinking of American law and politics from the premise that racial equality will require a more fundamental transformation than these constraints would permit, *and may in fact be unachievable* within the current American constitutional order. In this regard, I am evidently less hopeful than theorists of racial justice and democratic perfectionism who would "redefine rather than renounce"[2] redemptive politics, or for whom "practices of citizenship in friendship"[3] or rhetorics of "democratic individualism"[4] or full disclosure of the nation's shameful failure to live up to its core values would allow us to "achieve the greatness within reach."[5] My thinking here is influenced, rather, by critiques of constitutive racism in critical race theory and by the recent Afropessimistic turn in black radical thought. Adopting a line from the book of Jeremiah for the title of his classic text *And We Are Not Saved*, Derrick Bell leaves an opening for his titular claim to be read chiefly as a description of our present moment, and so as a call to make good on the promise of American equality: we are not saved, not now or not yet, without respect to any particular future state of affairs.[6] However, the force of Bell's argument, as a generative text of critical race theory, is in fact tied to his willingness to name and reckon with a more entrenched condition of black subjugation, and to contemplate the possibility of what he later would call "the permanence of racism in America."[7] Read this way, Jeremiah's line points to a failure that is ongoing and anticipates no end: we are not saved, not now and perhaps not ever, and a more forthright recognition of this condition will be necessary to spur more effective confrontations with a system designed to maintain injustice and domination. In this sense, to embrace an antiredemptive politics is to join Stephen Best and Saidiya Hartman in the judgment that (perhaps as early as 1787) "it was not too late to imagine an end to slavery, but it was too late to imagine the repair of its injury."[8] It is to acknowledge with Fred Moten that what "is supposed to be repaired is irreparable. It can't be repaired."[9]

In its most despairing form, the loss of redemptive potential renders domination not as ongoing possibility, but as ontological certainty. "The death of the black body," Frank Wilderson maintains, is "foundational to the life of American civil society," and so disrupts the emancipatory projects of other subordinated groups (workers, women, immigrants, the sexually nonconforming), for whom entry into civil society is a primary goal.[10] Blackness is inseparable from slavery, on this view, and so is excluded by definition from humanist ambitions. Antiblackness is constitutive of humanism's most basic categories, Wilderson claims, and recognition of this fact "throws the notion of humanity itself into crisis,"[11] deprives blackness of all "recourse to political or therapeutic resources,"[12] and replaces the quaint desire to build a better world with the more fundamental goal of "trying to destroy the world."[13]

As ontology, this conception of antiblackness is as far removed from the specific material conditions of racial domination as are the redemptive narratives of American exceptionalism that the theory would seek to supplant.[14] In place of unfounded hope, it offers dematerialized despair.[15] In place of the false universalism of liberals or the new Left, it supplies a version of black exceptionalism so uncompromising as to undermine seemingly all forms of coalitional politics, and perhaps all forms of politics entirely. It is unclear how such a position could be consistent with efforts to reorient antiracist discourse around the historical specificity and material conditions of racial formation. Indeed, it is not obvious why such a totalizing view should inspire anything beyond nihilism and unproductive despair.

Nonetheless, shorn of these ontological commitments, an Afropessimistic sensibility might inform both the historical analysis of antiblackness as a persistent premise of American social order and a direction of political engagement to exceed the boundaries of redemptive fantasy. Seen this way, the antiredemptive turn might generate a more productive form of despair, as holding out less hope for reparation clears space to consider new and conceivably more ambitious strategies or tactics.[16] Such a perspective may travel under the name of abolition.[17] It might authorize a turn toward global, anticolonial, or transnational movements against racial capitalism. Or, it could focus attention inward, toward intraracial solidarity, black nationalism, or multiracial alliances of intersectionally subordinated groups. Or, it might draw our focus downward to infrapolitical, everyday acts of survival and group care. As Saidiya Hartman has observed of such practices, "Redress does not or cannot restore or remedy loss."[18] And yet recognition of this state "implies neither resignation nor fatalism but a recognition of the enormity of the breach instituted by slavery and the magnitude of domination."[19] My interest here is, again, not to dictate terms or identify "solutions," but simply to illustrate a range of antiredemptive political possibility consistent with my suggestion that it is racial equality, not inequality, that violates constitutional norms.

In rejecting the project of national redemption, my approach also reveals a fundamental point of convergence between liberal and conservative constitutional visions that otherwise would appear to inhabit opposite ends of a spectrum. Whereas the conservative aim is to preserve or restore American values, championed as presumptively *innocent*, the liberal aspiration is to achieve an American tradition viewed as presumptively *perfectible*. Distinct versions of a common redemptive fantasy, both views require an embrace of America's fundamentally egalitarian nature as a condition of their legitimacy. As Jodi Melamed has shown, the nationalist imperative of official antiracisms functions to insulate from critique the role of US-led racial capitalism in perpetuating structural inequalities.[20] In either form, the promise of national redemption yields either an overly restrictive conception of racial equality or an overly optimistic understanding of what America is and might become. In contrast, my goal of moving beyond color-blindness and color-consciousness embraces the substantive goal of racial democracy without being tethered to the false promise of transcending race.

Throughout this book, I have tried both to identify color-blind constitutionalism as an element of racial formation and to steer criticism of color-blindness away from familiar arguments that would justify color-conscious alternatives. Framed in overly voluntaristic terms, the call for racial consciousness leaves in place two basic assumptions, both of which I reject. The first is that color-blindness describes an absence of racial awareness. Advocating for color-consciousness as a superior moral or legal alternative to color-blindness fails to contest this misleading assumption, and may in fact reinforce that view. The second is that we must choose between the two views, as if it were possible simply to *decide* whether to incorporate race into our decision-making. This voluntaristic assumption is deeply misleading, and not only because nonconsideration of race tends to reproduce institutional bias and structural inequality. It is also misleading in its failure to acknowledge that color-blind practices require a heightened awareness of race, institutionalized in law as a formal prohibition.

As we have seen, the peculiar form of race-consciousness that is produced through demands for nonconsideration of race drives social movements, structures individual identities, and supplies the basic logic of contemporary conservative legal strategy. Although framed in a language of equal rights and race-neutrality, the political mobilization against racial classification nonetheless creates and requires political organizations defined by their racial identities and committed to the advancement of white group rights.

Recognizing the paradoxical nature of such racially motivated attacks on race has the potential to disrupt the larger debate over whether race ought to be considered in matters of law and public policy. The question itself is deeply misleading in its suggestion that nonconsideration of race is a practical possibility, and politically dangerous in its assertion of white identity as racial absence. By demonstrating how color-blind rules produce race-conscious attitudes and behaviors, I hope to dislodge familiar debates from this stalemate. Rather than seeking to justify race-conscious remedies, I have tried to open the category of color-blindness to an awareness of its own racial commitments, born not from an absence of race but from its motivated rejection. Racial consciousness is an inevitable product of any society structured on lines of racial hierarchy and domination. But in demanding its recognition, we should take care not to reinforce the mistaken assumption that color-blind constitutionalism is any less structured by the logic of race, any closer to an ideal of racial neutrality, or in any way escapes its own mobilization of white intraracial solidarity.

In itself, racial consciousness is no more a problem than it is a choice. But in framing demands for the recognition of race as a justified departure from color-blindness, we risk losing sight of a more fundamental critique of its race-conscious logic. In equal protection law, the cost of failing to challenge color-blindness's underlying racial logic is to allow racial classification to signify as the introduction of race into an otherwise presumptively nonracial context. Understood as "playing the race card," this is what makes special rights "special"—and why efforts to achieve racial equality are experienced by many white Americans as a form of benevolence or gift or injury. In popular and legal discourse alike, this assumption treats color-blind constitutionalism as a narrowing of the scope for redress of racial injury: color-blindness discourse limits both what counts as discrimination and what tools may legitimately be used to contest it. And yet, by recognizing color-blind constitutionalism's race-conscious logic, these limits may be seen instead as powerful assertions of racial entitlement and *expansions* of the boundaries of what counts as discrimination against an aggrieved racial group, defined by its whiteness.

In color-blind constitutionalism we should learn to see an expansion of racial-consciousness rather than its suppression. But in doing so, we are forced to confront the depths of a problem that cannot be solved by living up to our national creed. Not just a holdover from America's redeemed or redeemable past, racial hierarchy and domination persist, institutionalized in the form of enforceable white rights. To regard racial equality as a constitutional *problem*—rather than its premise—is thus to turn away from James Baldwin's famous plea in "The Fire Next Time," "to end the racial nightmare, and achieve our country, and change the history of the world."[21] This is necessary not because changing the history of the world is impossible, but because doing so will require not the achievement of American values, but a decisive break from them, and a refounding upon principles of racial democracy.

NOTES

Chapter 1

1. This literature emerges on the popular scene in the late 1970s and assumes cultural dominance sometime in the 1980s. For key texts from the movement to establish a legal-cultural basis for color-blind constitutionalism, refer to Glazer, *Affirmative Discrimination*; Graglia, *Disaster by Decree*; Reynolds, "Affirmative Action"; Kull, *Color-Blind Constitution*; Eastland, "Affirmative Action"; Sleeper, *Liberal Racism*; Sternstrom and Sternstrom, *America*; Cohen, "Racial Preference." For foundational texts reacting against the color-blind view, and in defenses of "color-conscious" law and public policy, refer to Appiah and Gutmann, *Color-Conscious*; Sterba, "Defending Affirmative Action"; Peller, "Race Consciousness"; Gotanda, "Critique"; Lipsitz, *Possessive Investment*; Brown et al., *Whitewashing Race*; Bonilla-Silva, *Racism without Racists*; Haney-López, "Reactionary Color-Blindness"; Anderson, *Imperative of Integration*.

2. *Plessy v. Ferguson*, 163 U.S. 537 at 559 (1896) (Harlan, dissenting).

3. Kull, *Color-Blind Constitution*, 1.

4. *Parents Involved in Community Schools v. Seattle School District No. 1*, 127 S. Ct. 2738 at 2768 (2007).

5. In the aftermath of the Charleston massacre, for example, the *Wall Street Journal* editorial page concluded, "Today the system and philosophy of institutionalized racism identified by Dr. King no longer exists." Valerie Bauerlein, "The Charleston Shooting: An Echo of 52 Years Ago, but Also a Crucial Difference," *Wall Street Journal*, June 18, 2015.

6. Refer to Gotanda, "Critique"; Guinier and Torres, "A Critique"; Harris, "Whiteness as Property"; Lipsitz, *Possessive Investment*; Omi and Winant, *Racial Formation*; Peller, "Race Consciousness." More generally, see Essed and Goldberg, *Race Critical Theories*.

7. *Regents of the University of California v. Bakke*, 438 U.S. 265 at 407 (1978).

8. *Freeman v. Pitts*, 503 U.S. 467 at 494 (1992).

9. *Grutter v. Bollinger*, 539 U.S. 306 at 328 (2003).

10. *Shaw v. Reno*, 509 U.S. 630 (1993).

11. *Korematsu v. United States*, 323 U.S. 214 (1994); *Johnson v. California*, 543 U.S. 499 (2005).

12. Siegel, "Equality Talk," 1475.

13. *Fisher v. University of Texas at Austin*, 133 S. Ct. 2411 (2013); *Shelby County v. Holder*, 133 S. Ct. 2612 (2013).

14. *Grutter*, at 353 (Thomas, dissenting).

15. Brest, "In Defense," 1.

16. Brest, "In Defense," 15.

17. Turner, *Awakening to Race.*

18. Appiah and Gutmann, *Color-Conscious*, 178.

19. Dworkin, *Matter of Principle*, 294.

20. Aleinikoff, "Race-Consciousness"; Bell, *Racial Justice*; Colker, "Anti-Subordination"; Freeman, "Legitimizing Racial Discrimination"; Gotanda, "Critique"; Lawrence, "Crossburning"; Matsuda, "Public Response"; Sunstein, "Anticaste Principle."

21. Fiss, "Groups," 157.

22. Tussman and tenBroek, "Equal Protection"; Fiss, "Groups," 110–117. This view was famously articulated by Tussman and tenBroek.

23. *Hirabayashi v. United States*, 320 U.S. 81(1943). See Tussman and tenBroek, "Equal Protection," 353–355.

24. Fiss, "Groups," 119. See also Post, *Prejudicial Appearances*, 16–18.

25. Armour, "Race Ipsa Loquitur," 781.

26. *Grutter*, at 343 (O'Connor, dissenting). From *Grutter*: "We expect that 25 years from now, the use of racial preferences will no longer be necessary to further the interests approved today."

27. Fiss, "Groups," 129, 161. On the perilous rhetoric of symmetry in reverse-discrimination claims, see Haney-López, "Nation of Minorities."

28. *Shelley v. Kraemer*, 331 U.S. 803 at 1 (1947).

29. *Moose Lodge No. 107 v. Irvis*, 407 U.S. 163 (1972).

30. Taken to its logic conclusion, this observation anticipates potential conflicts between disparate impact analysis and antidiscrimination's prohibition against "disparate treatment" of racial groups. I discuss this conflict more thoroughly in chapter 5.

31. Abrams, "Groups." Notably, antisubordination scholars have been more eager to identify CRT as progeny than they have been interested in being so-claimed. If "Groups" serves as the founding text of antisubordination theory, CRT emerges from the writings of Derrick Bell and the student-led protests at Harvard Law School that followed Bell's departure in 1980. For a recount of this origin story, see Crenshaw et al., *Critical Race Theory*, xx–xxiii. See also Matsuda et al., *Words That Wound*, 4–5.

32. Freeman, "Legitimizing Racial Discrimination"; Spann, *Race against the Court.* On the dilemmas of reform, see Crenshaw, "Race, Reform and Retrenchment."

33. Kennedy, "Racial Critiques"; Farber and Sherry, "Telling Stories"; Ford, *Racial Culture.*

34. Delgado and Stefancic, *Critical Race Theory*, 9.

35. Matsuda, *Words That Wound*, 18–20.

36. Delgado and Stefancic, *Critical Race Theory*, 7. See also, Haney-López, "Social Construction of Race"; Haney-López, *White by Law*; Chang, "Critiquing Race."

37. Crenshaw et al., *Critical Race Theory*, xxvi.

38. On the formation of subaltern counterpublics, see Fraser, "Rethinking the Public Sphere." For further characterization of black political thought as a black counterpublic, see Dawson, *Black Visions*, 23–28.

39. For a review of this literature, see Ford, *Racial Culture*, 5–13. For a more philosophically robust demonstration of the nonessentialist foundations of black solidarity, refer to Shelby, *We Who Are Dark*.

40. Fiss, "Groups," 121.

41. For more on framing of this choice as a result of struggles to implement *Brown v. Board of Education*, refer to Siegel, "Equality Talk."

42. Holt, *Problem of Race*, 19.

43. On the concept of "racial practices," refer to Perry, *More Beautiful*.

44. Collins, *Black Sexual Politics*, 55. Similarly, for the theory of "preserving through transformation," refer to Siegel, "Equal Protection." For more on racial rearticulation, see Omi and Winant, *Racial Formation*, 99–101.

45. Lipsitz, *Possessive Investment*, 4.

46. Davis, *Problem of Slavery*; Morgan, *American Slavery*.

47. Bercovitch, *American Jeremiad*; Howard-Pitney, *Afro-American Jeremiad*; Shulman, *American Prophecy*. I discuss this literature in some detail in chapter 2.

48. Myrdal, *American Dilemma*.

49. Hochschild, *New American Dilemma*, 34 (emphasis supplied).

50. Coates, *The World and Me*, 103. As Coates has observed, "In America, it is traditional to destroy the black body—*it is heritage.*"

51. Hochschild, *New American Dilemma*, 8.

52. Mills, *Racial Contract*, 122.

53. Olson, *Abolition*, xv.

54. The remarkable rise to prominence of so-called alt-right white nationalism is a notable exception to this consensus. The political fate of these open appeals to the protection or preservation of "white culture" remains less than clear.

55. Balibar, *Ambiguous Identities*, 23; Bonilla-Silva, *Racism without Racists*. Balibar uses the phrase "racism without race" to analyze the shift from biological racism to racialized culture as a mode of social domination. The phrase "racism without racists" encapsulates Bonilla-Silva's account of white supremacy in a supposedly postracial age and supplies the title for his book.

56. Omi and Winant, *Racial Formation*, 16–23. Omi and Winant see this aspect of Myrdal's "ethnicity theory" as linked to its asserted analogy between racial groups and ethnic immigrants, which in turn lays the groundwork for the linked valorization of "model minorities" and demonization of racial cultural pathology. Also refer to Kim, "Racial Triangulation."

57. The concept of "racial innocence" traces to a line in Baldwin's open letter to his nephew that initiates "The Fire Next Time." Baldwin accuses (and will not forgive) his countrymen of a double crime: "They have destroyed and are destroying hundreds of thousands of lives and do not know it and do not want to know it." Understanding these acts of domination to be inseparable from the refusal of their knowledge, Baldwin famously declared, "It is *the innocence which constitutes the crime*" (334). On the concept of racial innocence, refer to Balfour, *Evidence of Things*; Shulman, *American Prophecy*; Turner, *Awakening to Race*; HoSang, *Racial Propositions*; Taylor, "Untimely Subjects."

58. Montagu, *Fallacy of Race*, 41.

59. Fredrickson, *Black Image*.

60. Morrison, *Playing in the Dark*, 46.

61. Melamed, *Represent and Destroy*, 219.

62. Dudziak, *Cold War Civil Rights*; Borstelmann, *Cold War.*

63. Dawson, *Blacks.*

64. Bell, "Two Masters," 470; Bell, "*Brown v. Board of Education*," 518; Bell, *Silent Covenants.*

65. Peller, "Race Consciousness," 760; Singh, *Black Is a Country.*

66. Bonilla-Silva, *Racism without Racists*, 181.

67. Haney-López, *Dog Whistle Politics.*

68. Steele and Aronson, "Stereotype Threat." See generally the work of Harvard University's Project Implicit. The literature on postintent racism is helpfully reviewed in chapter 1 of Perry, *More Beautiful.*

69. Lawrence, "Equal Protection"; Krieger, "Content of Our Categories"; Kang, "Trojan Horses"; Wang, *Discrimination by Default.*

70. Following Marx, critical legal studies scholarship tended to view the legitimation of class domination as law's central purpose in bourgeoisie societies (Unger, *Modern Society*; Fienman and Gabel, "Contract Law"). This insight is retained even in antireductionist adaptations that would resist Marx's purported economic determinism. Kennedy, *Legal Education*; McCann, "Equal Protection."

71. Omi and Winant, *Racial Formation*, 66–69. On Gramsci's relevance for the study of race, refer to Hall, "Gramsci's Relevance"; Apostolidis, *Breaks in the Chain.*

72. Omi and Winant, *Racial Formation*, 67.

73. Daria Roithmayr, for example, emphasizes the "self-reinforcing structural processes" by which racial inequality is "locked-in." *Reproducing Racism*, 9.

74. Washington, *American Negro.*

75. Du Bois, *Souls of Black Folk*, 3. See Holt, *Problem of Race*, 1. Holt herein reads Du Bois's line as both "prophecy" and "prediction."

76. Chesnutt, "Future American," 846–847.

77. Chesnutt, "Race Prejudice." Chesnutt herein makes a similar claim.

78. Chesnutt, "Future American," 850.

79. McWilliams, *Charles Chesnutt*, 51.

80. Chesnutt, "Future American," 862.

81. Chesnutt, "Race Prejudice."

82. In a fanciful thought experiment, Chesnutt envisions a scenario in which "the laws of the whole country were as favorable to this amalgamation as the laws of most Southern States are at present against it." This would amount to a criminalization of intraracial marriage, making it "a misdemeanor for two white or two colored persons to marry." Under such conditions, Chesnutt concludes, it would take just "three generations" before "there would be no perceptible trace of the blacks left." However sincerely Chesnutt might have anticipated America's mixed-race future, it is difficult not to read as satire this proposed prohibition of same-race marriage and procreation. Chesnutt, "Future American," 849–850.

83. *Adarand Constructors, Inc. v. Peña*, 515 U.S. 200 at 239 (1995) (Scalia, concurring). *Adarand* holds unconstitutional the use of race-based affirmative action in distribution of government employment contracts.

84. Glossing Raymond Williams, Daniel HoSang aptly observes, "The very power of hegemonic formations derives from their capacity to shape the terms on which they are opposed" (*Racial Propositions*, 22).

85. According to a popular slogan from the 2008 presidential campaign: "Rosa sat so that Martin could walk. Martin walked so that Barack could run. Barack ran so we could fly."

86. Carbado and Harris, "New Racial Preferences," 1147.

87. Carbado and Harris, "New Racial Preferences," 1148.

88. Carbado and Harris, "New Racial Preferences," 1200–1201.

89. Anderson, *Imperative of Integration*, 139.

90. Kennedy, *For Discrimination*, 18–19.

91. Delgado and Stefancic, *Critical Race Theory*, 7.

92. Bell, *Faces*.

Chapter 2

1. Motley, "In Memoriam," ix–xi.

2. While still living, Marshall was at times openly resistant to such acts of memorialization. On his reluctance to celebrate the Constitution on the occasion of its bicentennial, see Lebron, *Color of Our Shame*, 73–78.

3. *Parents Involved in Community Schools v. Seattle School District No. 1*, 127 S. Ct. 2783 (2007).

4. *Pasadena City Board of Education v. Spangler*, 427 U.S. 424 at 427 (1976) (Marshall dissenting); *Missouri v. Jenkins*, 515 U.S. 70 (1995) (Thomas concurring); *City of Richmond v. J.A. Croson, Co.*, 488 U.S. 469 (Marshall dissenting); *Adarand Constructors, Inc. v. Peña*, 515 U.S. 200 (Thomas concurring). On school desegregation; compare Marshall's opinion in *Pasadena* ("racial identifiability of a district's schools" constitutes "a condition that perpetuates the message of racial inferiority" condemned in *Brown*) to Thomas's in *Missouri* ("*Brown I* did not say that racially isolated schools were inherently inferior; the harm that it identified was tied purely to de jure segregation, not de facto segregation"). On affirmative action; compare Marshall's opinion in *Croson* (the Court's rejection of affirmative action "sounds a full-scale retreat from the Court's longstanding solicitude to race-conscious remedial efforts") to Thomas's in *Adarand* ("under our Constitution, the government may not make distinctions on the basis of race. . . . In my mind, government-sponsored racial discrimination based on benign prejudice is just as noxious as discrimination inspired by malicious prejudice").

5. Frymer, *Uneasy Alliances*; Kim, *Racial Logic*; Lowndes, *New Deal*.

6. Omi and Winant, *Racial Formation*, 117.

7. West, *Prophesy Deliverance*. The concepts of prophecy and redemption are notably associated with West and his theory of "prophetic Afro-American Christian thought." On the history of prophetic criticism, refer also to West, "Cultural Politics"; for recent thoughts on the black prophetic tradition, refer to West, *Prophetic Fire*.

8. Vogler and Markell, "Violence, Redemption," 1–10.

9. On the relationship between slavery and democracy in the American founding, refer to Morgan, *American Freedom*; Davis, *Problem of Slavery*.

10. Lincoln, "Second Inaugural Address," 686.

11. Lincoln was slow to arrive at this framing of the war as both a response to slavery and a source of national regeneration. On Frederick Douglass's tireless efforts to drive him to this position, see Blight, *Race and Reunion*, 15–18.

12. On the virtues of a "fallen" Constitution, see Balkin, *Constitutional Redemption*, 119–123.

13. Hughes, "America Again," 191.

14. Miller, *New England Mind*; Bercovitch, *American Jeremiad*; Howard-Pitney, *Afro-American Jeremiad*; Shulman, *American Prophecy*.

15. Shulman, *American Prophecy*, 22–23, 262.

16. Shulman, *American Prophecy*, 28.

17. Malcolm X, "Ballot," 26.

18. Singh, *Black Is a Country*, 4, 14.

19. Singh, *Black Is a Country*, 5.

20. Shulman, *American Prophecy*, 250.

21. Shulman, *American Prophecy*, xiii.

22. Shulman, *American Prophecy*, xiii.

23. Shulman, *American Prophecy*, 5.

24. Chris Lebron theorizes this condition as one of bad character, and its revelation as affective response of shame. *Color of Our Shame*.

25. Graber, *Constitutional Evil*.

26. Smith, *Civic Ideals*.

27. Morgan, *American Slavery*. On the similarly constitutive role of settler colonialism, refer to Rana, *Two Faces*.

28. Balkin, *Constitutional Redemption*.

29. Balkin, *Constitutional Redemption*, 228–230. Such a theory is more fully developed in his subsequent work, *Living Originalism*.

30. Ackerman, *We the People*.

31. Kramer, *The People Themselves*.

32. Frank, *Constituent Moments*, 249.

33. White, "Law as Rhetoric," 684.

34. White, "Law as Rhetoric," 691–692.

35. Cover, "*Nomos* and Narrative," 96–99.

36. On narrative and cultural approaches to the study of law, see especially Amsterdam and Bruner, *Minding the Law*; Brooks, "Narrative Transactions"; Kahn, *Cultural Study of Law*; Kairys, *Politics of Law*; Sarat and Simon, *Cultural Analysis*; West, *Narrative, Authority and Law*; White, *Justice as Translation*; White, *Legal Imagination*; Williams, *Alchemy*.

37. On the pervasiveness of this narrative in structuring civil rights memory, see Hall, "Long Civil Rights Movement," 91.

38. Kull, *Color-Blind Constitution*, 1–2.

39. Kull, *Color-Blind Constitution*, 1.

40. Bork, *Slouching towards Gomorrah*, 249.

41. Bork, *Slouching towards Gomorrah*, 247.

42. Glazer, *Affirmative Discrimination*, 3.

43. Glazer, *Affirmative Discrimination*, 31 (emphasis supplied).

44. Glazer, "Racial Quotas," 7.

45. Gotanda, "Critique." The "pastness" in this formulation nicely illustrates Gotanda's distinction between formal-race and historical-race.

46. Alexander and Alexander, "The New Racism," 9.

47. Graglia, *Disaster by Decree*, 13–14.

48. Abram, "Affirmative Action," 99 (emphasis supplied).

49. Sowell, *Civil Rights*, 37 (emphasis supplied).

50. See Freeman, "Legitimizing Racial Discrimination," 62; Ross, "Innocence and Affirmative Action," 43.

51. On the appropriation of civil rights rhetoric by anti-affirmative action groups, see Berry, "Vindicating Martin Luther King, Jr.," 137–144; Cose, *Color-Blind*, 101–106.

52. Reynolds, "Affirmative Action," 39–41.

53. *Croson*, at 529 (Marshall, dissenting). Justice Marshall writes: "Today's decision marks a deliberate and giant step backward in this Court's affirmative-action jurisprudence. Cynical of one municipality's attempt to redress the effects of past racial discrimination in a particular industry, the majority launches a grapeshot attack on race-conscious remedies in general."

54. Omi and Winant, *Racial Formation*.

55. A comprehensive review of this concept is provided by Gooding-Williams and Mills in "Post-racial Epoch."

56. Taylor, "Taking Post-racialism Seriously," 24. Taylor herein characterizes this version of the argument as "idiot post-racialism"—noting that its "many adherents" are "easier to find than the non-idiot variety."

57. Balfour, "Unthinking Racial Realism." Balfour positions reparations as a possible response to this aspect of postracial discourse, supplying a "counter-language that ties the analysis of the present to the historical conditions out of which it was produced," 46.

58. Haney-López, *Dog Whistle Politics*, 202.

59. Delgado, "Kill the Messengers," 173–174.

60. Lakoff, *Don't Think of an Elephant*.

61. Delgado, "Kill the Messengers," 171.

62. Delgado and Stefancic, *Critical Race Theory*; Matsuda, "Public Response," 18–20. Privileging perspectives "from the bottom," what Delgado and Stefancic call the "voice of color thesis," is a key element of critical race scholarship.

63. Delgado, "Kill the Messengers," 175–176.

64. Haney-López, *Dog Whistle Politics*, 220.

65. Haney-López, *Dog Whistle Politics*, 219–220.

66. Haney-López, *Dog Whistle Politics*, 220.

67. Delgado, "Kill the Messengers," 174.

68. In many ways, this insight parallels Michel Foucault's discussion of "the repressive hypothesis" in relationship to Victorian sexual regulations, in *History of Sexuality*. Imani Perry makes a similar connection in her discussion of racial surveillance in *More Beautiful*.

69. *Croson; Adarand*, at 227.

70. *Regents of the University of California v. Bakke*, 438 U.S. 265 (1978); *Grutter v. Bollinger* 539 U.S. 306 (2003); *Fisher v. Texas*, 570 U.S. ____ at 6 (2013); *Fisher v. Texas* 579 U.S. ____ at 7 (2016).

71. *Bakke*, at 307. In *Bakke*, Justice Powell dismisses "societal discrimination" as "an amorphous concept of injury that may be ageless in its reach into the past."

72. Ross, "Innocence and Affirmative Action," 552.

73. *Bakke*, at 299.

74. *Bakke*, at 307.

75. *Fullilove v. Klutznick*, 448 U.S. 488 at 530 (1980) (Stewart dissenting).

76. *Croson*, at 478–479.

77. *Croson*, at 505.

78. Cho, "Redeeming Whiteness," 73, 122.

79. Cho, "Redeeming Whiteness," 124.

80. *Fullilove*, at 523 (emphasis supplied) (Stewart, dissenting).

81. *Adarand*, at 240 (Thomas, concurring).

82. *Adarand*, at 245 (Stevens, dissenting).

83. *Shelby County v. Holder*, 570 U.S. ___ (2013).

84. Fannie Lou Hamer, Rosa Parks, and Coretta Scott King Voting Rights Act Reauthorization and Amendments Act of 2006, 120 Stat. 577 (2006). The act was also reauthorized in 1970, 1975, and 1982, without any change to the coverage formula.

85. *Shelby County*, at 13.

86. The Senate vote for reapproval was 98–0.

87. *Shelby County*, at 23 (Ginsburg dissenting).

88. *Shelby County*, at 30 (Ginsburg dissenting).

89. *Shelby County*, at 21 (emphasis supplied).

90. *Shelby County*, at 20.

91. *Shelby County*, at 20.

92. *Shelby County*, at 12-96, citing Respondent's original oral argument.

93. *Shelby County*, at 6, citing *Northwest Austin Municipal Utility District No. 1 v. Holder*, 557 U.S. 193 at 202 (2009).

94. Shelby *County*, at 12-96, citing Petitioner's original oral argument.

95. *Shelby County*, at 21 (emphasis supplied).

96. *Shelby County*, at 15.

97. *Shelby County*, at 33 (Ginsburg dissenting).

98. *Shelby County*, at 12-96, citing Respondent's original oral argument.

99. Matsuda, "Looking to the Bottom," 323; Crenshaw, "Race, Reform and Retrenchment," 101; Peller, "Race Consciousness," 758.

100. Peller, "Race Consciousness," 759–760, 820–844.

101. Peller, "Race Consciousness," 760.

102. Austin, "Performative-Constative," 3–13.

103. Michelman, "Racialism and Reason," 730.

104. Brown et al., *Whitewashing Race*, 197.

105. *Grutter*, at 353 (Thomas, dissenting).

106. *Bakke*, at 407 (Blackmun concurring in part, dissenting in part).

107. Van Alstyne, "Rites of Passage," 809–810.

108. *Parents Involved*, at 2768.

109. Van Alstyne, "Rites of Passage," 797. Elsewhere in his article, Van Alstyne describes affirmative action as "*Plessy v. Ferguson* all over again, in new and modish dress." The narrative conventions of color-blind constitutionalism are discussed in further detail in chapter 3.

110. Sabbagh, "Judicial Uses of Subterfuge," 411.

111. Sabbagh, "Judicial Uses of Subterfuge," 417–418.

112. Williams, *Seeing a Color-Blind Future*, 27.

113. Williams, *Seeing a Color-Blind Future*, 27–28.

114. Eastland, *Ending Affirmative Action*, 8 (emphasis supplied).

115. Ely, *Democracy and Distrust*.

116. *United States v. Carolene Products, Co.*, 304 U.S. 144 (1938).

117. Ely, *Democracy and Distrust*, 727. For this reason, Ely rejects the application of strict scrutiny in "reverse discrimination" cases, leaving aggrieved parties to engage the ordinary political processes; " 'special scrutiny' is not appropriate when White people have decided to favor Black people at the expense of White people. . . . It is not 'suspect' in a constitutional sense for a majority, any majority, to discriminate against itself."

118. *Korematsu v. United States*, 323 U.S. 214 at 216 (1944).

119. *Plessy v. Ferguson*, 163 U.S. 537 at 551 (1896). From *Plessy*: "We consider the underlying fallacy of the plaintiff 's argument to consist in the assumption that the enforced separation of the two races stamps the colored race with a badge of inferiority. If this be so, it is not by reason of anything found in the act, but solely because the colored race chooses to put that construction upon it."

120. *Korematsu*, at 223.

121. Irons, *Justice at War.*

122. *Korematsu*, at 233 (Murphy, dissenting). From *Korematsu:* "Such exclusion goes over 'the very brink of constitutional power' and falls into the ugly abyss of racism."

123. *Loving v. Virginia*, 388 U.S. 1 at 15 (1967).

124. Pascoe, *What Comes Naturally*, 287–306; Moran, *Interracial Intimacy*, 97–100. Pascoe herein explains Loving's emergence as a symbol of color-blind conservatism; Moran discusses *Loving*'s ambivalent rejection of race as biologically irrelevant.

125. *Loving*, at 7.

126. *Loving*, at 11.

127. *Bakke*, at 265.

128. *Bakke*, at 289–290.

129. Bybee, "Political Significance," 263–290; *Carolene Products*. Justice Powell's opinion contradicts *Carolene Products*.

130. *Grutter*, at 510.

Chapter 3

1. *Plessy v. Ferguson*, 163 U.S. 537 (1896). A number of books have been devoted to the history of the *Plessy* case. For a definitive legal history of the case, refer to Lofgren, *The Plessy Case*. For other excellent volumes having collect relevant historical documents, refer to Olsen, *Thin Disguise*; Thomas, *Plessy v. Ferguson*. For popular narrative histories of the case, refer to Medley, *We as Freemen*; Fireside, *Separate and Unequal*.

2. Primus, "Canon, Anti-Canon," 243, 248.

3. Primus, "Canon, Anti-Canon," 251.

4. Primus, "Canon, Anti-Canon," 284.

5. Krishnakumar, "Evolution," 800.

6. Krishnakumar, "Evolution," 800–801.

7. *Plessy*, at 538.

8. Hartman's reading of *Plessy* in *Scenes of Subjection*, 193–206, stands as a notable exception. I follow her lead in emphasizing *Plessy*'s continuity with *Dred Scott* rather

than its break, as well as Homer Plessy's ambiguous racialization and the legal process of racial determination.

9. Woodward, *Strange Career.*

10. Litwack, *Been in the Storm*, 261; Woodward, *Strange Career*, 17.

11. Welke, "Road to *Plessy.*"

12. Lofgren, *The Plessy Case*, 29. For a detailed account of transportation segregation prior to the *Plessy* decision, see *The Plessy Case*, 9–27.

13. Kull, *Color-Blind Constitution*, 113.

14. Lofgren, *The Plessy Case*, 3–4.

15. Kluger, *Simple Justice*, 74.

16. McClosky, *American Supreme Court*, 141; Ely, *Democracy and Distrust*, 163; Higginbotham, *Matter of Color*, 117.

17. *Dred Scott v. Sandford*, 60 U.S. 393 at 407 (1856).

18. *Plessy*, at 544.

19. The phrase "symmetrical equality" is not Brown's, but characterizes the logic of his argument. For a comparison of the argument's use in antimiscegenation cases and civil rights cases, see Bank, "Anti-miscegenation Laws," 303.

20. Kull, *Color-Blind Constitution*, 113–130; Lofgren, *The Plessy Case*, 61–93; Primus, "Canon, Anti-Canon," 288–293.

21. *Strauder v. West Virginia*, 100 U.S. 303 (1880). A list of those civil rights guaranteed by the Fourteenth Amendment is provided in *Strauder*: "The equality of the protection secured extends only to civil rights as distinguished from those which are political. . . . It opens the courts of the county to everyone, on the same terms, for the security of his person and property, the prevention and redress of wrongs, and the enforcement of contracts; it assures to everyone the same rules of evidence and modes of procedure . . . and in the administration of criminal justice it permits no different or greater punishments to be imposed upon one than such as is prescribed to all for like offences." For discussion of nineteenth-century understandings of social, civil, and political rights, refer also to Tushnet, "Politics of Equality."

22. *Strauder*, at 303. "Social rights . . . do not rest upon any positive law, though they are more potential in controlling the intercourse of individuals."

23. *Plessy*, at 544.

24. *Plessy*, at 543.

25. *Plessy*, at 551.

26. Du Bois, "Miscegenation," 467–471. The US census of 1890 reported the mulatto population at 1,132,060, or roughly 15 percent of the Negro population. Du Bois discusses the "doubtful validity" of these numbers and inevitability of racial admixture.

27. *Plessy*, at 559.

28. *Plessy*, at 554.

29. *Plessy*, at 555.

30. Przybyszewski, *Republic according to Harlan*, 99.

31. *Plessy*, at 561.

32. On Harlan's anti-Chinese racism, see also Chin, "The Plessy Myth," 156, 158. Chin herein argues: "Harlan was a faithful opponent of the constitutional rights of Chinese for much of his career on the Court . . . [and] Harlan's voting record as a whole . . . shows that his animosity towards the Chinese was fixed and strong."

33. *Plessy*, at 554.

34. Przybyszewski, *Republic according to Harlan*, 9. Harlan's racial attitudes were deeply paternalistic: In the aftermath of the Civil War, "Harlan was forced to choose between the two values on which paternalism rested: white supremacy and white forbearance from the abuse of power. He chose the latter and embraced legal equality of the races but never completely abandoned the idea of racial difference inherent in paternalism."

35. Black, "Lawfulness of Segregation Decisions," 421–422. For this reason, Black views *Plessy* as consistent with the antisubordination principle of *Strauder*: Their difference lies in *Plessy*'s implausible claim that "segregation did not really harm the Negro, except through his own choice."

36. Kull, *Color-Blind Constitution*, 116–118.

37. *Plessy*, at 544–545.

38. *Cooper v. Roberts*, 59 U.S. 173 at 198 (1855).

39. Kull, *Color-Blind Constitution*, 49.

40. Kull, *Color-Blind Constitution*, 51.

41. *Pace v. Alabama*, 106 U.S. 583 (1883).

42. *Pace*, at 585.

43. *Plessy*, at 545.

44. For further discussion of the connection between *Pace* and *Plessy*, see Moran, *Interracial Intimacy*, 80–81. On the role of antimiscegenation laws in the postemancipation "hardening of racial boundaries," see also Bardaglio, "Shameful Matches," 121. Bardaglio herein argues that such decisions run counter to the trend of courts deferring to the authority of contract in domestic relations and labor law.

45. Moran, *Interracial Intimacy*, 79.

46. *Plessy*, at 551.

47. Black, "Lawfulness of Segregation Decisions," 422 n. 8.

48. The inferior conditions of Jim Crow cars are widely documented, and Plessy's attorneys have been criticized for not making this a central aspect of their challenge; for further discussion, refer to Elliott, "Democratic Public." On the false promise of "equalization" in response to the "separate but equal" doctrine, refer to Lively, "Separate but Equal."

49. Berlin, *Slaves without Masters*.

50. Jordan, *White over Black*, xx.

51. Welke, "Road to *Plessy*," 269–270.

52. Friedman, "*Brown* in Context," 54–55. Calling Brown's argument in *Plessy* the "person-from-Pluto-approach," Friedman observes that "the legal system in the nineteenth century was replete with what we might call double systems, in which a yeasty and grimy reality lay under the surface of a smooth formality," and not only in regard to race. In regard to police brutality, for example, formalism's "surface posture of humility before legal rules" allowed for "winking at a bit of subterranean violence."

53. *Plessy*, at 562.

54. Przybyszewski, *Republic according to Harlan*, 109–114.

55. *Plessy*, at 544.

56. *Plessy*, at 559.

57. *Strauder*, at 308 (emphasis supplied).

58. Grinsell, "Prejudice of Caste," 339–347.

59. *Plessy*, at 559 (emphasis supplied).

60. *Plessy*, at 557 (emphasis supplied).

61. Compare Justice Thomas's dissent in *Grutter*, condemning the Court's "benighted notion that one can tell when racial discrimination benefits (rather than hurts) minority groups." *Grutter v. Bollinger*, 539 U.S. 306 at 24 (2003). Thomas concludes his opinion by quoting Harlan's "Our Constitution is color-blind" dissent in *Plessy*.

62. *Plessy*, at 560.

63. *Plessy*, at 562.

64. Primus, "Canon, Anti-Canon," 262.

65. Spear, "They Need Wives," 37.

66. Hall, *Africans in Colonia Louisiana*, 29–32, 200; Berlin, *Slaves without Masters*, 77.

67. Sterkx, *Free Negro*, 26–34; Fiehrer, *African Presence*.

68. Fischer, *Segregation Struggle*, 16–18.

69. Martin, "*Plaçage*." See also Fischer, *Segregation Struggle*, 15; Sterkx, *Free Negro in Louisiana*, 250.

70. Martin, "*Plaçage*," 57.

71. Hirsch and Logsdon, *Creole New Orleans*, 189.

72. Hirsch and Logsdon, *Creole New Orleans*, 190.

73. Hirsch and Logsdon, *Creole New Orleans*, 201. The two communities were divided by culture, language, and religion, but "a fundamental difference about race relations also caused friction between the two groups. Creole leaders resented racial separation even in private institutions and constantly nagged black as well as white recalcitrants about any adherence to the color line. Most of the Protestant leaders, however, had responded to racial discrimination . . . by forming their own all-black institutions where they could find solace and support. The reluctance of most black Creoles to . . . accept the norms of the American color line struck some black Americans as a denial of racial solidarity."

74. Hirsch and Logsdon, *Creole New Orleans*, 251–252.

75. Medley, *We as Freemen*, 139–140. The Separate Car Act imposed substantial costs on railroad companies, which were required to pay for and maintain separate coaches, although criticizing the laws would have risked public backlash. The Citizens' Committee secretly arranged for the cooperation of the East Louisiana Railroad Co. in bringing the case.

76. Gross, *Albion W. Tourgée*. Tourgée is remembered foremost for his works of fiction rather than his lawyering. For accounts of Tourgée's political life, see Olsen, *Carpetbagger's Crusade* and Elliott, *Color-Blind Justice*.

77. Trévigne, *Crusader*, cited by Medley, *We as Freemen*, 146.

78. Olsen, *Thin Disguise*, 11; Medley, *We as Freemen*, 162.

79. Elliott, "Democratic Public," 307 n. 48. Martinet, in communication to Tourgée, dismissed the assertion as "a lot of nonsense," cited in Olsen, *The Thin Disguise*, 12.

80. *Lochner v. New York*, 198 U.S. 45 (1905).

81. Bell, "Property Rights," 767.

82. Harris, "Whiteness as Property," 1747.

83. *Plessy*, at 549.

84. Tourgée, *Briefs*, 80, cited in Olsen, *Thin Disguise*, 80–103.

85. Tourgée, *Briefs*, 83.

86. Harris, "Whiteness as Property," 1750.

87. Tourgée, *Briefs*, 83–85.

88. Harris, "Whiteness as Property," 1710.

89. Harris, "Whiteness as Property," 1713.

90. Harris, "Whiteness as Property," 1711.

91. It should be added that noneconomic incentives have also played a role; many have "passed" out of love rather than money, when antimiscegenation laws would have prevented an interracial union. This may be seen most clearly in the phenomenon of "passing black" (usually so as to legitimize a romantic relation that would otherwise be considered interracial). For an example of an economic motive for "passing black," see *State v. Chavers*, 50 NC 11 (NC 1857).

92. Harris, "Whiteness as Property," 1779.

93. Tourgée, *Briefs*, 84.

94. Olsen, *Thin Disguise*, 56.

95. Harris, "Whiteness as Property," 1747 n. 179, cited by Lofgren, *The Plessy Case*, 31; Elliott, "Democratic Public," 307. Harris alludes to this letter, though none of these scholars include the remarkable lines that precede it. Such lines are quoted below.

96. Olsen, *Thin Disguise*, 56–57.

97. Olsen, *Thin Disguise*, 80.

98. Elliott, "Democratic Public," 306.

99. Tourgée, *Briefs*, 81.

100. Tourgée, *Briefs*, 81.

101. Tourgée, *Briefs*, 81.

102. Tourgée, *Briefs*, 81.

103. Tourgée, *Briefs*, 102–103, citing *Strauder*. The amendment guarantees "the right to exemption . . . from legal discriminations, implying inferiority in civil society, lessening the security of their enjoyment of the rights which others enjoy, and discriminations which are steps towards reducing them to the condition of a subject race."

104. Du Bois, *Dusk of Dawn*, 153; Medley, *We as Free Men*, 219. In 1905, Du Bois's Niagara Movement held a memorial service to honor three "Friends of Freedom": Frederick Douglass, William Lloyd Garrison, and Albion Winegar Tourgée.

105. *Plessy*, at 549.

106. *Plessy*, at 552.

107. *Chavers*, at 27.

108. *Chavers*, at 25.

109. *Chavers*, at 25.

110. *Gray v. Ohio*, 4 OH 353 (OH 1831).

111. *Gray*, at 355.

112. *Gray*, at 355.

113. *Monroe v. Collins*, 17 OH St. 665 (1867).

114. *Monroe*, at 679.

115. *Monroe*, at 679.

116. *Monroe*, at 679.

117. *Monroe*, at 680.

118. *Monroe*, at 681.

119. *Monroe*, at 688.

120. *Conlon v. Dean*, 14 MI Ct. App. 415 at 413 (MI 1986).

121. *Dean*, at 413.

122. *Dean*, at 424.

123. *Dean*, at 422.

124. *Dean*, at 424.

125. *Watson v. Jones*, 80 U.S. 679 at 538 (1871).

126. *Jones*, at 540.

127. *Jones*, at 542.

128. On the role of social performance in trials of racial determination, refer to Gross, "Litigating Whiteness"; Gross, *What Blood Won't Tell*.

Chapter 4

1. Novkov, "Conservative Attack," 196. Novkov makes a similar claim about the timing of color-blind conservatism's legal ascendency, noting that "conservative appropriations of colorblindness by state actors began well before the first lawsuits were filed challenging affirmative action plans."

2. Payne, "Whole United States," 83.

3. Bell, *Silent Covenants*, 130. Similarly, Bell locates *Brown*'s significance chiefly as "a symbol of the nation's ability to condemn racial segregation and put the unhappy past behind us."

4. Sarat, *Race, Law and Culture*, 4. Also refer to Irons, *Jim Crow's Children*.

5. Wilkinson, *From Brown to Bakke*, 11.

6. Wilkinson, *From Brown to Bakke*, 23.

7. Balkin, *Brown v. Board of Education*, 14. Also refer to Balkin, "Constitutional Theory."

8. Goluboff, *Lost Promise*, 7; *Parents Involved in Community Schools v. Seattle School District No. 1*, 127 S. Ct. 2738 at 2769 (2007), citing *North Carolina State Board of Education v. Swann*, 402 U.S. 43 at 6 (1971). Compare Goluboff's expansive definition of "Jim Crow as a system of both racial oppression and economic exploitation" with Justice Thomas's restrictive definition: "It is important to define segregation clearly and to distinguish it from racial imbalance. In the context of public schooling, segregation is the deliberate operation of a school system to 'carry out a governmental policy to separate pupils in schools solely on the basis of race.' "

9. Orfield and Eaton, *Dismantling Desegregation*, l; Orfield and Lee, *Historic Reversals*.

10. Rosenberg, *Hollow Hope*.

11. Klarman, "Backlash Thesis"; Klarman, *Jim Crow*.

12. My interest lies principally in *Brown*'s reception. I do not mean to endorse this general account of legal change, which has been criticized effectively by Garrow, "Hopelessly Hollow History." For a more nuanced and optimistic view of the Court's capacity to mobilize resources for affecting social change, refer to McCann, *Rights at Work*. On the central role of the NAACP's pre-*Brown* litigation against racial violence and its impact on subsequent civil rights organizing, see Francis, *Civil Rights*.

13. Goluboff, *Lost Promise*; Frymer, *Black and Blue*; Lee, "Hotspots in Cold War."

14. Bell, *Silent Covenants*; Bell, "Two Masters."

15. Critical race theorists have emphasized *Brown*'s implicit assumption of black inferiority in defining contact with white students as necessary for educational success. Refer to Brown, "Road Not Taken"; Culp, "Black People."

16. Irons, *Jim Crow's Children*, 177; Oh, "Discrimination and Distrust." Note a shift from the language of "segregation" in *Brown I* to "discrimination" in *Brown II*. For a defense of *Brown II*, see Wilkinson, *From Brown to Bakke*, 68–77.

17. Orfield and Eaton, *Dismantling Desegregation*; Chemerinsky, "Lost Opportunity," 999; Chemerinsky, "Segregation," 1620–1622.

18. Omi and Winant, *Racial Formation*, 67.

19. Payne, "Whole United States," 84.

20. Payne, "Whole United States," 85.

21. *Brown v. Board of Education of Topeka*, 349 U.S. 294 at 495 (1955).

22. *Brown*, at 493. From *Brown*: "Does segregation of children in public schools solely on the basis of race . . . deprive the children of the minority group of equal educational opportunities? We believe that it does."

23. Kluger, *Simple Justice*, 156–159. See within Kull's discussion of the Legal Defense Fund's consolidated brief and other briefs for appellants, including a typical example: "The Fourteenth Amendment has stripped the state of power to make race and color the basis for government action."

24. Schmidt, "*Brown* and Color-Blind Constitution," 208.

25. Cokorinos, *Assault on Diversity*; Delgado and Stefancic, *No Mercy*; Hollis-Brusky, *Ideas with Consequences*; Teles, *Conservative Legal Movement*.

26. Balkin, *Brown v. Board of Education*, 5.

27. Cho, "Redeeming Whiteness"; Omi and Winant, *Racial Formation*, 99–104; Siegel, "Rule of Love," 2178–2187. Compare Cho's logic of "transformation" with Omi and Winant's discussion of "rearticulation" and Siegel's "preservation-through-transformation."

28. Hall, "Long Civil Rights," 1234.

29. Lassiter and Crespino, *Southern Exceptionalism*; Sugrue, *Sweet Land of Liberty*; Countryman, *Up South*; Theoharris and Woodward, *Freedom North*; Singh, *Black Is a Country*.

30. Bartley, *Massive Resistance*, 320–339; Lassiter and Lewis, *Moderate's Dilemma*; Lassiter, *The Silent Majority*; Walker, *Ghost of Jim Crow*; Wilkinson, *From Brown to Bakke*, 78–127.

31. Bartley, *Massive Resistance*, 126–149. For a comprehensive defense of interposition by its fiercest champion, refer to Kilpatrick, *Southern Case*. See also Lassiter and Lewis, *Moderate's Dilemma*, 42.

32. Bartley, *Massive Resistance*, 77. Under Mississippi law: "It shall be unlawful for any member of the white or Caucasian race to attend any school of high school level or below wholly or partially supported by funds of the State of Mississippi which is also attended by a member or members of the colored or Negro race."

33. *Griffin v. County School Board of Prince Edward County*, 377 U.S. 218 (1964).

34. Lassiter and Lewis, *Moderate's Dilemma*; Cobb, *Selling of the South*.

35. Roche, *Restructured Resistance*; Lassiter and Lewis, *Moderate's Dilemma*, 104–133.

36. Webb, *Massive Resistance*, 29.

37. Lassiter and Lewis, *Moderate's Dilemma*, 14.

38. Lassiter and Lewis, *Moderate's Dilemma*, 44.

39. Walker, *Ghost of Jim Crow*, 14.

40. Bartley, *Massive Resistance*, 74.

41. Coates and Paul, *School Segregation Decision*, 38.

42. Coates and Paul, *School Segregation Decision*, section 3.

43. *Brown*, at 300.

44. *Brown*, at 300.

45. *Brown*, at 300.

46. *Brown*, at 301.

47. Irons, *Jim Crow's Children*, 173.

48. Bartley, *Massive Resistance*, 78.

49. Klarman, *Jim Crow*, 330.

50. Coates and Paul, *School Segregation Decision*, 88.

51. Coates and Paul, *School Segregation Decision*, 92 (emphasis supplied).

52. Coates and Paul, *School Segregation Decision*, 100–101.

53. Walker, *Ghost of Jim Crow*, 44.

54. Irons, *Jim Crow's Children*, 190.

55. Hershman, *Moderate's Dilemma*, 106.

56. Lassiter, *Silent Majority*, 4.

57. Lassiter, *Silent Majority*, 8.

58. Kull, *Color-Blind Constitution*, 171–181. Parker's opinion receives a sympathetic treatment by Kull. More critical receptions can be found in Wilkinson, *From Brown to Bakke*, 81–82, and in Irons, *Jim Crow's Children*, 174–177.

59. *Briggs v. Elliott*, 132 F. Supp. 776 at 777 (EDSC 1955).

60. *Green v. County School Board of New Kent County*, 391 U.S. 430 (1968); *North Carolina State Board of Education v. Swann*, 402 U.S. 43 at 1 (1971).

61. *Green*, at 437 (emphasis supplied).

62. *Green*, at 439.

63. *Green*, at 435.

64. Sowell, *Civil Rights*, 68.

65. Glazer, *Affirmative Discrimination*, 83.

66. *Swann*, at 6.

67. *Swann*, at 15.

68. *Swann*, at 6.

69. *Swann*, at 22–23.

70. *Swann*, at 24.

71. *Swann*, at 26.

72. *Swann*, at 25.

73. *Swann*, at 24.

74. *Swann*, at 28.

75. *Swann*, at 30.

76. *Swann*, at 37.

77. *Swann*, at 43.

78. *N.C.Gen.Stat. § 115-176.1 (Supp. 1969)*, cited by *Swann*, at 44–45.

79. *Swann*, at 45–46.

80. *McDaniel v. Barresi*, 402 U.S. 39 at 41 (1971). In the process of remediating segregation, from *McDaniel*, "steps will almost invariably require that students be assigned 'differently because of their race.' Any other approach would freeze the status quo that is the very target of all desegregation processes."

81. Freeman, "Legitimizing Racial Discrimination," 1099–1102.

82. *Swann*, at 28.

83. *Swann*, at 31–32.

84. Kluger, *Simple Justice*, 683–699; Irons, *Jim Crow's Children*, 163; Klarman, *Jim Crow*, 313–314. Kluger herein discusses Chief Justice Warren's pursuit of unanimity; Irons discusses "the cost of unanimity;" Klarman discusses the gradualism of *Brown II* as price of unanimity.

85. *Keyes v. School District No. 1, Denver, Colorado*, 413 U.S. 189 at 209 (1973).

86. *Keyes*, at 258 (Rehnquist dissenting).

87. Orfield and Eaton, *Dismantling Desegregation*, 40–45.

88. *Keyes*, at 220.

89. *Keyes*, at 224 (Powell dissenting).

90. Jeffries, *Justice Powell, Jr.* 140–141.

91. Jeffries, *Justice Powell, Jr.*, 174–177.

92. *Keyes*, at 189 (Powell dissenting) (emphasis supplied).

93. Jacobs, *Getting around Brown*; Lipsitz, "Getting around *Brown*."

94. *Milliken v. Bradley*, 418 U.S. 717 at 745 (1974).

95. *Milliken*, at 741–742.

96. Orfield and Eaton, *Dismantling Desegregation*, 10–13.

97. Irons, *Jim Crow's Children*, 246.

98. Orfield and Eaton, *Dismantling Desegregation*, 293.

99. *Milliken*, at 723 (emphasis supplied).

100. *United States v. Rodwell*, 338 F. Supp. 780 at 587 (N.D. Cal. 1972); *Milliken*, at 723.

101. Clotfelter, *After Brown*, 75–100; Denton, "Persistence of Segregation"; Farley, "Residential Segregation"; Hochschild, *New American Dilemma*, 55–70; HoSang, *Racial Propositions*; Massey and Denton, *American Apartheid*, 53–90; Orfield and Eaton, *Dismantling Desegregation*, 291–330; Powell et al., *A Dream Deferred*; Ryan, "Schools," 249, 275–284; Sugrue, *Origins*.

102. *Milliken*, at 770 (White dissenting).

103. *Milliken*, at 762 (Douglass dissenting).

104. *Milliken*. at 756 n. 2 (Stewart concurring). See also *Columbus Board of Education v. Penick*, 433 U.S. 499 at 512 (1979) (Rehnquist dissenting). Justice Rehnquist herein characterizes residential segregation as resulting from "a mélange of past happenings prompted by economic considerations, private discrimination, discriminatory school assignments, or a desire to reside near people of one's own race or ethnic background."

105. Lipsitz, *Possessive Investment*, 35.

106. Arguably, the separation of right from remedy in *Brown I* and *II* made this move possible. After *Milliken I* rendered integration no longer a viable option, *Milliken II* (1972), permitted federal courts to require increased funding to improve the quality of Detroit's segregated schools. Refer to *Missouri v. Jenkins*, 515 U.S. 70 (1995); the Court of *Jenkins* severely restricted this "equalization" remedy.

107. Orfield and Eaton, *Dismantling Desegregation*, 19. See *Freeman v. Pitts*, 503 U.S. 467 at 495–196 (1992) (emphasis supplied). Kennedy's majority opinion in *Freeman* follows as such: "But though we cannot *escape our history*, neither must we overstate its consequences in fixing legal responsibilities."

108. *Board of Education of Oklahoma City v. Dowell*, 498 U.S. 237 at 238 (1991).

109. *Dowell*, at 261 (Marshall dissenting).

110. *Dowell*, at 255 (Marshall dissenting).

111. *Dowell*, at 248.

112. *Dowell*, at 247.

113. *Dowell*, at 249.

114. Chemerinsky, "Lost Opportunity."

115. Kluger, *Simple Justice*, X.

116. For an advancing of the "backlash thesis," refer to Klarman, "Backlash Thesis"; Edsall and Edsall, *Chain Reaction*. For recent criticisms of the theory, refer to Lowndes, "Backlash Thesis"; Weaver, "Frontlash."

117. Lipsitz, *Possessive Investment*, 35. As Lipsitz puts it, it was "as if whites were innocent victims of remedies for a disease that did not even exist."

118. *Freeman v. Pitts*, 503 U.S. 467 at 500 (1992) (Scalia concurring).

Chapter 5

1. Wright, "Color-Blind Theories," 213, 218.

2. Wright, "Color-Blind Theories," 221.

3. *Civil Rights Cases*, 109 U.S. at 3 (1883).

4. *Civil Rights Cases*, at 25 (emphasis supplied).

5. *Civil Rights Cases*, at 61. The obviousness of this point is registered in Justice Harlan's satirical use of understatement, writing in dissent: "It is, I submit, scarcely just to say that the colored race has been the special favorite of the laws."

6. *Grutter v. Bollinger*, 539 U.S. at 306 (2003).

7. *Gratz v. Bollinger*, 539 U.S. at 244 (2003).

8. *Regents of the University of California v. Bakke*, 438 U.S. at 265 (1978).

9. *Fisher v. University of Texas at Austin* 579 U.S. ___ (2016). In *Fisher*, the question concerned whether an affirmative action program modeled on the one upheld in *Grutter* should be considered "narrowly tailored" if the University of Texas could accomplish its diversity goals by using a "Top 10% Plan" that does not classify individuals by race.

10. *Grutter*, at 332.

11. *Grutter*, at 326, citing *Adarand Constructors, Inc. v. Peña*, 515 U.S. 200 at 227 (1995). From *Grutter*: "It follows from this principle that 'government may treat people differently because of their race only for the most compelling reasons." Under strict scrutiny analysis, legislation must be narrowly tailored to achieve a compelling state interest; under ordinary judicial review, it need only be rationally related to a permissible state interest.

12. *Bakke*, at 296.

13. *Bakke*, at 295.

14. *Bakke*, at 296.

15. *Bakke*, at 298. On the language of "innocence" in affirmative action discourse, see Ross, "Innocence and Affirmative Action," 297, and Post and Rogin, *Race and Representation*, 29.

16. *Bakke*, at 307.

17. *Bakke*, at 307 (emphasis supplied).

18. *Bakke*, at 307.

19. *Bakke*, at 313.

20. *Bakke*, at 313.

21. *Bakke*, at 317. Also refer to Lawrence's criticism of the diversity rationale's depoliticized race concept in "Two Views."

22. See Schuck, "Affirmative Action," 34–47. Schuck argues that racial diversity fails to produce educational benefits, is a weak proxy for "viewpoint diversity," and leads to "intellectual Balkanization."

23. See Lawrence, "Two Views," 942–958. Lawrence further argues that "diversity" rationales fail to challenge racial subordination.

24. *City of Richmond v. J.A. Croson, Co.*, 488 U.S. 469 at 480 (1989).

25. *Bakke*, at 499.

26. *Bakke*, at 500.

27. *Bakke*, at 518 (Kennedy concurring).

28. *Bakke*, at 519 (Kennedy concurring).

29. *Bakke*, at 520 (Scalia concurring).

30. *Grutter*, at 388 (emphasis supplied). Justice Kennedy would echo this association of affirmative action with national destruction in his dissent: "Preferment by race, when resorted to by the State, can be the most divisive of all policies, containing within it *the potential to destroy confidence in the Constitution and the idea of equality.*"

31. *Adarand*, at 227.

32. *Adarand*, at 237.

33. *Adarand*, at 239 (emphasis supplied) (Scalia concurring).

34. *Adarand*, at 239.

35. *Adarand*, at 240 (Thomas concurring).

36. Frymer and Skrentny, "Instrumental Affirmative Action," 677.

37. Karst and Horowitz, "Affirmative Action," 955–974; Anderson, *Imperative of Integration*.

38. Dworkin, *Matter of Principle*, 294–295; Michelman, "Racialism and Reason," 723, 732.

39. Loury, "America's Moral Dilemma," 90–94; Appiah and Gutmann, *Color-Conscious*, 109.

40. *Grutter*, at 341, citing *Bakke*, at 298. From O'Connor: "We acknowledge that 'there are serious problems of justice connected with the idea of preference itself.'"

41. *Grutter*, at 342.

42. *Grutter*, at 342.

43. *Grutter*, at 343. Note that *Grutter* was decided twenty-five years after *Bakke*.

44. *Grutter*, at 346 (Ginsburg concurring).

45. *Grutter*, at 342, citing *Croson*, at 510.

46. Refer to my discussion in chapter 1.

47. The organization took its name from Malcolm X's famous phrase, for which BAMN is an acronym: By Any Means Necessary. For more on BAMN, see Brown-Nagin, "Affirmative Action," 1436.

48. *Grutter*, at 330–333.

49. Brown-Nagin, "Affirmative Action," 1441–1442.

50. Crenshaw, "Race, Reform and Retrenchment," 1379.

51. On the role of institutional support structures and the rise of conservative legal movements, see Hollis-Brusky, *Ideas with Consequences*; Teles, *Conservative Legal Movement*.

52. King and Smith, *Still a House Divided*, 10.

53. Crenshaw, "Race, Reform and Retrenchment," 1346 (emphasis supplied).

54. Karst and Horowitz, "Affirmative Action," 959.

55. For more on "white identity politics," refer to Lipsitz, *Possessive Investment*.

56. Keck, "From *Bakke*," 419.

57. Refer to Sarat and Scheingold, *Cause Lawyering*.

58. Keck, "From *Bakke*," 425.

59. Dreyfuss and Lawrence, *Bakke Case*, 113.

60. Loury, "America's Moral Dilemma," 93.

61. Loury, "America's Moral Dilemma," 93.

62. Dudas, "Rights and Regulation," 161.

63. Elizabeth Chuck, "Meet the Supreme Court Matchmaker: Edward Blum," NBC News, June 11, 2013.

64. *Students for Fair Admissions v. Harvard* (1:14-cv-14176-DJC (D. Mass.)); *Students for Fair Admissions v. University of North Carolina* (1:14-cv-00954-TDS-JLW (M.D. N.C.)).

65. *Students for Fair Admissions*, accessed March 1, 2017, (https://studentsforfairadmissions.org/about/).

66. *Students for Fair Admissions*, accessed March 1, 2017, (https://studentsforfairadmissions.org) (emphasis supplied).

67. Lawrence, "Two Views," 928–976. For just this reason, some left critics reject the diversity rational as offering a depoliticized race-concept that prioritizes the instrumental value of ethnic difference (in educating white students) over that of social injustice.

68. *Grutter*, at 49–50.

69. *Grutter*, at 306 (Rehnquist dissenting). According to Justice Rehnquist, the "alleged goal of 'critical mass' is simply a sham."

70. *Croson*, at 552 (Marshall dissenting).

71. *Parents Involved in Community Schools v. Seattle School District No. 1*, 551 U.S. 701 at 712 (2007).

72. *Parents Involved*, at 711.

73. *Parents Involved*, at 720–721, citing *Milliken v. Bradley*, 418 U.S. 717 (1974); *Freeman v. Pitts*, 503 U.S. 467 (1992); *Board of Education of Oklahoma City v. Dowell*, 498 U.S. 237 (1991).

74. Ryan, "Schools," 132. Ironically, the significance of the decision in regard to public policy is muted by the fact that "racial integration is not on the agenda of most school districts, and has not been for over twenty years."

75. *Parents Involved*, at 725–733 III, B.

76. *Parents Involved*, at 726, citing *Freeman*, at 494; *Grutter*, at 330. From *Freeman*: "Racial balance is not to be achieved for its own sake"; from *Grutter*: "Outright racial balancing is patently unconstitutional."

77. *Parents Involved*, at 732.

78. *Parents Involved*, at 746.

79. *Parents Involved*, at 772 (Thomas concurring).

80. *Parents Involved*, at 748. From *Parents Involved:* "The segregationists in *Brown* embraced the arguments the Court endorsed in *Plessy*. Though *Brown* decisively rejected those arguments, today's dissent replicates them to a distressing extent. . . . This approach is just as wrong today as it was a half-century ago."

81. *Parents Involved*, at 778.

82. *Parents Involved*, at 749, citing *North Carolina State Board of Education v. Swann*, 402 U.S. 43 (1971).

83. *Parents Involved*, at 750.

84. *Parents Involved*, at 773–774.

85. Spann, "Disintegration"; Fischbach et al., "Race at the Pivot Point."

86. *Swann*, at 16.

87. *Parents Involved*, at 738.

88. *Parents Involved*, at 788. Kennedy's opinion has been criticized for rejecting Seattle's race-conscious remedies "on utterly unclear grounds" and failing to offer a clear account of what alternatives he would accept. Nussbaum, "Constitutions and Capabilities," 92 – 93. For a more sympathetic reading of Kennedy's opinion, see Gerken, "Justice Kennedy."

89. *Parents Involved*, at 782.

90. *Parents Involved*, at 788.

91. *Grutter*, at 388. Recall that Kennedy's dissent was also based on a narrow-tailoring objection, in which he denounced the Court's standard of review as "nothing short of perfunctory."

92. *Parents Involved*, at 788–789.

93. *Parents Involved*, at 789.

94. *Parents Involved*, at 796, 862. Note Justice Ginsburg's herein citation of Judge Boudin, and Justice Kennedy's response to this objection.

95. *Parents Involved*, at 797.

96. *Ricci v. DeStefano*, 129 S. Ct. 2658 (2009).

97. *Ricci*, at 2691 (Ginsburg dissenting).

98. *Ricci*, at 2664.

99. *Ricci*, at 2691 (Ginsburg dissent).

100. *Civil Rights Act 1991*, 42 USC § 2000e-2(a)(2); *Griggs v. Duke Power Co.*, 401 U.S. 424 (1971).

101. The new policy required applicants to pass a standardized intelligence test, or to have graduated from high school.

102. *Washington v. Davis*, 426 U.S. 229 (1976).

103. Freeman, "Legitimizing Racial Discrimination."

104. *Civil Rights Act 1991*, 42 USC § 2000e-2(k)(1)(A)(i).

105. Harris and West-Faulcon, "Reading *Ricci*."

106. Refer to Primus, "Equal Protection." Primus herein raises and refutes the concern that disparate impact contradicts current equal protection doctrine.

107. *Ricci*, at 2682–2683 (Scalia concurring).

108. *Ricci*, at 2674 (emphasis supplied).

109. *Ricci*, at 2673 (emphasis supplied).

110. *Parents Involved*, at 788 (Kennedy concurring).

111. *Ricci*, at 2677.

112. That Justice Kennedy uses this point to distinguish himself from the *Parents Involved* plurality underscores his judgment that Chief Justice Roberts's opinion could plausibly be read in this way.

113. *Ricci*, at 2674.

114. King and Smith, *Still a House Divided*, 95.

115. King and Smith, *Still a House Divided*, 96–97.

Chapter 6

1. In an interview with Don Lemon, presidential candidate Donald Trump declared, "I am the least racist person that you have ever met." Gregory Krieg, "Trump: 'I'm Doing Good for the Muslims,'" *CNN*, December 10, 2015. As president, Trump has repeated this claim: "Number one, I am the least anti-Semitic person that you've ever seen in your entire life. Number two, racism, the least racist person." Reuters, February 16, 2017; http://www.reuters.com/video/2017/02/16/trump-says-he-is-the-least-racist-person?videoId=371135921).

2. Shulman, *American Prophecy*, 252.

3. Allen, *Talking to Strangers*, 156.

4. Turner, *Awakening to Race*, 120–123.

5. Lebron, *Color of Our Shame*, 152.

6. From Jer. 8:20: "The harvest is past, the summer is ended, and we are not saved."

7. This line supplies the subtitle of Bell's subsequent book, *Faces at the Bottom of the Well: On the Permanence of Racism in America*.

8. Best and Hartman, "Fugitive Justice," 1.

9. Harney and Morten, "*The Undercommons*," 152.

10. Wilderson, "Gramsci's Black Marx," 223.

11. Wilderson, "Gramsci's Black Marx," 235.

12. Wilderson, "Afro-Pessimism," 5.

13. "We're Trying to Destroy the World: An Interview with Frank B. Wilderson, III," by Jared Bell, Todd Steven Burroughs, and Dr. Hate for IMIXWHATILIKE, October 1, 2014, (https://imixwhatilike.org/2014/10/01/frankwildersonandantiblackness-2/).

14. See Michael Dawson's convincing critique of Wilderson, "Hidden in Plain Sight," 157–159.

15. Cornel West famously described hopelessness and despair as "the most basic issue now facing black America: the *nihilistic threat to its very existence*." *Race Matters*, 19.

16. My thinking about the productive uses of despair has benefited greatly from conversations with Kirstine Taylor.

17. Davis, *Abolition Democracy*; Olson, *Abolition of White Democracy*; Dilts, *Punishment and Inclusion*.

18. Hartman, *Scenes of Subjection*, 76.

19. Hartman, *Scenes of Subjection*, 51.

20. Melamed, *Represent and Destroy*.

21. Baldwin, "Fire Next Time," 105.

BIBLIOGRAPHY

Abram, Morris B. "Affirmative Action: Fair Shakers and Social Engineers." *Harvard Law Review* 99, no. 6 (1986): 1312–1326.

Abrams, Kathryn R. "'Groups' and the Advent of Critical Race Scholarship." *Issues in Legal Scholarship* 2 (2003): 1–11.

Ackerman, Bruce A. *We the People: Transformations.* Cambridge, MA: Belknap Press of Harvard University Press, 1998.

Aleinikoff, T. Alexander. "A Case for Race-Consciousness." *Columbia Law Review* 91, no. 5 (1991): 1060–1125.

Alexander, Eliane A. and Lawrence A. Alexander. "The New Racism: An Analysis of the Use of Racial and Ethnic Criteria in Decision-Marking." *San Diego Law Review* 9, no. 2 (1972): 190–263.

Alexander, Michelle. *The New Jim Crow: Mass Incarceration in the Age of Colorblindness.* New York: New Press, 2010.

Allen, Danielle S. *Talking to Strangers: Anxieties of Citizenship since* Brown v. Board of Education. Chicago: University of Chicago Press, 2004.

Amsterdam, Anthony G. and Jerome Bruner. *Minding the Law: How Courts Rely on Storytelling, and How Their Stories Change the Way We See the Law—and Ourselves.* Cambridge, MA: Harvard University Press, 2002.

Anderson, Elizabeth. *The Imperatives of Integration.* Princeton: Princeton University Press, 2010.

Apostolidis, Paul. *Breaks in the Chain: What Immigrant Workers Can Teach America about Democracy.* Minneapolis: University of Minnesota Press, 2010.

Appiah, Kwame Anthony and Amy Gutmann. *Color-Conscious: The Political Morality of Race.* Princeton: Princeton University Press, 1996.

Armour, Jody D. "Race Ipsa Loquitur: Of Reasonable Racists, Intelligent Bayesians, and Involuntary Negrophobes." *Stanford Law Review* 46 (1994): 781–816.

Austin, J. L. "Performative-Constative." In *The Philosophy of Language*, edited by John R. Searle, 3–13. Oxford: Oxford University Press, 1972.

Baldwin, James. "The Fire Next Time." In *The Price of the Ticket: Collected Nonfiction*, edited by Steven Olswang, 333–380. New York: St. Martin's Press, 1985.

Balfour, Lawrie. *The Evidence of Things Not Said: James Baldwin and the Promise of American Democracy*. Ithaca, NY: Cornell University Press, 2000.

Balfour, Lawrie. "Unthinking Racial Realism: A Future for Reparations?" *Du Bois Review* 11, no. 1 (2014): 43–56.

Balibar, Etienne. *Race, Nation, Class: Ambiguous Identities*. London: Verso, 1991.

Balkin, Jack M. *Constitutional Redemption: Political Faith in an Unjust World*. Cambridge, MA: Harvard University Press, 2011.

Balkin, Jack M. "What *Brown* Teaches Us about Constitutional Theory." *Virginia Law Review* 90, no. 6 (2004): 1537–1577.

Balkin, Jack M. *What* Brown v. Board of Education *Should Have Said: The Nation's Top Experts Rewrite America's Landmark Civil Rights Decision*. New York: New York University Press, 2002.

Bank, Steven A. "Anti-miscegenation Laws and the Dilemma of Symmetry: The Understanding of Equality in the Civil Rights Act of 1875." *University of Chicago Law School Roundtable* 2 (1995): 303–344.

Bardaglio, Peter. "'Shameful Matches': The Regulation of Interracial Sex and Marriage in the South before 1900." In *Sex, Love, Race: Crossing Boundaries in North America*, edited by Martha Hodes, 112–140. New York: New York University Press, 1999.

Bartley, Numan V. *The Rise of Massive Resistance: Race and Politics in the South during the 1950's*. Baton Rouge: Louisiana State University Press, 1999.

Bell, Derrick A., Jr. *And We Are Not Saved: The Elusive Quest for Racial Justice*. New York: Basic Books, 1987.

Bell, Derrick A., Jr. "*Brown v. Board of Education* and the Interest-Convergence Dilemma." *Harvard Law Review* 93 (1979): 518–533.

Bell, Derrick A., Jr. "Serving Two Masters: Integration Ideals and Client Interests in School Desegregation Litigation." *Yale Law Review* 85, no. 4 (1976): 470–516.

Bell, Derrick A., Jr. *Silent Covenants:* Brown v. Board of Education *and the Unfulfilled Hopes for Racial Reform*. New York: Oxford University Press, 2005.

Bercovitch, Sacvan. *The American Jeremiad*. Madison: University of Wisconsin Press, 1978.

Berlin, Ira. *Slaves without Masters: The Free Negro in the Antebellum South*. New York: Pantheon, 1974.

Berry, Mary Frances. "Vindicating Martin Luther King, Jr.: The Road to a Color-Blind Society." *Journal of Negro History* 81, no. 1 (1996): 137–144.

Best, Stephen and Saidiya Hartman. "Fugitive Justice." *Representations* 92, no. 1 (2005): 1–15.

Black, Charles L., Jr. "The Lawfulness of Segregation Decisions." *Yale Law Journal* 69 (1960): 421–430.

Blight, David W. *Race and Reunion: The Civil War in American Memory*. Cambridge, MA: Belknap Press of Harvard University Press, 2001.

Bonilla-Silva, Eduardo. *Racism without Racists: Color-Blind Racism and the Persistence of Racial Inequality in America*. New York: Rowman and Littlefield, 2003.

Bork, Robert H. *Slouching towards Gomorrah: Modern Liberalism and American Decline*. New York: Regan Books, 1996.

Borstelmann, Thomas. *The Cold War and the Color Line: American Race Relations in the Global Arena*. Cambridge, MA: Harvard University Press, 2001.

Brest, Paul. "In Defense of the Antidiscrimination Principle." *Harvard Law Review* 90 (1976): 1–54.

Brooks, Peter. "Narrative Transactions: Does the Law Need a Narratology?" *Yale Journal of Law and the Humanities* 18, no. 1 (2006): 1–28.

Brooks, Roy L. *Racial Justice in the Age of Obama.* Princeton: Princeton University Press, 2009.

Brown, Kevin. "The Road Not Taken in *Brown*: Recognizing the Dual Harm of Segregation." *Virginia Law Review* 90, no. 6 (2004): 1579–1599.

Brown, Michael K., Martin Carnoy, Elliott Currie, Troy Duster, David B. Oppenheimer, Marjorie M. Shultz, and David Wellman. *Whitewashing Race: The Myth of a Color-Blind Society.* Berkeley: University of California Press, 2003.

Brown-Nagin, Tomiko. "Elites, Social Movements and the Law: The Case of Affirmative Action." *Columbia Law Review* 105, no. 5 (2005): 1436–1528.

Bybee, Keith J. "The Political Significance of Legal Ambiguity: The Case of Affirmative Action." *Law and Society Review* 34, no. 2 (2000): 263–290.

Carbado, Devon W. and Cheryl I. Harris. "New Racial Preferences." *California Law Review* 96, no. 5 (2008): 1139–1214.

Carr, Leslie. *"Color-Blind" Racism.* Thousand Oaks, CA: Sage Publications, 1997.

Chang, Robert. "Critiquing 'Race' and Its Uses: Critical Race Theory's Uncompleted Argument." In *Crossroads, Directions, and a New Critical Race Theory*, edited by Francisco Valdes, Jerome McCristal Culp, and Angela P. Harris, 87–97. Philadelphia: Temple University Press, 2002.

Chemerinsky, Erwin. "Lost Opportunity: The Burger Court and the Failure to Achieve Equal Educational Opportunity." *Mercer Law Review* 45 (1994): 999–1015.

Chemerinsky, Erwin. "The Segregation and Resegregation of American Public Education: The Court's Role." *North Carolina Law Review* 81 (2003): 1597–1622.

Chesnutt, Charles. "The Future American." In *Charles W. Chesnutt: Stories, Novels, and Essays*, edited by Werner Sollors, 845–863. New York: Library of America, 2002.

Chesnutt, Charles. "Race Prejudice; Its Causes and Its Cure." *Alexander's Magazine* 1 (1905): 21–26. The Charles Chesnutt Digital Archives (http://www.chesnuttarchive. org/Works/Essays/race.html).

Chin, Gabriel. "The Plessy Myth: Justice Harlan and the Chinese Cases." *Iowa Law Review* 82 (1996): 151–182.

Cho, Sumi K. "Redeeming Whiteness in the Shadow of Internment: Earl Warren, *Brown*, and a Theory of Racial Redemption." *Boston College Third World Law Journal* 19 (1998): 73–170.

Clotfelter, Charles T. *After* Brown: *The Rise and Retreat of School Desegregation.* Princeton: Princeton University Press, 2006.

Coates, Albert and James C. N. Paul. *School Segregation Decision: A Report to Governor of North Carolina on the Decision of the Supreme Court of the United States on the 17th of May 1954.* Chapel Hill, NC: Institute of Government, 1954.

Coates, Ta-Nehisi. *Between the World and Me.* New York: Spiegel and Grau, 2015.

Cobb, James C. *On the Selling of the South: The Southern Crusade for Industrial Development, 1936–1980.* Urbana: University of Illinois Press, 1993.

Cohen, Carl and James P. Sterba. *Affirmative Action and Racial Preference: A Debate.* Oxford: Oxford University Press, 2003.

Cokorinos, Lee. *Assault on Diversity: An Organized Challenge to Racial and Gender Justice.* New York: Rowman and Littlefield, 2003.

Cole, David. *Enemy Aliens: Double Standards and Constitutional Freedoms in the War on Terrorism.* New York: New Press, 2003.

Colker, Ruth. "Anti-subordination above All: Sex, Race, and Equal Protection." *New York University Law Review* 61 (1986) 1003–1057.

Collins, Patricia H. *Black Sexual Politics: African Americans, Gender, and the New Racism.* New York: Routledge, 2005.

Cose, Ellis. *Color-Blind: Seeing beyond Race in a Race-Obsessed World.* New York: Harper Perennial, 1998.

Countryman, Matthew J. *Up South: Civil Rights and Black Power in Philadelphia.* Philadelphia: University of Pennsylvania Press, 2007.

Cover, Robert M. "The Supreme Court 1982 Term: Foreword: Nomos and Narrative." *Harvard Law Review* 97, no. 4 (1983): 4–68.

Crenshaw, Kimberlé. "Race, Reform, and Retrenchment: Transformation and Legitimation in Anti-discrimination Law." *Harvard Law Review* 101, no. 7 (1998): 1331–1387.

Crenshaw, Kimberlé, Neil Gotanda, Gary Peller, and Kendall Thomas, eds. *Critical Race Theory: The Key Writings That Formed the Movement.* New York: The New Press, 1996.

Culp, Jerome, Jr. "Black People in the White Face: Assimilation, Culture, and the *Brown* Case." *William and Mary Law Review* 36, no. 2 (1994): 665–683.

Davis, Angela. *Abolition Democracy: Beyond Prison, Empire, and Torture.* New York: Seven Stories Press, 2005.

Davis, Angela. *Are Prisons Obsolete?* New York: Seven Stories Press, 2003.

Davis, David Brion. *The Problem of Slavery in the Age of Revolution.* Oxford: Oxford University Press, 1999.

Dawson, Michael C. *Black Visions: The Roots of Contemporary African-American Political Ideologies.* Chicago: University of Chicago Press, 2003.

Dawson, Michael C. *Blacks in and out of the Left.* Cambridge, MA: Harvard University Press, 2013.

Delgado, Gary. "Kill the Messengers: Can We Achieve Racial Justice without Mentioning Race?" In *Racial Formation in the Twenty-First Century*, edited by Daniel HoSang, Oneka LaBennett, and Laura Pulido, 162–182. Berkeley: University of California Press, 2010.

Delgado, Richard and Jean Stefancic. *Critical Race Theory: An Introduction.* New York: New York University Press, 2001.

Delgado, Richard and Jean Stefancic. *No Mercy: How Conservative Think Tanks and Foundations Changed America's Social Agenda.* Philadelphia: Temple University Press, 1996.

Denton, Nancy A. "The Persistence of Segregation: Links between Residential Segregation and School Segregation." *Minnesota Law Review* 80 (1995): 795–824.

Dilts, Andrew. *Punishment and Inclusion: Race, Membership, and the Limits of American Liberalism.* New York: Fordham University Press, 2014.

Dreyfuss, Joel and Charles Lawrence III. *The* Bakke *Case: The Politics of Inequality.* New York: Harcourt Brace Jovanovich, 1979.

Du Bois, W. E. B. *Dusk of Dawn: An Essay toward an Autobiography of a Race Concept.* New York: Schocken, 1940.

Du Bois, W. E. B. "Miscegenation." In *Interracialism: Black-White Intermarriage in American History, Literature, and Law*, edited by Werner Sollors, 461–472. Oxford: Oxford University Press, 2000.

Du Bois, W. E. B. *The Souls of Black Folk.* New York: Oxford University Press, 2007.

Dudas, Jeffrey R. "Rights and Regulation in Bush's America; or, How the New Right Learned to Stop Worrying and Love Equal Rights." In *The Intersection of Rights and Regulation: New Directions in Socio-Legal Scholarship,* edited by Bronwen Morgan, 153–166. Brookfield, VT: Ashgate, 2007.

Dudziak, Mary L. *Cold War Civil Rights: Race and the Image of American Democracy.* Princeton: Princeton University Press, 2000.

Dworkin, Ronald. *A Matter of Principle.* Cambridge, MA: Harvard University Press, 1986.

Eastland, Terry. "The Case against Affirmative Action." *William and Mary Law Review* 34 (1992): 33–51.

Eastland, Terry. *Ending Affirmative Action.* New York: Basic Books, 1997.

Edsall, Mary D. and Thomas B. Edsall, eds. *Chain Reaction: The Impact of Race, Rights, and Taxes on American Politics.* New York: Norton, 1992.

Elliott, Mark. *Color-Blind Justice: Albion Tourgée and the Quest for Racial Equality from the Civil War to* Plessy v. Ferguson. New York: Oxford University Press, 2008.

Elliott, Mark. "Race, Color Blindness, and the Democratic Public: Albion W. Tourgée's Radical Principles in *Plessy v. Ferguson.*" *Journal of Southern History* 67, no. 2 (2001): 287–330.

Ely, John Hart. *Democracy and Distrust: A Theory of Judicial Review.* Cambridge, MA: Harvard University Press, 1980.

Essed, Philomena and David Theo Goldberg, eds. *Race Critical Theories: Text and Context.* Hoboken, NJ: Wiley-Blackwell, 2001.

Farber, Daniel A. and Suzanna Sherry. "Telling Stories out of School: An Essay on Legal Narratives." *Stanford Law Review* 45 (1993): 807–855.

Farley, Reynolds. "Residential Segregation and Its Implications for School Integration." *Law and Contemporary Problems* 39 (1975): 164–193.

Fiehrer, Thomas M. "The African Presence in Colonial Louisiana: An Essay on the Continuity of Caribbean Culture." In *Louisiana's Black Heritage*, edited by Robert R. MacDonald, John R. Kemp, and Edward F. Hass, 3–31. New Orleans: Louisiana State Museum Press, 1979.

Fienman, Jay M. and Peter Gabel. "Contract Law as Ideology." In *The Politics of Law: A Progressive Critique*, edited by David Kairys, 497–510. New York: Basic Books, 1998.

Fireside, Harvey. *Separate and Unequal: Homer Plessy and the Supreme Court Decision That Legalized Racism.* New York: Carroll and Graf, 2004.

Fischbach, Jonathan, Will Rhee, and Robert Cacace. "Race at the Pivot Point: The Future of Race-Based Policies to Remedy De Jure Segregation After *Parents Involved in Community Schools.*" *Harvard Civil Rights–Civil Liberties Law Review* 43, no. 2 (2008): 491–538.

Fischer, Roger A. *The Segregation Struggle in Louisiana, 1862–77.* Urbana: University of Illinois Press, 1974.

Fiss, Owen M. "Groups and the Equal Protection Clause." *Philosophy and Public Affairs* 5, no. 2 (1976): 107–177.

Ford, Richard T. *Racial Culture: A Critique*. Princeton: Princeton University Press, 2005.

Foucault, Michel. *The History of Sexuality*, vol. 1: *An Introduction*. New York: Vintage, 1990.

Francis, Megan Ming. *Civil Rights and the Making of the Modern American State*. Cambridge: Cambridge University Press, 2014.

Frank, Jason. *Constituent Moments: Enacting the People in Post-Revolutionary America*. Durham, NC: Duke University Press, 2010.

Fraser, Nancy. "Rethinking the Public Sphere: A Contribution to the Critique of Actually Existing Democracy." *Social Text* 25 (1990): 56–80.

Fredrickson, George M. *The Black Image in the White Mind: The Debate on Afro-American Character and Destiny, 1817–1914*. New York: Harper and Row, 1971.

Freeman, Alan David. "Legitimizing Racial Discrimination through Antidiscrimination Law: A Critical Review of Supreme Court Doctrine." *Minnesota Law Review* 62 (1978): 1049–1119.

Friedman, Lawrence. "*Brown* in Context." In *Race, Law, and Culture: Reflections on Brown v. Board of Education*, edited by Austin Sarat, 49–73. Oxford: Oxford University Press, 1997.

Frymer, Paul. *Black and Blue: African Americans, the Labor Movement, and the Decline of the Democratic Party*. Princeton: Princeton University Press, 2007.

Frymer, Paul. *Uneasy Alliances: Race and Party Competition in America*. Princeton: Princeton University Press, 2010.

Frymer, Paul and John D. Skrentny. "The Rise of Instrumental Affirmative Action: Law and the Significance of Race in America." *Connecticut Law Review* 36 (2004): 677–723.

Garrow, David J. "Hopelessly Hollow History: Revisionist Devaluing of *Brown v. Board of Education*." *Virginia Law Review* 80 (1994): 151–160.

Gerken, Heather K. "Justice Kennedy and the Domains of Equal Protection." *Harvard Law Review* 121 (2007): 104–130.

Gilmore, Ruth Wilson. *Golden Gulags: Prisons, Surplus, Crisis, and Opposition in Globalizing California*. Berkeley: University of California Press, 2007.

Glazer, Nathan. *Affirmative Discrimination: Ethnic Inequality and Public Policy*. New York: Basic Books, 1975.

Glazer, Nathan. "Racial Quotas." In *Racial Preference and Racial Justice: The New Affirmative Action Controversy*, edited by Russell Nieli, 3–29. Lanham, MD: National Book Network, 1991.

Goluboff, Risa. *The Lost Promise of Civil Rights*. Cambridge, MA: Harvard University Press, 2007.

Gooding-Williams, Robert and Charles W. Mills. "Race in a 'Post-racial' Epoch?" *Du Bois Review* 11, no. 1 (2014): 1–8.

Gotanda, Neil. "A Critique of 'Our Constitution Is Color-Blind.'" *Stanford Law Review* 44 (1991): 1–68.

Graber, Mark A. *Dred Scott and the Problem of Constitutional Evil*. Cambridge: Cambridge University Press, 2006.

Graglia, Lino. *Disaster by Decree: The Supreme Court Decisions on Race and the Schools*. Ithaca, NY: Cornell University Press, 1976.

Greenberg, Jack. *Crusaders in the Courts: How a Dedicated Band of Lawyers Fought for the Civil Rights Revolution.* New York: Basic Books, 2004.

Grinsell, Scott. "'The Prejudice of Caste': The Misreading of Justice Harlan and the Ascendency of Anticlassification." *Michigan Journal of Race and Law* 15 (2010): 317–367.

Gross, Ariela J. "Litigating Whiteness: Trials of Racial Determination in the Nineteenth-Century South." *Yale Law Journal* 108 (1998): 109–186.

Gross, Ariela J. *What Blood Won't Tell: A History of Race on Trial in America.* Cambridge, MA: Harvard University Press, 2010.

Gross, Theodore L. *Albion W. Tourgée.* New York: Twayne, 1963.

Guinier, Lani and Gerald Torres. "A Critique of Colorblindness." In *The Miner's Canary: Enlisting Race, Resisting Power, Transforming Democracy,* 32–66. Cambridge, MA: Harvard University Press, 2003.

Gutmann, Amy and Kwame Anthony Appiah. "Responding to Racial Injustice." In *Color Conscious: The Political Morality of Race,* 106–178. Princeton: Princeton University Press, 1996.

Hall, Gwendolyn Midlo. *Africans in Colonial Louisiana: The Development of Afro-Creole Culture in the Eighteenth Century.* Baton Rouge: Louisiana State University Press, 1995.

Hall, Jacquelyn Dowd. "The Long Civil Rights Movement and the Political Uses of the Past." *Journal of American History* 91 (2005): 1233–1263.

Hall, Stuart. "Gramsci's Relevance for the Study of Race and Ethnicity," *Critical Dialogues in Cultural Studies.* London: Routledge, 1996.

Haney-López, Ian F. *Dog Whistle Politics: How Coded Racial Appeals Have Reinvented Racism and Wrecked the Middle Class.* New York: Oxford University Press, 2015.

Haney-López, Ian F. "A Nation of Minorities: Race, Ethnicity, and Reactionary Color-Blindness." *Stanford Law Review* 59 (2007): 985–1063.

Haney-López, Ian F. "The Social Construction of Race: Some Observations on Illusion, Fabrication, and Choice." *Harvard Civil Rights–Civil Liberties Law Review* 29 (1994): 1–62.

Haney-López, Ian F. *White by Law: The Legal Construction of Race.* New York: New York University Press, 1996.

Harney, Stefano and Fred Moten. *The Undercommons: Fugitive Planning and Black Study.* Brooklyn, NY: Minor Compositions for Autonomedia, 2013.

Harris, Cheryl I. "Whiteness as Property." *Harvard Law Review* 106, no. 8 (1993): 1707–1791.

Harris, Cheryl I. and Kimberly West-Faulcon. "Reading Ricci: Whitening Discrimination, Racing Test Fairness." *UCLA Law Review* 58 (2010): 73–165.

Hartman, Saidiya V. *Scenes of Subjection: Terror, Slavery, and Self-Making in Nineteenth-Century America.* New York: Oxford University Press, 1997.

Hartz, Louis. *The Liberal Tradition in America.* New York: Harcourt Brace, 1920.

Hershman, James H., Jr. "Massive Resistance Meets Its Match: The Emergence of a Pro-Public School Majority." In *Moderate's Dilemma: Massive Resistance to School Desegregation in Virginia,* edited by Matthew D. Lassiter and Andrew B. Lewis, 104–133. Charlottesville: University of Virginia Press, 1998.

Higginbotham, A. Leon. *In the Matter of Color: Race and the American Legal Process: The Colonial Period.* Oxford: Oxford University Press, 1978.

Hirsch, Arnold R. and Joseph Logsdon, eds. *Creole New Orleans: Race and Americanization.* Baton Rouge: Louisiana State University Press, 1992.

Hochschild, Jennifer L. *The New American Dilemma: Liberal Democracy and School Desegregation.* New Haven: Yale University Press, 1984.

Hollis-Brusky, Amanda. *Ideas with Consequences: The Federalist Society and the Conservative Counterrevolution.* Oxford: Oxford University Press, 2015.

Holt, Thomas C. *The Problem of Race in the Twenty-First Century.* Cambridge, MA: Harvard University Press, 2002.

HoSang, Daniel. *Racial Propositions: Ballot Initiatives and the Making of Postwar California.* Berkeley: University of California Press, 2010.

Howard-Pitney, David. *The Afro-American Jeremiad: Appeals for Justice in America.* Philadelphia: Temple University Press, 1990.

Hughes, Langston. "Let America Be America Again." In *The Collected Poems of Langston Hughes*, edited by Arnold Rampersad and David Roessel, 189–191. New York: Random House, 1995.

Irons, Peter. *Jim Crow's Children: The Broken Promise of the* Brown *Decision.* New York: Penguin, 2004.

Irons, Peter. *Justice at War: The Story of the Japanese-American Internment Cases.* Berkeley: University of California Press, 1993.

Jacobs, Gregory S. *Getting around* Brown: *Desegregation, Development, and the Columbus Public Schools.* Columbus: Ohio State University Press, 1998.

Jeffries, John C., Jr. *Justice Lewis F. Powell Jr.* New York: Charles Scribner, 1994.

Jordan, Winthrop D. *White over Black: American Attitudes towards the Negro, 1550–1812.* Chapel Hill: University of North Carolina Press, 1968.

Kahn, Paul W. *The Cultural Study of Law.* Chicago: University of Chicago Press, 1999.

Kairys, David, ed. *The Politics of Law: A Progressive Critique.* New York: Pantheon, 1982.

Kang, Jerry. "Trojan Horses of Race." *Harvard Law Review* 118, no. 5 (2005): 1489–1593.

Karst, Kenneth L. and Harold W. Horowitz. "Affirmative Action and Equal Protection." *Virginia Law Review* 60, no. 6 (1974): 955–974.

Katznelson, Ira. *When Affirmative Action Was White: The Untold History of Racial Inequality in Twentieth-Century America.* New York: Norton, 2005.

Keck, Thomas. "From *Bakke* to *Grutter*: The Rise of Rights-Based Conservatism." In *The Supreme Court and American Political Development*, edited by Ronald Kahn and Ken I. Kersch, 414–442. Lawrence: University of Kansas Press, 2006.

Kennedy, Duncan. *Legal Education and the Reproduction of Hierarchy: A Polemic against the System.* New York: New York University Press, 2007.

Kennedy, Randall L. "Racial Critiques of Legal Academia." *Harvard Law Review* 102, no. 8 (1989): 1745–1819.

Kilpatrick, James. *The Southern Case for School Segregation.* New York: Crowell-Collier, 1962.

Kim, Claire Jean. "Racial Triangulation of Asian Americans." *Politics and Society* 27 (1999): 105–138.

Kim, Thomas P. *The Racial Logic of Politics: Asian Americans and Party Competition.* Philadelphia: Temple University Press, 2006.

King, Desmond S. and Rogers M. Smith. *Still a House Divided: Race and Politics in Obama's America*. Princeton: Princeton University Press, 2011.

Klarman, Michael J. "How *Brown* Changed Race Relations: The Backlash Thesis." *Journal of American History* 81 (1994): 81–118.

Klarman, Michael. *Jim Crow to Civil Rights: The Supreme Court and the Struggle for Racial Equality*. New York: Oxford University Press, 2004.

Kluger, Richard. *Simple Justice: The History of* Brown v. Board of Education *and Black America's Struggle for Equality*. New York: Vintage, 1977.

Kramer, Larry. *The People Themselves: Popular Constitutionalism and Judicial Review*. New York: Oxford University Press, 2004.

Krieger, Linda Hamilton. "The Content of Our Categories: A Cognitive Bias Approach to Discrimination and Equal Employment Opportunity." *Stanford Law Review* 47, no. 6 (1995): 1161–1248.

Krishnakumar, Anita S. "On the Evolution of Canonical Dissent." *Rutgers Law Review* 52 (2000): 781–826.

Kull, Andrew. *The Color-Blind Constitution*. Cambridge, MA: Harvard University Press, 1992.

Lakoff, George. *Don't Think of an Elephant! Know Your Values and Frame the Debate: The Essential Guide for Progressives*. White River Junction, VT: Chelsea River, 2004.

Lassiter, Matthew D. *The Silent Majority: Suburban Politics in the Sunbelt South*. Princeton: Princeton University Press, 2006.

Lassiter, Matthew D. and Joseph Crespino. *The Myth of Southern Exceptionalism*. Oxford: Oxford University Press, 2009.

Lassiter, Matthew D. and Andrew B. Lewis, eds. *Moderate's Dilemma: Massive Resistance to School Desegregation in Virginia*. Charlottesville: University of Virginia Press, 1998.

Lawrence, Charles R., III. "Crossburning and the Sound of Silence: Anti-subordination Theory and the First Amendment." *Villanova Law Review* 37, no. 4 (2001): 787–804.

Lawrence, Charles R., III. "The Id, the Ego, and Equal Protection: Reckoning with Unconscious Racism." *Stanford Law Review* 39, no. 2 (1987): 317–388.

Lawrence, Charles R., III. "Two Views of the River: A Critique of the Liberal Defense of Affirmative Action." *Columbia Law Review* 101 (2001): 928–975.

Lebron, Christopher J. *The Color of Our Shame: Race and Justice in Our Time*. Oxford: Oxford University Press, 2013.

Lee, Sophia. "Hotspots in a Cold War: The NAACP's Postwar Workplace Constitutionalism, 1948–1964." *Law and History Review* 26, no. 2 (2008): 327–377.

Lincoln, Abraham. "Second Inaugural Address." In *Lincoln: Speeches and Writings, 1859–1865*, edited by Don E. Fehrenbacher, 686. New York: Library of America, 1989.

Lipsitz, George. "Getting around *Brown*: The Social Warrant of the New Racism." In *Remembering* Brown *at Fifty: The University of Illinois Commemorates* Brown v. Board of Education, edited by Orville Vernon Burton and David O'Brien, 38–63. Urbana: University of Illinois Press, 2009.

Lipsitz, George. *The Possessive Investment in Whiteness: How White People Profit from Identity Politics*. Philadelphia: Temple University Press, 1998.

Litwack, Leon F. *Been in the Storm So Long: The Aftermath of Slavery*. New York: Vintage, 1979.

Lively, Donald E. "Separate but Equal." In *Race and Constitutional Law*, 89–108. Westport, CT: Praeger, 1992.

Lofgren, Charles. *The* Plessy *Case: A Legal-Historical Interpretation.* New York: Oxford University Press, 1987.

Loury, Glenn C. "America's Moral Dilemma: Will It Be Color Blindness or Racial Equality?" *Journal of Blacks in Higher Education* 27 (2000): 90–94.

Lowndes, Joseph E. *From the New Deal to the New Right: Race and the Southern Origins of Modern Conservatism.* New Haven: Yale University Press, 2008.

McCann, Michael W. *Judging the Constitution: Critical Essays on Judicial Lawmaking.* Glenview, IL: Scott Foresman, 1989.

McCann, Michael W. *Rights at Work: Pay Equity Reform and the Politics of Legal Mobilization.* Chicago: University of Chicago Press, 1994.

Malcolm X. "The Ballot or the Bullet." In *Malcolm X Speaks: Selected Speeches and Statements*, edited by George Breitman, 23–44. New York: Grove Press, 1996.

Martin, Joan. "*Plaçage* and the Louisiana *Gens de Couleur Libre*: How Race and Sex Defined the Lifestyles of Free Women of Color." In *Creole: The History and Legacy of Louisiana's Free People of Color*, edited by Sybil Kein, 57–70. Baton Rouge: Louisiana State University Press, 2000.

Massey, Douglass S. and Nancy A. Denton. *American Apartheid: Segregation and the Making of the Underclass.* Cambridge, MA: Harvard University Press, 1993.

Matsuda, Mari J. "Looking to the Bottom: Critical Legal Studies and Reparations." *Harvard Civil Rights–Civil Liberties Law Review* 22, no. 2 (1987): 323–388.

Matsuda, Mari J. "Public Response to Racist Speech: Considering the Victim's Story." In *Words That Wound: Critical Race Theory, Assaultive Speech, and the First Amendment*, edited by Mari J. Matsuda, Charles R. Lawrence III, Richard Delgado, and Kimberlé Crenshaw, 17–18. Boulder, CO: Westview Press, 1993.

Matsuda, Mari J., Charles R. Lawrence, III, Richard Delgado, and Kimberlé Crenshaw, eds. *Words That Wound: Critical Race Theory, Assaultive Speech, and the First Amendment.* Boulder, CO: Westview Press, 1993.

McClosky, Robert. *The American Supreme Court.* Chicago: University of Chicago Press, 2010.

McWilliams, Dean. *Charles W. Chesnutt and the Fictions of Race.* Athens: University of Georgia Press, 2002.

Medley, Keith W. *We as Freemen:* Plessy v. Ferguson. Gretna, LA: Pelican, 2003.

Melamed, Jodi. *Represent and Destroy: Rationalizing Violence in the New Racial Capitalism.* Minneapolis: University of Minnesota Press, 2011.

Michelman, Frank I. "Foreword: 'Racialism' and Reason." *Michigan Law Review* 95 (1997): 723–740.

Miller, Perry. *The New England Mind: The Seventeenth Century.* New York: Macmillan, 1939.

Mills, Charles W. *The Racial Contract.* Ithaca, NY: Cornell University Press, 1997.

Montagu, Ashley. *Man's Most Dangerous Myth: The Fallacy of Race.* Walnut Creek, CA: Rowman and Littlefield, 1997.

Moran, Rachel F. *Interracial Intimacy: The Regulation of Race and Romance.* Chicago: University of Chicago Press, 2001.

Morgan, Edmund S. *American Slavery, American Freedom.* New York: Norton, 2003.

Morrison, Toni. *Playing in the Dark: Whiteness and the Literary Imagination*. Cambridge, MA: Harvard University Press, 1992.

Motley, Constance Baker. "Remarks of Judge Motley." In "In Memoriam: Honorable Thurgood Marshall, Proceedings of the Bar and Officers of the Supreme Court of the United States, Vol. 10," presented by the United States Supreme Court, ix–xi. Washington, DC, November 15, 1993.

Murakawa, Naomi. *The First Civil Right: How Liberals Built Prison America*. Oxford: Oxford University Press, 2014.

Murakawa, Naomi. "The Origins of the Carceral Crisis: Racial Order as 'Law and Order' in Postwar American Politics." In *Race and American Political Development*, edited by Joseph Lowndes, Julie Novkov, and Dorian T. Warren, 234–255. New York: Routeldge, 2008.

Myrdal, Gunnar. *The American Dilemma: The Negro Problem and Modern Democracy*. New York: Harper, 1994.

Novkov, Julie. "The Conservative Attack on Affirmative Action: Toward a Legal Genealogy of Color Blindness." In *The Politics of Inclusion and Exclusion: Identity Politics in Twenty-First Century America*, edited by David F. Ericson, 177–206. New York: Routledge, 2011.

Nussbaum, Martha. "The Supreme Court 2006 Term: Foreword: Constitutions and Capabilities: 'Perception' against Lofty Formalism." *Harvard Law Review* 121 (2007): 4–97.

Oh, Reginald. "Discrimination and Distrust: A Critical Linguistic Analysis of the Discrimination Concept." *Journal of Constitutional Law* 7, no. 3 (2005): 837–866.

Olsen, Otto H. *Carpetbagger's Crusade: The Life of Albion Winegar Tourgée*. Baltimore: Johns Hopkins University Press, 1965.

Olsen, Otto H., ed. *The Thin Disguise: Turning Point in Negro History:* Plessy v. Ferguson. *A Documentary Presentation, 1864–1896*. New York: Humanities Press, 1967.

Olson, Joel. *The Abolition of White Democracy*. Minneapolis: University of Minnesota Press, 2004.

Omi, Michael and Howard Winant. *Racial Formation in the United States: From the 1960s to the 1990s*. New York: Routledge, 1994.

Orfield, Gary and Susan E. Eaton. *Dismantling Desegregation: The Quiet Reversal of Brown v. Board of Education*. New York: New Press, 1996.

Orfield, Gary and Chungmei Lee. *Historic Reversals, Accelerating Resegregation, and the Need for New Integration Strategies*. Special report prepared for the Civil Rights Project / Proyecto Derechos Civiles, UCLA, August 2007.

Pascoe, Peggy. *What Comes Naturally: Miscegenation Law and the Making of Race in America*. Oxford: Oxford University Press, 2009.

Payne, Charles. "'The Whole United States is Southern!': *Brown v. Board* and the Mystification of Race." *University of Pennsylvania Journal of Constitutional Law* 7, no. 3 (2005): 837–866.

Peller, Gary. "Race-Consciousness." *Duke Law Journal* 39, no. 4 (1990): 758–847.

Perry, Imani. *More Beautiful and More Terrible: The Embrace and Transcendence of Racial Inequality in the United States*. New York: New York University Press, 2011.

Post, Robert C. *Prejudicial Appearances: The Logic of American Antidiscrimination Law*. Durham, NC: Duke University Press, 2001.

Post, Robert C. and Michael Paul Rogin, eds. *Race and Representation: Affirmative Action*. New York: Zone Books, 1998.

Powell, John A., Gavin Kearney, and Vina Kay, eds. *In Pursuit of a Dream Deferred: Linking Housing and Education Policy*. New York: Peter Lang, 2001.

Primus, Richard A. "Canon, Anti-canon, and Judicial Dissent." *Duke Law Journal* 48 (1998): 243–303.

Primus, Richard A. "Equal Protection and Disparate Impact: Round Three." *Harvard Law Review* 117 (2003): 494–587.

Przybyszewski, Linda. *The Republic According to John Marshall Harlan*. Chapel Hill: University of North Carolina Press, 1999.

Rana, Aziz. *The Two Faces of American Freedom*. Cambridge, MA: Harvard University Press: 2010.

Roche, Jeff. *Restructured Resistance: The Sibley Commission and the Politics of Desegregation in Georgia*. Athens: University of Georgia Press, 1998.

Reynolds, William Bradford. "Affirmative Action and Its Negative Repercussions," *Annals of the American Academy of Political and Social Science* 523 (1990): 39–41.

Roithmayr, Daria. *Reproducing Racism: How Everyday Choices Lock In White Advantage*. New York: New York University Press, 2014.

Rosenberg, Gerald. *The Hollow Hope: Can Courts Bring About Social Change?* Chicago: University of Chicago Press, 1993.

Ross, Thomas. "Innocence and Affirmative Action." *Vanderbilt Law Review* 43, no. 2 (1990): 297–315.

Ryan, James E. "Schools, Race, and Money." *Yale Law Journal* 109 (1999): 249–316.

Sabbagh, Daniel. "Judicial Uses of Subterfuge: Affirmative Action Reconsidered." *Political Science Quarterly* 118, no. 3 (2003): 411–436.

Sarat, Austin, ed. *Race, Law, and Culture: Reflections on* Brown v. Board of Education. Oxford: Oxford University Press, 1997.

Sarat, Austin and Jonathan Simon. *Cultural Analysis, Cultural Studies, and the Law*. Durham, NC: Duke University Press, 2003.

Schmidt, Christopher. "*Brown* and the Colorblind Constitution." *Cornell Law Review* 94 (2008): 203–238.

Schuck, Peter H. "Affirmative Action: Past, Present, and Future." *Yale Law and Policy Review* 20 (2002): 1–96.

Shelby, Tommie. *We Who Are Dark*. Cambridge, MA: Harvard University Press, 2005.

Shulman, George. *American Prophecy: Race and Redemption in American Political Culture*. Minneapolis: University of Minnesota Press, 2008.

Siegel, Reva. "Equality Talk: Antisubordination and Anticlassification Values in Constitutional Struggles over *Brown*." *Harvard Law Review* 117 (2004): 1470–1547.

Siegel, Reva. "'The Rule of Love': Wife Beating as Prerogative and Privacy." *Yale Law Journal* 105 (1996): 2117–2207.

Siegel, Reva. "Why Equal Protection No Longer Protects: The Evolving Forms of Status-Enforcing State Action." *Stanford Law Review* 49 (1997): 1111–1148.

Singh, Nikhil Pal. *Black Is a Country: Race and the Unfinished Struggle for Democracy*. Cambridge, MA: Harvard University Press, 2004.

Sleeper, Jim. *Liberal Racism*. New York: Viking Press, 1997.

Smith, Rogers M. *Civil Ideals: Conflicting Visions of Citizenship in U.S. History.* New Haven: Yale University Press, 1997.

Sowell, Thomas. *Civil Rights: Rhetoric or Reality?* New York: William Morrow, 1984.

Spann, Girardeau A. "Disintegration." *University of Louisville Law Review* 46 (2008): 565–630.

Spann, Girardeau A. *Race against the Court: The Supreme Court and Minorities in Contemporary America.* New York: New York University Press, 1993.

Spear, Jennifer M. "'They Need Wives': Métissage and the Regulation of Sexuality in French Louisiana." In *Sex, Love, Race: Crossing Boundaries in North America*, edited by Martha Hodes, 35–59. New York: New York University Press, 1999.

Steele, Claude M., and Joshua Aronson. "Stereotype Threat and the Intellectual Test Performance of African-Americans." *Journal of Personality and Social Psychology* 69 (1995): 797–811.

Sterkx, H. E. *The Free Negro in Ante-bellum Louisiana.* Madison, NJ: Fairleigh Dickinson University Press, 1972.

Sugrue, Thomas J. *The Origins of the Urban Crisis: Race and Inequality in Postwar Detroit.* Princeton: Princeton University Press, 1996.

Sugrue, Thomas J. *Sweet Land of Liberty: The Forgotten Struggle for Civil Rights in the North.* New York: Random House, 2009.

Sunstein, Cass R. "The Anticaste Principle." *Michigan Law Review* 92, no. 8 (1994): 2410–2455.

Taylor, Kirstine. "Untimely Subjects: 'White Trash' and the Politics of Modernization, 1944–1969." *American Quarterly* 67 (2015): 55–79.

Taylor, Paul C. "Taking Post-racialism Seriously: From Movement Mythology to Racial Formation." *Du Bois Review* 11, no. 1 (2014): 9–25.

Teles, Steven M. *The Rise of Conservative Legal Movement: The Battle for Control of the Law.* Princeton: Princeton University Press, 2008.

Theoharis, Jeanne and Komozi Woodward, eds. *Freedom North: Black Freedom Struggles outside the South, 1940–1980.* New York: Palgrave Macmillan, 2003.

Thernstrom, Stephan and Abigail Thernstrom. *America in Black and White: One Nation, Indivisible.* New York: Simon and Schuster, 1999.

Thomas, Brook. *Plessy v. Ferguson: A Brief History with Documents.* Boston: Bedford Books, 1997.

Tourgée, Albion W. "Brief for Homer A. Plessy." In *The Thin Disguise: Turning Point in Negro History: Plessy v. Ferguson. A Documentary Presentation, 1864–1896*, edited by Otto H. Olsen, 80–103. New York: Humanities Press, 1967.

Turner, Jack. *Awakening to Race: Individualism and Social Consciousness in America.* Chicago: University of Chicago Press, 2012.

Tushnet, Mark. "The Politics of Equality in Constitutional Law." *Journal of American History* 74, no. 3 (1987): 884–903.

Tussman, Joseph and Jacobus tenBroek. "The Equal Protection of the Laws." *California Law Review* 37, no. 3 (1949): 341–381.

Unger, Roberto Mangabeira. *Law in Modern Society: Toward a Criticism of Social Theory.* New York: Free Press, 1997.

Van Alstyne, William. "Rites of Passage: Race, the Supreme Court, and the Constitution." *University of Chicago Law Review* 46 (1979): 775–810.

Vogler, Candace A. and Patchen Markell. "Violence, Redemption and the Liberal Imagination." *Public Culture* 15 (2003): 1–10.

Walker, Anders. *The Ghost of Jim Crow: How Southern Moderates Used* Brown v. Board *to Stall Civil Rights*. Oxford: Oxford University Press, 2009.

Wang, Lu-in. *Discrimination by Default: How Racism Becomes Routine*. New York: New York University Press, 2006.

Washington, Booker T. *The Future of the American Negro*. Boston: Small, Maynard, 1900.

Weaver, Vesla M. "Frontlash: Race and the Development of Punitive Crime Policy." *Studies in American Political Development* 21 (2007): 230–265.

Webb, Clive. *Massive Resistance: Southern Opposition to the Second Reconstruction*. Oxford: Oxford University Press, 2005.

Welke, Barbara Y. "When All the Women Were White, and All the Blacks Were Men: Gender, Class, Race, and the Road to *Plessy*." *Law and History Review* 13, no. 2 (1995): 261–316.

West, Cornel. "The New Cultural Politics of Difference." *Humanities as Social Technology* (MIT Press) 53 (1990): 93–109.

West, Cornel. *Prophesy Deliverance!* Louisville, KY: Westminster John Knox Press, 2002.

West, Cornel and Christa Buschendorf. *Black Prophetic Fire*. Boston: Beacon Press, 2015.

West, Robin. *Narrative, Authority, and Law*. Ann Arbor: University of Michigan Press, 1993.

White, James Boyd. *Justice as Translation: An Essay in Cultural and Legal Criticism*. Chicago: University of Chicago Press, 1990.

White, James Boyd. "Law as Rhetoric, Rhetoric as Law: The Arts of Cultural and Communal Life." *University of Chicago Law Review* 52, no. 3 (1985): 684–702.

Wilderson, Frank, III. "Afropessimism and the End of Redemption," *Occupied Times* March 30, 2016, 225–240.

Wilderson, Frank, III. "Gramsci's Black Marx: Whither the Slave in Civil Society?" *Social Identities* 9, no. 2 (2003): 225–240.

Wilkinson, J. Harvie. *From* Brown *to* Bakke: *The Supreme Court and School Integration: 1954–1978*. Oxford: Oxford University Press, 1979.

Williams, Patricia. *The Alchemy of Race and Rights*. Cambridge, MA: Harvard University Press, 1991.

Williams, Patricia. *Seeing a Color-Blind Future: The Paradox of Race*. New York: Farrar, Straus and Giroux, 1998.

Woodward, C. Vann. *The Strange Career of Jim Crow*. Oxford: Oxford University Press, 1955.

Wright, J. Skelly. "Color-Blind Theories and Color-Conscious Remedies." *University of Chicago Law Review* 47, no. 2 (1980): 213–245.

INDEX

Note: References to tables are denoted by 't' in italics following the page number